Studies in
Modern French History

Aristocratic families in republican France, 1870–1940

Manchester University Press

Studies in
Modern French History
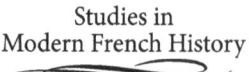

Edited by
Mark Greengrass and Pamela Pilbeam

This series is published in collaboration with the UK Society for the Study of French History. It aims to showcase innovative short monographs relating to the history of the French, in France and in the world since c.1750. Each volume speaks to a theme in the history of France with broader resonances to other discourses about the past. Authors demonstrate how the sources and interpretations of modern French history are being opened to historical investigation in new and interesting ways, and how unfamiliar subjects have the capacity to tell us more about the role of France within the European continent. The series is particularly open to interdisciplinary studies that break down the traditional boundaries and conventional disciplinary divisions.

Titles already published in this series

Catholicism and children's literature in France: The comtesse de Ségur (1799–1874)
Sophie Heywood

The Society for the
Study of French History

Aristocratic families in republican France, 1870–1940

ELIZABETH C. MACKNIGHT

Manchester University Press

Copyright © Elizabeth C. Macknight 2012

The right of Elizabeth C. Macknight to be identified as the author of this work has been asserted by her in accordance with the Copyright, Designs and Patents Act 1988.

Published by Manchester University Press
Altrincham Street, Manchester M1 7JA, UK
www.manchesteruniversitypress.co.uk

British Library Cataloguing-in-Publication Data is available

Library of Congress Cataloging-in-Publication Data is available

ISBN 978 1 5261 0680 3 *paperback*

First published by Manchester University Press 2012

This edition first published 2017

The publisher has no responsibility for the persistence or accuracy of URLs for any external or third-party internet websites referred to in this book, and does not guarantee that any content on such websites is, or will remain, accurate or appropriate.

Printed by Lightning Source

To the memory of my grandmothers

Contents

List of figures	*page* ix
Acknowledgements	xi
List of abbreviations	xiii
Introduction	1
1 Nobility, titles, and genealogy	15
2 Marriage	40
3 Property and inheritance	65
4 Serving the household	92
5 Paternity and politics	117
6 Aristocratic motherhood	145
7 Children's worlds	170
8 Space and memory, loss and nostalgia	196
Conclusion	219
Appendix	233
List of archival sources	245
Index	249

List of figures

1. Armand de Gramont, duc de Guiche (1900)
   Photograph by Paul Nadar. © Ministère de la culture – Médiatheque du patrimoine, dist. RMN/auteur de la photo *page* 55
2. Élaine Greffulhe (1900)
   Photograph by Paul Nadar. © Ministère de la culture – Médiatheque du patrimoine, dist. RMN/auteur de la photo 56
3. Stables at the prince de Radziwill's Parisian residence (1884)
   Photograph by Paul Nadar. © Ministère de la culture – Médiatheque du patrimoine, dist. RMN/auteur de la photo 102
4. The princesse de Radziwill's *cabinet de toilette* (1884)
   Photograph by Paul Nadar. © Ministère de la culture – Médiatheque du patrimoine, dist. RMN/auteur de la photo 105
5. Boy sketching, by Paul-César Helleu (c.1900)
   Reproduced with permission from Les Amis de Paul-César Helleu 171
6. The général marquis de Galliffet (1893)
   Photograph by Paul Nadar. © Ministère de la culture – Médiatheque du patrimoine, dist. RMN/auteur de la photo 190

7 The *grand salon* at the château d'Ermenonville (1884)
  Photograph by Paul Nadar. © Ministère de la culture –
  Médiatheque du patrimoine, dist. RMN/auteur de la photo   200

8 Alcove in the prince's bedroom at the château de
  Chalais (1977)
  Photograph by Daniel Bontemps. © Ministère de la culture –
  Médiatheque du patrimoine, dist. RMN/auteur de la photo   213

Acknowledgements

My principal debt of gratitude is to the aristocratic families whose *archives privées* became the focus of my work as a historian. I extend a special thank you to those families. Although research and writing are solitary pursuits, my time in the archives has not been a lonely one. I deeply appreciate the help of all the staff at the Archives nationales and Archives départementales who in snow, rain, or sunshine welcomed *l'Australienne*. The idea for this book came from questions posed by Robert Nye in response to my doctoral dissertation on elite Parisian women's sociability. I am very grateful to Robert for his encouragement and support as the new project gradually unfolded. Siân Reynolds provided a valuable steer, urging me to investigate noblemen's experiences in order to bring greater depth and balance to my writing about gender. Peter McPhee contributed detailed, critical comment on drafts and has guided my development as a historian of France with patience, care, and generosity. The manuscript has also benefited from careful reading by Mark Greengrass, Campbell Macknight, Linda Mitchell, and Pamela Pilbeam. I have endeavoured to follow their very helpful suggestions for improvement. Of course, any errors in the book remain my responsibility alone.

Grants that facilitated my research in French archives came from the University of Melbourne, Goddard Sapin-Jaloustre Trust, French Government, Carnegie Trust for the Universities of Scotland, and the University of Aberdeen. Chapter 4 is based on an article first published in *French History* which is reproduced in modified form with permission from Oxford University Press. Short extracts from an article in *Historical*

Reflections/Réflexions Historiques and a chapter in *Material Women 1750–1950* are reproduced with permission from Berghahn and Ashgate. With the guidance and care of archivists, every effort has been made to contact families, where appropriate, about my translation of archival material for this book. I very much appreciate the patience and assistance from staff at Manchester University Press.

For their friendship and kindness, I wish to thank Béatrice Bronnert, Paul Davis, Juliet Flesch, Hélène Hiquily, Andrew Mackillop, Ros Minchin, Kirsty Munro, and Aude Sowerwine. I am fortunate that Daniel Nethery is willing to continue our long conversation in different parts of the world and he helped to secure permissions for the book's illustrations. Luke Gartlan has been a trusted companion and gave me the dictionary. Michael and Caroline Hubbard helped me to realise that a corner of southwest France is a place to feel at home. Finally, for this project and for the ongoing wonder of an academic life, I have relied constantly on the support of my own family. Campbell, Lorraine, and Thomas Macknight inspire and encourage me through their love, creativity, and commitment to intellectual endeavours. At a perennial distance in geographic terms, they have never been far from my thoughts during the research and writing of this book.

List of abbreviations

AD	Archives départementales
AN	Archives nationales
ANF	Association d'entraide de la Noblesse Française
AP	Archives privées
LFF	Ligue des Femmes Françaises
LPF	Ligue Patriotiques des Françaises
extr.	nobility of 'extraction'
lett.	ennobled by letters
par ch.	ennobled by office
XIX	nineteenth-century nobility

Introduction

In her memoirs the comtesse de Pange (née Pauline de Broglie) described her childhood in a French aristocratic household at the beginning of the twentieth century: 'I lived in a closed world that wished to ignore the passing of time and to preserve to the extreme its customs and its illusions.'[1] What was it like to grow up in such a world and why did aristocratic families like the Broglie wish 'to ignore the passing of time'? How did girls and boys of the nobility interact with their parents and other relatives? What role did servants play in children's upbringing? Were parents involved and interested in their children's education and where, or to whom, did they look for models?

To answer these questions this book documents the daily life, concerns, and dynamics of aristocratic families in the France of the Third Republic. The decision to focus on this seventy-year period, from 1870 to 1940, was driven by curiosity to understand nobles' responses to the re-establishment and gradual consolidation of a republican regime after the fall of the Second Empire. During the Third Republic there were many changes in legislation that reconfigured the relationship between the state and French citizens on matters pertaining to childrearing and education, marriage, property ownership, paternal authority, and birth control. In the 1880s for example the republican government passed new laws for free, obligatory, secular state schooling (1880–82); for divorce (1884); and for state protection of juvenile delinquents (1889). Early in the twentieth century came a tax on inheritance (1901); an extension to married women's property rights (1908); a new law on paternity suits (1912); a tax on income (1914); and new laws that made abortion a criminal offence

(1920, 1923). It took some time, of course, for these and other legislative changes to filter into society and take effect within daily practices. The extent of their impact on families at all levels of French society remains difficult to measure today.[2]

Reflected in the government's reforms were some far-reaching developments that engaged public interest across the nineteenth century. Efforts to improve hygiene and raise the birth rate, increased migration affecting rural and urban economies, and debates over the rights of women and citizenship were among the longstanding considerations that shaped decisions on policy. Arguably the most significant driver for new legislation, however, was the republican commitment to the principle of secularism (*laïcité*). During the 1789 Revolution trenchant disputes over this principle had divided the French population. The resulting violence was grafted deep into collective memories, particularly in the west of France where communities of the Vendée sought to defend the traditional structures of the Catholic Church through armed struggle against republican forces. Although the 1801 Concordat helped to ease religious–secular tensions, key issues such as the Church's role in education were repeatedly reopened for discussion. In the early decades of the Third Republic the government and local authorities pushed hard to bring secularism into greater practical effect. Priests were banned from teaching in public schools and from education supervisory bodies (1879). Crucifixes were removed from nearly all Paris hospitals (1890). The 1901 Law on Associations required religious congregations to change their ties to Rome or risk dissolution by force. In 1905, spurred by the turmoil of the Dreyfus Affair and exposure of Radicals' targeting of Catholics in the army and civil service, the government passed the Law for the Separation of Church and State.

These government actions fuelled a resurgence of hostility between anticlerical republicans and segments of the Catholic population who were resolutely opposed to the regime and bitter about the changes it had wrought. Catholic reactions to the republicans' secularising campaign were complex, not least because of fragmentation in the support for monarchism. Historians have investigated Pope Leo XIII's policy of *ralliement* in the 1890s that aimed to bring about reconciliation between the Catholic Church and the French state. They have uncovered a range of public demonstrations and initiatives through which clergy, members of religious orders, and groups of lay Catholics protested against and sought to minimise the effectiveness of the new laws.[3] What has been less studied to date is the manner in which opposition and resistance to secularism became manifest in domestic practices and daily decision-making by individuals and families.

To address the implications of legislative change under the Third Republic by focusing on the nobility is to swim against the tide of historical scholarship that has examined such change from republican and middle-class perspectives. The three decades before 1914 are usually interpreted as an unstable period that witnessed the 'triumph' of republicanism underpinned by the increasing political, social, and cultural dominance of the bourgeoisie. In this modernising France of the Third Republic, where 'progress' is generally associated with the ambitions, tastes, networks, and financial resources of bourgeois elites, what happened to the French nobility? It would be easy to take at face value the comtesse de Pange's statement 'I lived in a closed world' and assume that nobles shrank into the background of public affairs, becoming increasingly irrelevant to the life of the French nation. Indeed this is exactly the assumption historians have made in representing the aristocracy as 'defeated' by the bourgeoisie and the 'least important' group in French society by the late nineteenth century.[4]

This book argues that in the context of political, social, and economic challenges arising under the Third Republic nobles actively sought to defend their interests and projects, adopting strategies to counter republican initiatives and to sustain conservative rearguard action against the regime. There were only some five thousand aristocratic families in France at the turn of the century making up less than one per cent of the national population. Yet in spite of these small numbers nobles continued to exercise a disproportionate amount of authority, prestige, and influence in French society, playing leadership roles in the military, diplomatic service, cultural patronage, charity, and political activities of all kinds. The survival of the French nobility has long rested upon its ability to adapt to changing circumstances whilst preserving the integrity of the aristocratic lifestyle and traditions. A central purpose of this book is to show the ways in which gender and class were implicated in that process of adaptation taking place within families.

Pierre Bourdieu defined class as 'the unity hidden under the diversity and multiplicity of the set of practices' through which distinctive lifestyles are constituted.[5] This definition, whilst it does not discount the relevance of income and political affiliations to class identity, does move away from fixed economic categories. Since the 1960s historians have also recognised the limitations of such categories and focused more on cultural practices and experience to study class formation. One of the contributing factors to that transformation has been the insistence by feminist scholars that gender be made 'a category of historical analysis'.[6]

Historians who write specifically on the bourgeoisie or the nobility in modern France document the fluidity between these social strata that rendered cultural practices, and hence class distinctions, complex and interconnected. Jean Lhomme argued in an influential study that the elites of the bourgeoisie secured the dominant position in nineteenth-century French society, drawing nobles into their orbit whilst surpassing them in terms of political and financial clout. Natalie Petiteau has countered by showing that those who received titles after 1808 embraced the lifestyle and ideals of the *ancienne noblesse* 'to escape becoming middle-class (*embourgeoisement*) and uphold the nobility of their name'.[7] Éric Mension-Rigau uncovers evidence of cultural differences between aristocratic and bourgeois elites persisting into the late twentieth century. His findings reinforce David Higgs's conclusion about the resilience of the nineteenth-century nobility: 'Egalitarianism and individual accomplishment could never outweigh a society based on distinguished families that preserved the values of the past.'[8]

Central to this historical debate is the exercise of power for which Bourdieu provided significant analytical tools. Bourdieu's wide-ranging research turned on 'the idea that struggles for recognition are a fundamental dimension of social life and that what is at stake in them is an accumulation of a particular form of capital'.[9] He analysed social life as a series of 'fields' in which a person's ability to detain certain types and amounts of capital (economic, cultural, social, and symbolic) determined their position within a social group. A useful illustration of Bourdieu's concepts is found in André-Jean Tudesq's classic study of *les grands notables* in the France of the 1840s. Tudesq showed how superior wealth was only one form of capital (economic) that underpinned the status and power of these upper-class men: 'The grand magnate *has* possessions, *has* knowledge, *has* connections, *has* a family, *has* an office which gives him part of public authority ... he *has* a name and often a title, he is a notable as a function of what he *has*.'[10] Familiarity with command of capital was manifest in behaviours and attitudes that for the most part operated below the level of conscious thought. Bourdieu called those behaviours and attitudes the 'habitus' and they derived from conditioning begun in infancy.[11]

For elites in various parts of Europe historians have investigated configurations of capital to explain continuities as well as gradual evolution in class dynamics. Whilst not all agree with Arno Mayer's thesis, that the old landed aristocracies maintained their supremacy to 1914, they have found common use for the concept of 'active symbiosis' between the nobility and haute bourgeoisie that accompanied amalgamation of these formerly separate social strata.[12] Within this emerging upper class the numbers and population density of nobles varied from country to country. Prior to about 1800 some historians emphasise sharp differences in the wealth, lifestyle, and habitation of nobles; others argue that diversity diminished, making the European aristocracy more cohesive by the nineteenth century.[13] One of the most enduring commonalities among nobles is reverence for lineage. The aristocratic preoccupation with bloodlines has nourished scholarly reflections upon memory, identity, and culture. Increasingly too there is work being done on gender and kinship.[14]

When historians write about nobles there is a tendency to focus on the public exercise of power, for example on the battlefield or at court. Yet in order to understand how and why nobles occupied a range of public roles it is necessary to turn the microscope on to the internal workings of their families and investigate the ways in which aristocratic domestic practices articulated with the nobility's wider political, social, and cultural undertakings. For it is within the domestic environment that nobles underwent most of the conditioning that informed their daily actions and decisions. In their own homes, surrounded by furniture inherited from their ancestors and with servants to attend to their needs, nobles gained their earliest appreciation of ownership and authority. With the embedding of that appreciation in childhood came the very first thrill of power.

This book documents the familial world in order to explain how the articulation between nobles' domestic culture and gendered public roles and activities operated in the France of the Third Republic. Aristocratic command of different types of capital was not readily relinquished after 1870. Nobles continued to hold on to symbolic and material resources that were recognised as valuable and specific to them not only in France but also across Europe and in other parts of the world. Titles and honorific privileges, ancestral estates, the social cachet of 'distinction', high-level networks reaching to royal and imperial courts all contributed to nobles' sense of belonging to a superior 'race'. The stronghold for this accumulation of capital was the aristocratic family, which may be defined as 'simultaneously a lineage, a historical legacy tied to specific fiefs, a nuclear family, a kin group interwoven with other equally ambitious dynasties, and a financial enterprise'.[15] Not surprisingly, therefore, it was on matters pertaining to family that some of the most intense and prolonged 'struggles for recognition' took place under the bourgeois-led republican regime. In responding to legislative changes introduced by the government nobles had a range of strategies at their disposal, all of which involved the deployment of different forms of capital. Moreover, it was precisely because many of the republican reforms threatened to undercut nobles' ability to exercise their capital that aristocratic families resisted those reforms in a whole manner of ways within and outside their homes. Since this is an account of 'struggles' there are examples of weakening and failure as well as of strengthening and success. Nobles were neither passive nor of little importance within the Third Republic in seeking to defend their way of life, convictions, and identities.

Three core scholarly aims inform my writing about aristocratic families. First, this book represents a history of nobles in which the experiences of both sexes are fully integrated. I have sought to balance male and female perspectives across most aspects of familial activity and decision-making as well as through all stages of the human lifecycle. The interrelationship of gendered roles and the manner in which men and women negotiated the consequences of those roles on a daily basis are documented and discussed. In this respect I have followed the example set by Suzanne Desan, Julie Hardwick, and others who are incorporating understandings of gender and power into the history of families. In 1999 Megan Doolittle wrote: 'families continue to remain sidelined in the rich and lively theoretical resources developed by gender historians'.[16] Despite path-breaking research since then, particularly on masculinities and fathering, there are still calls for further work to be done.[17] Aristocratic involvement in politics took many different forms, for men and for women, so a broad definition of what constituted the political has been adopted. Issues that historians have termed 'private' or 'family-related' are often omitted from historical narratives of politics under the Third Republic. By contrast, this book demonstrates that decision-making on such issues was of a political nature.[18]

My second aim is to contribute to the historical knowledge of familial relationships and emotions from an empirical grounding in archival research. During the 1960s and 1970s Philippe Ariès, Edward Shorter, and Lawrence Stone advanced the notion that the modern nuclear family was more affective than pre-industrial kin groupings. Strong emotional ties were possible in families, it was argued, only once life expectancy was prolonged, contraception improved, and a division between workplace and home was enshrined along with ideals of companionate marriage.[19] This 'sentiments' approach to the history of families triggered intense debate and led to revision by demographers, historians, and ethnographers of the 'comfortable fit between the modern family and modern industrial society'.[20] Yet the nineteenth-century bourgeois stereotype of family life as a private emotional haven has endured in popular perception even as historians have qualified its accordance with realities. Since the 1980s many new approaches and themes have developed around the study of the family, and class remains vital to scholars' debate. The notion that middle-class prescriptions and practices had a 'trickle-up effect' is one of the 'assumptions about families in the past [that] must be taken apart and questioned'.[21]

Sex and intimacies of all kinds are not left out of this book. Without attention to those core aspects of life the account would be incomplete.[22] I agree with Steven Ozment that portrayals of family life are best developed 'in as direct a dialogue as possible with the subjects themselves' so that the family and the world around it are seen 'through the eyes of individual household members'.[23] Letters, notes, and other personal documents in archives contain a rich marrow of emotional experiences. When historians ignore, belittle, or rely on second-hand reports to avoid grappling with such evidence the theories and categories they construct for human relations are liable to be hollow ones. Without assuming they provide a complete picture for any society, the words individuals used in correspondence may help us to recognise 'the emotional signature of an age'.[24]

My third aim is to show the results of a different research path than the one more commonly pursued by those historians who consult public archives and published sources. This book exploits the numerous collections (*fonds*) of nobles' papers classed as *archives privées* which have been little used by historians of modern France, even by those working on French elites since 1789. André-Jean Tudesq, who was certainly no stranger to archival research, did not believe *archives privées* were of much relevance for illuminating matters of pertinence to France as a whole. '*Archives privées*, of which we do not mistake the interest, have brought to our study, and can bring to any study conducted at the national level, only a supplement of information.' The use of such sources, he continued, posed difficulties of access but might be 'possible and fruitful, especially in studies relating to a more limited regional context than the one which we have adopted'.[25] This book serves as a counterweight to the narrow circumscription of the value of *archives privées* for writing modern French history. That most historians of nineteenth- and twentieth-century France have chosen not to investigate the evidence on nobles in these archives, or have hesitated to extend their observations beyond the regional level suggested by Tudesq, means that comparatively little information about aristocratic families has so far penetrated historical debate.

The empirical base for this study consists principally of *fonds* in the Archives privées (AP) series at the Archives nationales in Paris. Created in June 1949, the AP series comprises over 660 *fonds* produced by individuals, businesses, families, associations, political parties, and unions. From these, forty-four were chosen for research because they pertain to aristocratic families and include materials from the period of the Third Republic. Additionally I consulted two other *fonds* from the AP series relating to individuals who were in regular contact with nobles: the abbé Mugnier and Gabriel Astruc. Further information on aristocratic families was located in two *fonds* from the series AB XIX Papiers d'érudits. These pertain to the ministerial officials of the French Seal (*référendaires au Sceau de France*) and to a leading genealogist, the vicomte Albert Révérend. To extend my research beyond the archival sources available in Paris, I also investigated the *fonds* of aristocratic families classed in the E and J series in seventeen Archives départementales (a couple of *fonds* were also located in the F series). Permission for access, where it was required, was granted in all cases; limits to time and resources presented the only real and inevitable constraints.[26] This book, therefore, is not a study of 'Parisian' nobility; nor is it a study of nobles within one region of France.[27] Various works have enhanced our understanding of aristocratic patterns of habitation that cannot be compartmentalised in terms of an urban–rural binary.[28] The aristocratic families whose *fonds* I have examined originated from diverse geographic regions of France. Some continued to live in their region of origin; many established homes in other regions.

Since the 1990s *archives privées* have begun to receive greater attention in France through publications and colloquia designed to refresh their profile and to increase public awareness of their scope and significance.[29] The importance of these archives has not always been so well recognised, nor has their communication and conservation been prioritised. 'For a long time, *archives privées* were treated with suspicion, they did not enter the state's collections through regular and official channels.'[30] In part, the low level of interest towards *archives privées* can be explained by the fact that archivists in the nineteenth century were primarily concerned with the preservation and communication of state records, which is reflected in the arrangement of collections including the chronological markers used. In part too, it is a reflection of French pride in having fashioned a democratic nation and the desire to promote the historic accomplishments of the 1789 Revolution that included the abolition of feudalism and the legal status of nobility. Although in the twenty-first century not all the *fonds* in the AP, E, and J series pertain to aristocratic families, there remains a close cultural association between *archives privées* and the world of landed wealth and ancient privileges.

In extreme circumstances, anti-aristocratic sentiment in France has resulted in the deliberate destruction of archives. Such was the case with the Cabinet des Ordres du Roi created by Pierre Clairambault at the end of the seventeenth century. In 1792 this collection was transferred from the Couvent des Grands-Augustins to the Bibliothèque nationale in the rue de Richelieu. At the order of the archivist of the First Republic, Armand-Gaston Camus, nearly two thousand volumes, or over half the Cabinet des Ordres du Roi including hundreds of *preuves de noblesse*, were burned. Camus was also responsible for drafting the law of 7 Messidor An II (25 June 1794) that legitimated the act of destruction. Under the terms of this law, many titles, deeds, and other documents of a feudal nature were removed, seized, and destroyed across France.[31] Not surprisingly, the law of 7 Messidor An II has been a controversial subject for archivists who interpret the intentions behind and results of its application very differently. On the one hand it has been positively described as the 'fundamental charter' of archival organisation in France up until the archives law of 3 January 1979. On the other it is characterised as a purely utilitarian measure implemented in an incompetent fashion. 'Only the lack of personnel and resources prevented the damage from being more serious.'[32]

The increase in professional knowledge of *archives privées* has been paralleled by an increase in legal regulations for their preservation and communication. In 1855 the archivist Henri Bordier wrote of family archives scattered in residences all over France: 'it is impossible today to know, even approximately, what these types of stores contain'.[33] The romantic image of a lone scholar delving into piles of neglected papers consigned to a back room, attic, or basement remains appealing (not least to historians themselves!) but the experience of archival research is generally very different today. During the interwar decades in France legal regulations and procedures were established for the modes of entry and cataloguing of *fonds* in state collections. The broad principles of the approach taken to archives were the same then as for monuments and works of art deemed to be of national historic interest.[34]

Within the AP, E, and J series all the different types of nobility known in France are represented. By examining archival sources it becomes possible, and indeed a necessary part of the research process, to distinguish these types from one another. Nevertheless, it would be misleading to begin labelling the *fonds* under separate categories. This is because within each *fonds*, and even within a single archival box, there are often documents relating to individuals of different lineages, nationalities, regional affiliations, political allegiances, and religious sensibilities. Some of the *fonds* consulted are named after just one nobleman or noblewoman; some contain documents relating to multiple branches of one aristocratic family; some contain documents on several different families who resided in or had some other link with the property where the collection was originally kept (*fonds d'un chartrier seigneurial*).[35]

Attention to differences within and between *fonds* must be coupled with attention to commonalities. Those commonalities become increasingly apparent the further one probes into the AP, E, and J series. On the basis of the research undertaken, this book draws conclusions about cultural practices and experiences that were characteristic of aristocratic families. Yet it does so with an eye for the particular. The writing of the book could not have been approached otherwise since it is the very uniqueness of archival documents that has made research so compelling. Authenticity in a project such as this lies somewhere between recreating for the reader what is general to aristocratic families and what is particular to the life of an individual noble located within one family. Of course there is – or happily always seems to be – a never-ending amount of archival digging to be done. At some point, however, the historian must come away from the archives, in a physical sense, and start to write.

Notes

1 Comtesse Jean de Pange, *Comment j'ai vu 1900* (Paris, 1962), preface. For an excellent study of scientific achievements and sibling experience within the Broglie family see Mary Jo Nye, 'Aristocratic culture and the pursuit of science: the de Broglies in modern France', *Isis* 88 (1997), 397–421.

2 Véronique Antomarchi, *Politique et famille sous la IIIe République 1870–1914* (Paris, 2000); Catherine Rollet-Echalier, *La Politique à l'égard de la petite enfance sous la Troisième République* (Paris, 1990).

3 On republican legislation and Catholic reactions see, for example, John McManners, *Church and State in France 1870–1914* (London, 1972); Maurice Larkin, *Religion, Politics and Preferment in France since 1890: La Belle Époque and its Legacy* (Cambridge, 1995); Judith F. Stone, 'Anticlericals and *bonnes soeurs*: the rhetoric of the 1901 Law of Associations', *French Historical Studies* 23 (2000), 103–28; Bruno Duriez, Étienne Fouilloux, Denis Pelletier, Nathalie Viet-Depaule (eds), avec la collaboration de Tangi Cavalin, *Les Catholiques dans la République 1905–2005* (Paris, 2005); Bruno Dumons, *Les Dames de la Ligue des Femmes Françaises (1901–1914)* (Paris, 2006).
4 See, for example, Gordon Wright, *France in Modern Times: From the Enlightenment to the Present* 3 ed. (London, 1981), pp. 284–5; Jean-Marie Mayeur and Madeleine Rebérioux, *The Third Republic from Its Origins to the Great War, 1871–1914*, trans. J. R. Foster (Cambridge, 1988), pp. 5–41, 58, 65; Charles Sowerwine, *France since 1870: Culture, Politics and Society* (New York, 2001), pp. 6–8, 27–39.
5 Pierre Bourdieu, *Distinction: A Social Critique of the Judgement of Taste*, trans. Richard Nice (London, 2000), p. 101.
6 Joan Wallach Scott, 'Gender: a useful category of historical analysis' in *Gender and the Politics of History* (New York, 1988), pp. 28–50. On cultural practices and experience among the bourgeoisie, see Carol E. Harrison, *The Bourgeois Citizen in Nineteenth-Century France: Gender, Sociability, and the Uses of Emulation* (Oxford, 1999), pp. 5–9.
7 Natalie Petiteau, *Élites et mobilités: la noblesse d'Empire au XIXe siècle (1808–1914)* (Paris, 1997), p. 391; Jean Lhomme, *La Grande Bourgeoisie au pouvoir (1830–1880). Essai sur l'histoire sociale de la France* (Paris, 1960). See also Adeline Daumard, *Les Bourgeois et la bourgeoisie en France* (Paris, 1987), pp. 174–9.
8 David Higgs, *Nobles in Nineteenth-Century France: The Practice of Inegalitarianism* (Baltimore, 1989), p. 222; Éric Mension-Rigau, *Aristocrates et grands bourgeois: éducation, traditions, valeurs* (Paris, 1994), pp. 16–17.
9 Pierre Bourdieu, *In Other Words: Essays Towards a Reflexive Sociology* (1990) trans. in Jen Webb, Tony Schirato, and Geoff Danaher, *Understanding Bourdieu* (Crow's Nest, 2002), p. 71.
10 André-Jean Tudesq, *Les Grands Notables en France (1840–1849)* (1964) trans. in Peter McPhee, *A Social History of France 1789–1914* 2 ed. (New York, 2004), p. 109.
11 Among the criticisms made of Bourdieu's early work was that it paid limited attention to gender and this is a matter he sought to address in later studies. Pierre Bourdieu, *Masculine Domination*, trans. Richard Nice (Cambridge, 2001); Pierre Bourdieu, 'Symbolic Violence' in Roger Célestin, Éliane DalMolin, and Isabelle de Courtivron (eds), *Beyond French Feminisms: Debates on Women, Politics, and Culture in France, 1981–2001* (New York, 2003), pp. 23–6.

12 The term 'active symbiosis' was coined by Joseph Schumpeter. Arno J. Mayer, *The Persistence of the Old Regime: Europe to the Great War* (New York, 1981), pp. 11–12. For responses to Mayer see, for example, Seymour Becker, *Nobility and Privilege in Late Imperial Russia* (Dekalb, 1985), pp. 3–7; Anthony L. Cardoza, *Aristocrats in Bourgeois Italy: The Piedemontese Nobility, 1861–1930* (Cambridge, 1997), pp. 1–12; Jesus Cruz, *Gentlemen, Bourgeois and Revolutionaries: Political Change and Cultural Persistence among the Spanish Dominant Groups 1750–1850* (Cambridge, 1996), pp. 3–15, 172.

13 To compare views and for the numbers and density of nobles, see M. L. Bush, *Rich Noble, Poor Noble* (Manchester, 1988), pp. 6, 7–29, 174; Jonathan Dewald, *The European Nobility, 1400–1800* (Cambridge, 1996), pp. xvi, 22–7; H. M. Scott (ed.), *The European Nobilities in the Seventeenth and Eighteenth Centuries* 2 vols (London, 1995).

14 Jaroslaw Dumanowski, 'La Famille, le lignage, la parenté – questions autour de la noblesse' in Jaroslaw Dumanowski and Michel Figeac (eds), *Noblesse française et noblesse polonaise. Mémoire, identité, culture XVI–XXe siècles* (Pessac, 2006), pp. 613–18; Josette Pontet, Michel Figeac, and Marie Boisson (eds), *La Noblesse de la fin du XVIe au début du XXe siècle: un modèle social?* 2 vols (Anglet, 2002). On gender and kinship see for example Linda E. Mitchell, *Portraits of Medieval Women: Family, Marriage and Politics in England 1225–1350* (New York, 2003); Amy Livingstone, *Out of Love for My Kin: Aristocratic Family Life in the Lands of the Loire, 1000–1200* (Ithaca, 2010).

15 Caroline Castiglione, 'Accounting for affection: battles between aristocratic mothers and sons in eighteenth-century Rome', *Journal of Family History* 25 (2000), 39.

16 Megan Doolittle, 'Close relations? Bringing together gender and family in English history', *Gender and History* 11 (1999), 543. See also Louise A. Tilly, 'Women's history and family history: fruitful collaboration or missed connection?', *Journal of Family History* 12 (1987), 303–15.

17 Suzanne Desan, *The Family on Trial in Revolutionary France* (Berkeley, 2004); Julie Hardwick, *The Practice of Patriarchy: Gender and the Politics of Household Authority in Early Modern France* (University Park, 1998); Suzanne Desan and Jeffrey Merrick (eds), *Family, Gender, and Law in Early Modern France* (University Park, 2009). John Tosh's superb work set a benchmark for exploration of the emotive territory of fatherhood: *A Man's Place: Masculinity and the Middle-Class Home in Victorian England* (New Haven, 1999). See also Barbara Hobson (ed.), *Making Men into Fathers: Men, Masculinities and the Social Politics of Fatherhood* (Cambridge, 2002).

18 My approach to the study of politics follows Siân Reynolds, *France Between the Wars: Gender and Politics* (London, 1996), p. 156; Desan, *The Family on Trial*, pp. 11–12.

19 Philippe Ariès, *L'Enfant et la vie familial sous l'ancien régime* (Paris, 1960); Edward Shorter, *The Making of the Modern Family* (New York, 1975); Law-

rence Stone, *The Family, Sex, and Marriage in England,* 1500–1800 (New York, 1977). For overviews and critical responses see Patrick H. Hutton, *Philippe Ariès and the Politics of French Cultural History* (Amherst, 2004), ch. 6; Steven Ozment, *Ancestors: The Loving Family in Old Europe* (Cambridge, 2001).

20 Leonore Davidoff, Megan Doolittle, Janet Fink, and Katherine Holden, *The Family Story: Blood, Contract and Intimacy 1830–1960* (London, 1999), p. 31.

21 Davidoff, et al., *The Family Story*, p. 18. For the significance of class compare Peter Gay, *The Bourgeois Experience* 2 vols (Oxford, 1984, 1986); Martine Segalen, *Love and Power in the Peasant Family: Rural France in the Nineteenth Century*, trans. Sarah Matthews (Oxford, 1983); Margaret H. Darrow, 'French noblewomen and the new domesticity, 1750–1850', *Feminist Studies* 5 (1979), 41–65. On approaches and themes see the introduction to Desan and Merrick, *Family, Gender, and Law*, pp. xi–xxvi; David I. Kertzer and Marzio Barbagli (eds), *The History of the European Family* 3 vols (New Haven, 2002).

22 See the apology to readers in David Cannadine, *The Decline and Fall of the British Aristocracy* (London, 2005), p. 7.

23 Steven Ozment, *Flesh and Spirit: Private Life in Early Modern Germany* (New York, 2001), pp. x–xi.

24 Georg Steinhausen quoted in Ozment, *Ancestors*, p. 106. See also Barbara Rosenwein, 'Worrying about emotions in history', *American Historical Review* 107 (2002), 921–45; Barbara Rosenwein, *Emotional Communities in the Early Middle Ages* (Ithaca, 2006); Susan J. Matt, 'Current emotion research in history: or, doing history from the inside out', *Emotion Review* 3 (2011), 117–24.

25 André-Jean Tudesq, *Les Grands Notables en France (1840–1849). Étude historique d'une psychologie sociale* vol. 1 (Paris, 1964), p. 15.

26 The conditions for reading the *archives privées* in the Archives nationales are in most cases the same as for other series, but researchers are not allowed to photograph or photocopy the documents. Similar restrictions apply to some *fonds* in departmental archives, particularly those that require permission to access. This meant that documents had to be transcribed onsite, requiring a greater investment of time spent in the archives.

27 On nobles in Paris see Mathieu Marraud, *La Noblesse de Paris au XVIIIe siècle* (Paris, 2000); Anne Martin-Fugier, *La Vie élégante ou la formation du Tout-Paris 1815–1848* (Paris, 1990). Regional studies include Claude-Isabelle Brelot, *La Noblesse réinventée: les nobles de Franche-Comté de 1814 à 1870* 2 vols (Paris, 1992); Jean-Marie Wiscart, *La Noblesse de la Somme au dix-neuvième siècle* (Amiens, 1994). Claude-Isabelle Brelot provides a useful survey of different approaches to the study of nobles in 'Où en est l'histoire des noblesses' *Bulletin Centre Pierre Léon* 4 (1995), 3–12.

28 Social science scholars were among the first to open up new paths of investigation on French nobles' habitation: Michel Pinçon and Monique Pinçon-Charlot, *Dans les beaux quartiers* (Paris, 1989); Monique de Saint-Martin, *L'Espace de la noblesse* (Paris, 1993); Claude-Isabelle Brelot (ed.), *Noblesses et*

villes (1780–1950) Actes du colloque de Tours 17–19 mars 1994 (Tours, 1995). On European nobilities and the urban-rural binary, see Bush, *Rich Noble, Poor Noble*, ch. 6.

29 The marquis de Vogüé argued for the significance of these archives in 'Discours sur l'importance des archives de famille', *Annuaire-bulletin de la Société d'Histoire de France* 28 (1891), 89–105. Works produced since the 1990s include Françoise Hildesheimer, *Les Archives privées. Le traitement des archives personnelles, familiales, associatives* (Paris, 1990); René Favier (ed.), *Archives familiales et noblesse provinciale: Hommage à Yves Soulingeas* (Grenoble, 2006); Christine Nougaret and Pascal Even (eds), *Les Archives privées: manuel pratique et juridique* (Paris, 2008). Importantly, there is now an Association Française pour la Protection des Archives Privées. See Odon de Quinsonas-Oudinot, 'Aux côtés des services publics, l'action associative', *La Gazette des Archives* 201 (2005), 26–31.

30 Suzanne d'Huart, Chantal de Tourtier-Bonazzi and Claire Sibille, *État sommaire des fonds d'archives privées. Séries AP (1 à 629 AP) et AB XIX* (Paris, 2004), p. 3. On modes of entry, see Jean Favier (ed.) assisté de Danièle Neirinck, *La Pratique archivistique française* (Paris, 2008), pp. 76–9; Jean Sablou, 'Les Archives privées dans les Archives départementales', *La Gazette des Archives* 85 (1974), 89–103; Suzanne d'Huart, 'Les Archives privées aux Archives Nationales', *La Gazette des Archives* 85 (1974), 79–88.

31 Jean-Philippe Gérard, *Répertoire des ressources généalogiques et héraldiques du Départment des Manuscrits de la Bibliothèque Nationale de France* (Versailles, 2003), p. 38; Sophie Coeuré and Vincent Duclert, *Les Archives* (Paris, 2001), p. 17.

32 Michel Duchein, 'Requiem pour trois lois défuntes', *La Gazette des Archives* 104 (1979), 12–16; Pierre Santoni, 'Archives et violence: à propos de la loi du 7 messidor an II', *La Gazette des Archives* 146–7 (1989), 199–214.

33 Henri Bordier, *Les Archives de la France* (Geneva, 1978), p. 356.

34 Favier, *La Pratique archivistique*, pp. 70–9; Chantal de Tourtier-Bonazzi, 'La loi du 3 janvier 1979 et les archives privées', *La Gazette des Archives* 107 (1979), 261–70.

35 On archival practices pertaining to *fonds* see Françoise Hildesheimer, *Les Archives, pourquoi? comment?* (Paris, 1984), pp. 23–37, 119–20.

1

Nobility, titles, and genealogy

When does a family begin? That's the first question to ask.[1]

In his book *Papiers de famille*, René de La Croix de Castries, born in 1908, offers a nobleman's insights into the compulsion to trace one's family roots. As he explains, the question of when a family begins has long held particular resonance for the nobility in France. Genealogical research on aristocratic families traditionally served the purpose of establishing the origins and legitimacy of noble titles. In 1666 Louis XIV instigated the *grandes recherches de noblesse* in order to separate anyone who had usurped noble status from the ranks of genuine nobility. Thirty years later, following an edict of 1696, Charles René d'Hozier was employed to collect the armorial bearings of nobles, towns, communities, and provinces of the kingdom for the purposes of taxation. Persons who professed noble status were required by the edict to register their armorial bearings for a fee of twenty *livres*. Hozier confronted a mammoth task in establishing the *Armorial général de France*, which consists of thirty-four volumes of text and thirty-five volumes of coloured armorial bearings preserved in the Bibliothèque nationale de France. No doubt the compiler was keenly aware of the deficiencies of the work and perhaps annoyed at those individuals who were too vain, poor, or recalcitrant to register. Hozier's credentials as a genealogist of the French aristocracy, a profession inherited from his father Pierre, meant he understood better than most people the intricate web of social and blood ties that lay behind some 110,000 registered armorial bearings, of which perhaps 20,000 belonged to nobles.

To facilitate work on the *Armorial*, Charles René d'Hozier developed the principle at the end of the seventeenth century that 'proof' of nobility lay in documents such as wills and deeds that showed a person had six generations of noble ancestors. That meant, as a rule of thumb, being able to identify a noble ancestor living in 1400. The year 1400 was a fairly arbitrary marker and over the course of the eighteenth and nineteenth centuries it came to appear less meaningful as a determining date. This was partly because the proportion of the French aristocracy who could actually furnish a document identifying a noble ancestor living in 1400 was growing smaller. Many 'new' titles were conferred before 1789 by kings of France, and also by Napoleon I during the First Empire. It was the Emperor himself who in 1808 reintroduced titles to France, for the legal status of nobility had been abolished by decree on 19 June 1790 during the French Revolution.

In France nobility was understood to be a personal *quality* inherited or acquired in specific ways: by birth, by office, or by letters. This was different from the situation in England, for example, where one could become aristocratic only by appointment to the House of Peers.[2] When the French Revolution broke out in 1789 it is estimated that there were between 17,000 and 26,000 noble families in France. The number of noble individuals is thought to have been between 110,000 and 120,000. Ennoblement by office (*l'anoblissement par charge*) was the most common route into the nobility; in the eighteenth century alone some 5,500 individuals were ennobled by office compared with around a thousand individuals ennobled by letters (*l'anoblissement par lettres*). There also exists a separate category of nobility, said to be of 'extraction', whose noble origins date from 'time immemorial'.[3] René de La Croix de Castries, writing in the early 1970s, observed that this latter type of nobility carries a tantalising air of mystery, which he illustrates by citing the case of his own family. 'Whilst the first great ancestor, Guillaume de la Croix, born around 1430, is perfectly identified and there are abundant documents concerning him, one is less sure about [the noble status of] his ancestors.'[4]

The question, then, of when a family begins quickly leads to a second related question: with whom does a family begin? For a member of the French aristocracy, the answer is, virtually without exception, a person of the male sex. 'He is identified by indisputable documents; he becomes the head of a line.'[5] Generally speaking in France nobility could be transmitted only through the father. Transmission of nobility by the mother (*la noblesse utérine*) was very restricted. It was permitted in some regions of eastern France, notably in Champagne and in Brie at least until the sixteenth century, and there were special cases where authorisation from the king was required. An edict of Charles V in 1370 suppressed *la noblesse utérine* by imposing a fee (*le droit de franc fief*) on nobles born of a commoner father and a noble mother for the purchase of real estate. This edict, together with the Salic law excluding women from the throne, effectively meant that the transmission of nobility was kept to the male bloodline.[6]

Before the French Revolution nobility was a significant legal concept, not least because of the rights and privileges attached to it including exemption from some forms of taxation. This helps to explain why since the decree of 19 June 1790 nobility has not been re-created in French law. The titles established by Napoleon were technically speaking 'nobiliary' and the word 'nobility' is not used anywhere in the legal texts of the Napoleonic decrees. Subsequent political rulers opted for or against the legal recognition of titles. They were recognised under the Bourbon Restoration in 1814, abolished under the Second Republic in 1848, recognised again under the Second Empire in 1852, and ceased to be conferred following a decision made in 1875 by the President of the Third Republic. The status of titles, then, was subject to constant evolution through the nineteenth century. By contrast, from the French Revolution to the present day, French courts have consistently maintained that the legal concept of nobility is incompatible with the principle of the equality of all citizens before the law set down in the 1789 Declaration of the Rights of Man and Citizen.

Society has made this revolutionary principle incompatible with social convention. Since the nineteenth century people have used the collective term *la noblesse d'Empire* when referring to the group of individuals who received titles from Napoleon I via letters patent. Similarly, the collective term *l'ancienne noblesse* has continued to be applied to those whose aristocratic lineage predates the French Revolution. In this way the social construct of nobility has far outlasted the legal concept. So too, the implicit and explicit hierarchical relationships which derive from it have proved very durable. Historically it has been in nobles' interests to perpetuate and to defend the hierarchical ordering of society. Nobles have also been conscious of social gradations within their own class.[7]

In France one had to be noble to bear a title but most nobles were in fact untitled (*la noblesse simple*). There was no relationship between the bearing of a title and the antiquity of the lineage. Until the early nineteenth century a title of nobility was simply a rank attached to certain pieces of land. When Louis XVIII assumed the throne under the Bourbon Restoration (1814–30) it became possible also to acquire a hereditary title that was not attached to any land but was purely an appendage of the family name. Protection of the rights to a title in France was and remains a matter for the civil courts; in theory, titles are subject to the same legal protection against usurpation as the family name. Verification of the rights to a title, on the other hand, was and remains a matter for a branch of the executive. This is because titles have resulted from the exercise of the sovereign's will and so questions arising over the meaning and intent of sovereign acts need to be resolved either by the sovereign or by his modern equivalent.[8] Across the nineteenth century successive bureaucratic bodies were put in charge of verifying rights to noble titles. In 1808 Napoleon I set up a Conseil du Sceau des Titres. Louis XVIII replaced this body with a Commission du Sceau in 1814, which was abolished in 1830 and its decision-making powers transferred to the Ministère de la Justice. Napoleon III recreated the Conseil du Sceau under the Second Empire but this was again abolished in 1872 when its offices and functions were transferred back to the Ministère de la Justice where they have remained.

Most noble titles, including some very old and illustrious ones, were conferred in recognition of services performed, on the battlefield or in state affairs, and 'proof' of their legitimacy lies in letters patent or imperial decree. For an individual to have his right to a noble title verified in the Third Republic, he had to present the documents proving its creation to the appropriate office within the Ministère de la Justice, along with identity documents such as birth certificates to show that he had the right to bear the title according to the rules of transmission. Until 1947 the office that received the documents was the Bureau du Sceau de France and the ministerial officials with responsibility for claims to titles were known as *référendaires au Sceau*. The Bureau then prepared a report for a board, which transmitted its opinion to the minister, who, if the verification was successful, issued a resolution (*un arrêté*) that authorised the inscription of the individual on the Registre du Sceau. Once this was done the individual could have the title inserted on any legal document such as a passport or an identity card. The *arrêté* was valid solely for that person so the procedure had to be repeated in the next generation for the individual's heir. There were some technical and terminology differences that applied in the case of a foreign title (*un titre étranger*). By decree of 5 March 1859 a foreign title held by a French citizen was deemed to be not transmissible and 'authorisation' of a foreign title was granted only in very exceptional cases. Yet a French citizen could apply for 'recognition' of a foreign title, for which the procedure was the same as for the 'verification' of a French title.[9]

Why invest the time, money and energy to go through such a bureaucratic process? To what extent did nobles consider it important, a century after the legal status of nobility had been abolished, to prove their rights to bear a noble title? Were there additional hurdles to establishing the legitimacy of any particular title, for instance, a papal honour, in republican France governed according to secular, democratic principles? These types of questions cannot be answered, of course, by reconstructing or examining family trees. Nevertheless, the answers are connected with aristocratic genealogies and, as we shall see, knowledge about those genealogies was valuable not only to nobles but also to a range of non-noble professionals in turn-of-the-century France such as editors, journalists and lawyers. To understand the significance of that knowledge, and the variety of ways in which it was applied, we need to consider how titles were regarded within the political and social context of the Third Republic.

Between 1870 and 1875 there was great uncertainty in France over whether a monarchy would be restored or a republican regime installed definitively. In February 1875 the proposal for a constitutional law to establish the Third Republic received a majority vote. Three months later, on 10 May 1875, President MacMahon is reported to have declared that titles would no longer be conferred. He did not go so far as to abolish them as had been done on 29 February 1848, just one day after the Second Republic was proclaimed. The Emperor Napoleon III's decree of 24 January 1852, re-establishing titles under the Second Empire, was never overturned. But President MacMahon's 1875 decision on titles was not made public in the manner one might expect it to have been. It was not published and, despite the efforts of researchers and archivists to trace the text of the decision, it has never been located in the archives of the Ministère de l'Intérieur, or in the archives of the Elysée, or in the archives of the Chancellery.[10] MacMahon was a duc, like a number of other leading politicians of his day, so the phrase 'The Republic of the Dukes' is often used to describe the regime under his presidency. He and his advisers were very aware of the social capital that a noble title represented in the world of European diplomacy. France in 1875 firmed up its constitutional status as a republic, but its European neighbours were monarchic or imperial states with continuing traditions of court ceremony. To receive and be received with dignity and respect mattered in the diplomatic profession, which is why the rules governing the use of titles on official correspondence and at receptions were so complicated and so precise. After MacMahon's presidency there were some unsuccessful attempts to get rid of titles altogether. In 1882 Beauquier, deputy for Doubs, put forward proposals to abolish titles and to amend Article 259 of the Penal Code which declared the usurpation of titles illegal. Neither of these proposals was followed through. Then in 1905 the French government legislated for the Separation of Church and State, thus bringing to an end the Concordat with the Roman Catholic papacy established by Napoleon I. This was a major sign that the republican regime was on a firmer footing than it had been in the 1870s. The following year, on 14 December 1906, the government decreed that it would neither create new titles nor authorise the bearing of foreign titles, including honorific titles granted by the pope.

One of the paradoxes of these developments with regard to titles was that signs of nobility were keenly sought after in French society. This was not a new phenomenon, for practices such as buying a château, adding the particle *de* to one's name, and mimicking aristocratic habits had been going on for centuries among the upper middle class.[11] Even after President MacMahon's 1875 decision there continued to be a great many non-aristocratic individuals in the Republic who aspired to become or to marry a noble. Among the wealthier bourgeoisie, particularly, the ambition to cultivate social acquaintance with members of the nobility, usually with a view to marital alliance, reinforced certain features of class relations. It promoted curiosity about the possibility of attaining aristocratic 'distinction'. It also instilled a markedly competitive air into elite sociability, dramatised to great effect by Proust in the snobbery manifest by Madame Verdurin and her circle. During the three decades before 1914 many new annuals began to be published which were marketed as definitive guides to aristocratic high society. The differences between these works, in terms of the numbers of people listed and their social background, are indicative of the late nineteenth-century obsession with defining the membership of *le Tout-Paris*.[12]

Certainly the size of the noble population in France had declined dramatically since the late eighteenth century. In 1900 it is estimated that there were 5,033 aristocratic families. Conversely, the numbers of individuals usurping noble titles – falsely calling themselves 'comte' or 'marquis', for example – had been steadily growing, despite the fact that usurpation constituted a breach of Article 259 of the Penal Code. The number of 'false nobles' in France has been estimated at five hundred thousand by the twentieth century, although very few were ever prosecuted. Towards the end of the Third Republic nobles responded to this problem of usurpation by initiating some rearguard action to protect their families' names and titles. In 1932 the Association d'entraide de la Noblesse Française (ANF) was founded with one of its purposes being to certify, by the application of very strict rules of transmission, the noble ancestry of those on its register. This prestigious non-profit organisation was given formal government recognition as being of public utility on 29 July 1967.[13]

Aristocratic titles and genealogies, then, were not simply a matter of antiquarian interest in the France of the Third Republic. Politically and socially the question of who was or was not a noble, and who had the right to bear a title, were matters that occupied not just nobles themselves but also the president, government ministers, lawyers, and other professionals. There is humour, to be sure, in Proust's depiction of the duc de Guermantes dazzling the Narrator with his intimate knowledge of genealogical intricacies designed to pulverise any suspicion that his family was not the bluest of the 'bluebloods'. The novelist was making a serious point, however, skilfully exposing truths about class and race along with all their complex ramifications in the political and social environment he meticulously recreated in his great work. To take up that point let us examine how nobles actually negotiated the legislative hurdles and other challenges arising from titles in republican France between 1870 and 1940.

In July 1911 a man dubbed 'the last genealogist of France' died. The vicomte Albert Révérend left behind a widow, who perhaps collected some of the eulogies published in over twenty French and foreign newspapers that commended her deceased husband for his remarkable skills and dedication to his job as director of the *Annuaire de la noblesse de France*. Révérend was a leading nineteenth-century authority on French aristocratic genealogies whose books remain standard reference works today.[14] His death came as a blow to many, including a man to whom it must have seemed an especially bitter twist of fate, the prince Henri de Béarn. For just over a decade, before Révérend's untimely death, the prince and the director of the *Annuaire* had collaborated in the search for a title. Strictly speaking, it was the documents to 'prove' a title they were after for there was no doubt in either of the men's minds that Henri de Béarn was the legal inheritor of the title 'prince de Chalais'. It was just that the 'proof' was elusive.

The search commenced in 1901 when Béarn wrote to Révérend about his desire to revive the ancient title of prince de Chalais, in the interests of his blossoming diplomatic career and with a view to his eventual marriage. The princely title was linked to another form of title, 'Spanish grandee', and Béarn, who was already a French prince, wanted to have his right to be known as the prince de Chalais and Spanish grandee recognised in France. In practical terms there were two main obstacles for Béarn to achieve his desire. The first obstacle lay in the constitution of a dossier, a burdensome enough task as anyone who has had dealings with French bureaucracy will know. The second obstacle lay in the payment of a large sum of money to cover the costs of rights to the title, payable to the Spanish Treasury (40,000 pesetas); rights to the official seal (*dell Sello Real*, 800 pesetas); and charges for the work of a specialist on Spanish aristocratic genealogies, Monsieur Francisco de Béthencourt, who was to undertake the necessary translations, legal duties, and compiling of a dossier in Madrid. Informed of the need to pay a large sum of money, Béarn, who was comparatively short on available cash but not on determination, was able to make an initial outlay of 40,000 francs paid over the course of 1903. In light of the prince's willingness to 'sacrifice' such a large sum of money, Révérend, for his part, agreed to a delay in receiving full payment of his 'honorary' charges for all the work required to ensure Béarn would have the title of prince de Chalais recognised in France and with it obtain the privileges associated with being a first-class Spanish grandee.[15]

One of the most famous and unusual of those privileges was the right to remain covered in the sovereign's presence at the Spanish court, not an insignificant gesture of status for an ambitious nineteenth-century French diplomat. There was another interesting aspect to this Spanish dignity too. Whereas in France, generally, an aristocratic title could be passed down only through the male line, Spanish law authorised the descent of aristocratic titles and honours through the women of an aristocratic house (known as the 'distaff' side). This was of particular import for Béarn, who stood to inherit the Chalais title through his mother. In May 1873 Cécile de Talleyrand-Périgord married the prince Gaston de Béarn, Henri's father. She had inherited the Chalais title from her childless uncle, Élie Roger de Talleyrand-Périgord. Originally King Louis XIII had incorporated the ancient title, with several other titles, on letters patent for Daniel de Talleyrand-Périgord in 1613. To it was attached, in 1714, the first-class *grandeza* of Spain, an honour that Henri de Béarn succeeded in having conferred afresh on himself by Alfonso XIII, King of Spain, on 7 April 1904.[16]

In 1903, when Béarn agreed to pay a large sum of money to have the Chalais title and *grandeza* recognised in France, he was serving as a secretary to the French Embassy in Washington, and he was looking to marry. It was a distinctly eligible and handsome bachelor who cast his eye around Washington high society and had many an eye cast upon him in return. But was it his looks that were the cause for attention or the gossip circulating about his inherited Spanish dignities that would be shared by a future wife? As the *Washington Times* reminded readers in June 1904: 'hundreds of foreign men not half so agreeable and manly as the prince de Béarn have come to America and carried away our nicest girls, and the prince, if he came for this purpose, may yet win a wife'.[17]

In May 1905 Béarn did become engaged; his fiancée was Miss Béatrice Winans, daughter of Mr and Mrs Ross Winans of Baltimore, Maryland, and of Newport, Rhode Island. Béatrice's paternal grandfather had been responsible for the construction of the first Russian railway line (Line Nicolaï, from Petersburg to Moscow) while her mother was the great-niece of the artist James McNeill Whistler and had other relations among the landed gentry in England. Writing to Révérend on the 18 May 1905, informing him of the engagement, Béarn stated: 'it is pleasing to think that thanks to your work and to your efforts, I can today offer this young woman a great and indisputable position and I undertake to express anew our deep gratitude.'[18]

What had been Révérend's 'work and efforts' up to that point? Let us return to the subject of the dossier. Between 1901 and 1905 Révérend had kept up a steady correspondence with Béarn informing him of the progress that he and Béthencourt were making in having the Chalais title and *grandeza* recognised. Béthencourt was the director of the *Annales de la Nobleza de España* and an old friend of Révérend. Being in the same line of work, and confronting similar challenges, the pair had an agreement to perform reciprocal services for one another, which was of direct benefit to their clients. Béthencourt was not short on words in explaining to Révérend the terrible difficulties he was encountering in Madrid, dealing with the proverbial slowness of Spanish bureaucracy and getting the royal seal and all the ancillary documentation together. On receiving a telegram from the prince, concerning his engagement to Miss Winans, Béthencourt wrote in grudging humour to Révérend: 'not a letter nor a word more [from 'young Béarn']: it's not much to ask in return for all I do for him. But do please give him my congratulations.'[19]

Révérend took a rather more generous view of the prince, of whom he seemed over the years to become quite fond. His letters to Béarn, which were always courteous and friendly in tone, must have encouraged the aristocrat to expand his ambitions for stature in the world of European diplomacy. For Béarn began to make more and more demands on Révérend. In a letter dated 22 September 1903 the prince charged

Révérend with the task of constituting another dossier with a view to his admission to the Bavarian Order of Saint-George. On 15 September 1904 he added to this task his inscription in the almanach of the court of Bavaria with a view to obtaining the Cross of Saint-George. Completion of these two tasks required Révérend to make a detailed study of the prince de Béarn's sixteen *quartiers* of nobility. More instructions followed. Commencing in the autumn of 1903 Révérend undertook a number of trips to Vienna and to Gotha with the purpose of negotiating on the prince's behalf inscription of the Chalais title in the *Almanach de Gotha*. Then, on 18 August 1904, Béarn charged Révérend with the task of inscription in the *Almanach de la Guya*, the insertion of a notice in Béthencourt's *Annales de la Nobleza de España*, and an examination of the question of family arms relating to the Spanish titles of Viena and Cantabrie. In his letter of 15 September 1904, Béarn asked Révérend to undertake negotiations and to furnish the necessary justifications for obtaining the Order of Malta on his behalf. As the prince's wedding date approached, in the spring of 1905, Révérend was given the responsibility of communicating the news to the press, to ensure up-to-date information was published regarding the groom's various dignities and honours, not all of which had been conclusively established. Révérend also had to get those dignities and honours registered on the prince's personal identity documentation.[20]

It was the Chalais title that proved most tricksy. In June 1906 the Ministère des Affaires Étrangères opposed the use of this title on official certificates. This was just six months before the government ruling of 14 December that it would no longer create new titles or authorise foreign titles. A French nobleman trying to confirm that he was a Spanish prince was bound to run into difficulties. Since Béarn wanted the Chalais title to appear, alongside other Spanish titles, on the birth certificate of his daughter, the first of two children he had with Béatrice, the minister demanded by letter of 4 February 1907 that appropriate justifications be provided. The case for recognition of the Chalais title in France was to occupy Révérend for the next three years. In that time he made numerous interventions at the French Chancellery, performed research in at least four departmental archives in southwest France, made several business trips to Madrid, corresponded with numerous officials in France and in Spain, ensured erroneous notices in the *Annuaire diplomatique* were corrected, and kept Béarn up to date with all his activities and progress by letter.

With unfailing politeness, Révérend did from time to time, and especially in the spring of 1907, gently remind Béarn that he was awaiting payment of 'honorary' fees. Révérend had agreed to keep those fees to a minimum because of the large sum payable to the Spanish Treasury for title rights. Béarn, in his letters through the autumn of 1906, wrote of experiencing huge losses and financial difficulties, asking for extra time before paying Révérend for his work. Money was sent through sporadically and this was quickly absorbed in travel and accommodation expenses incurred by Révérend as he moved about from archive to archive. The researcher occasionally suffered influenza and he was not a young man, as he reminded the prince by letter on 10 January 1907: 'I am old and you are just entering into life; I was very happy given my memories of your father to help you with my advice and to facilitate at minimum expense the regularisation of your titles ... I remain devoted to the historical work that I have begun for you.'[21]

Révérend went further in explaining his concern for posterity in a letter dated 8 February 1909. In it he laid the blame for various problems he encountered squarely on previous generations of nobles whose 'fatal negligence' in not regularising titles did nothing to assure their security for successors. Perhaps Révérend's professional forerunner, Charles René d'Hozier, would have agreed, given his experience of compiling the *Armorial général de France* in the late seventeenth century. The refusal of some nobles back then to pay twenty *livres* for the registration of their armorial bearings offers a clue to the aristocratic *mentalité* that considered a title of nobility an inheritable and inalienable 'right', not something you paid for. The prince de Béarn may have personally liked the vicomte Révérend, and judging by the two men's letters they got along well, but they were not social equals. They both knew, too well, that the prince's illustrious noble ancestry stretched back to the personage of Centule, sovereign of Béarn in 819, and that this bloodline was linked to that of the ancient Gascony house of Galard by virtue of François de Galard's marriage to Jeanne de Béarn on 12 November 1508. It was this marriage that had prevented the surname Béarn from becoming extinct in the sixteenth century. Descendants of François and Jeanne took the full surname Galard de Brassac de Béarn to which was added, in future generations, the Spanish title of the prince de Viana, held by the prince Gaston de Béarn. Henri, the aspiring young French diplomat married to a rich American woman, was as 'blue-blooded' an aristocrat as it was possible to be.

What separated Révérend from Hozier was a span of three centuries during which revolutions had taken place that brought fundamental changes to political and social life in France. In the first decade of the twentieth century, when France was into its third republican regime, Révérend pointed a finger at another group of people causing problems for him in regularising the prince's titles. 'It is certain,' he wrote to Béarn on 8 February 1909, 'that in the Department of Protocol the pen-stroke of the spiteful and vindictive bourgeois, who has not dared to cross the path of pseudo nobility, is as tactless as possible in its form and is not made for raising [the French chancellery bureaucrats] in the eyes of other [European] chancelleries.'[22] France, one of the few European countries not ruled by a monarch in the years preceding the outbreak of the first World War, was a very different place from the France of Louis XIV.

Révérend's persistence in research, despite bouts of illness and troubles in obtaining money from Béarn, eventually paid off. Early in the summer of 1910, as the result of repeat trips to Madrid, Révérend found a vital document that he knew was the key to success in concluding the 'Affaire de Chalais'. The document was the royal ordinance of 1722, relating to the title of the prince de Chalais and to its devolution through the female line, which had been preserved in the archives of the Parlement de Bordeaux. On receiving the news in Peking, where he had been sent on diplomatic posting, Béarn replied joyfully to Révérend:

> Bravo! For your magnificent success. After so many years of struggle, of efforts and of research, to find at last the extraordinary document that proves definitively the thesis you have always supported must have been for you a veritable satisfaction. It is tremendous news for me, because thanks to you I will arrive at establishing in an indisputable manner my family titles and give to my son a brilliant and incontestable position. Your trip to Madrid has provided more than we hoped for since the recognition of the title in Spain alone would not have had the value of the ordinance that you have so happily discovered. We could not have wished for more if we had written this act ourselves. Everything is contained in it: the recognition of the title, the link to the *grandeza*, the extraordinary exception made for the transmissible female grandees [*les grandesses*] specially consecrated to Chalais. One wonders, what admirable concern for the future animated the writer of this ordinance? It is simply incredible and I really don't see how the Bureau du Sceau can oppose us. I am infinitely grateful for all the trouble to which you have gone to arrive at this result that definitively establishes my rights, and I ask you to accept, as a testimony of my gratitude, a diamond worth 10,000 francs to go with the sum that I sent you in November 1908.[23]

Correspondence between Béarn and Révérend appears to have ended five months later in November 1910. The exhausting research trips to

NOBILITY, TITLES, AND GENEALOGY   27

Madrid, and bad seasonal conditions there, had compromised the old man's health. After a few months of sickness he died in July 1911, exactly one year after discovering the royal ordinance of 1722. Révérend's physical decline and death prevented him from definitively concluding the Affaire de Chalais and from receiving full financial remuneration for a decade of difficult and painstaking work. He seems not to have accepted the diamond worth 10,000 francs, perhaps out of embarrassment at the offer of so valuable a gift.

In 1911 the widow Révérend (née Bru) made a formal request for 25,000 francs payment from the prince for the honorary charges owing to her husband on his death. In her eyes this sum, which was certainly modest for the work undertaken, constituted a 'debt of honour'. She had, as she informed Béarn, read the congratulatory letter he addressed to her husband on 4 July 1910. 'You [prince] well knew how much the vicomte Révérend travelled over the years to locate your titles. How much money he spent. How much trouble he brought on himself in order to bring you satisfaction.' All the paperwork relating to the Chalais title, she assured him, was at the Bureau du Sceau awaiting the minister's signature.[24]

When the elderly woman died, on 18 March 1923, the debt of 25,000 francs had still not been paid, largely because some very important documents Béarn believed to be in her possession had not yet been recovered by him. They included a decree on parchment with the Royal Seal of Her Majesty the Queen Isabella of Spain dated 7 July 1868; the personal seal on letters patent of His Majesty Alfonso XIII dated 7 April 1904; copies of a decree issued on 23 December 1717 by His Majesty Philippe V; a copy of the royal ordinance of 1722 ruling the devolution of the grandee title; an extract of a royal ordinance of 26 December 1818; a study of Béarn's sixteen *quartiers* of nobility; and a receipt for 40,000 pesetas paid to the Spanish Treasury.

Madame Révérend seems to have tried to deliver these documents in person, two years after her husband's death, by visiting the prince's home in Paris on 15 May 1913. Béarn, in a letter sent the following day, expressed his regret at not being there to receive her, explaining that at the present time, in a climate of acute international tension, he was obliged to work very long days at the Ministère des Affaires Étrangères, returning home late in the evening for dinner. 'My *maître d'hôtel* told me that you are leaving soon for the countryside and that you will not return to Paris until the autumn. I therefore ask if you would be so obliging as to send me the documents that are part of my family archives . . . I would like to try to complete, whilst there is still time, the work that Monsieur the vicomte Révérend was not able to finish, and for this I will need those documents.'[25]

Béarn never did complete Révérend's work. In August 1923 the Affaire de Chalais passed into the hands of lawyers. Monsieur Mottet, acting for the widow Révérend's successor, drew up an account of the whole business that was passed to the prince. Highly disgruntled by the 'inaccuracies' of this account, Béarn wrote to his lawyer Léopold Moreau to set the story straight, claiming, amongst other things, that the motive for one of Révérend's trips to Madrid, in March 1905, had been personal rather than connected with his research for the Chalais title. He also stated that the widow Révérend had asked him for money as a form of charity, given her precarious situation, and that he had shown himself willing to come to her aid in memory of her husband, on condition that, in return, he would obtain the important documents loaned to Révérend. The case went to a tribunal and was settled in June 1926 through the expert mediation of a judiciary administrator, Monsieur Louis David. The prince came into the possession of all the documents belonging to his family archive, including a large quantity of original birth and marriage certificates, and paid, in addition to his legal expenses, 2,000 francs to end the 'transaction' definitively.[26]

Without doubt there is something exceptional about the search for 'proof' of the Chalais title conducted on behalf of the prince Henri de Béarn, by 'the last genealogist of France'. The lawyers, to whom the Affaire de Chalais devolved, observed that the vicomte Albert Révérend 'appears more like an artist preoccupied by his art than by pecuniary satisfaction'. Dozens of eulogies published after the researcher's death testified to Révérend's 'notoriety, erudition and talent'.[27] Béarn must have known that the vicomte Révérend was the sole person capable of conducting, and willing to conduct, research of this kind with scrupulous honesty, tact, and professionalism. They were both driven men, ambitious in different ways. Both knew that the title of first-class Spanish *grandeza*, and its associated privileges, were held by only a handful of 'blue-blooded' French noblemen at the turn of the century.[28]

There was an element of bad luck in the timing of Révérend's research and dealings with the French bureaucracy, coinciding as they did with the republican government taking a harder line on foreign titles. Between 1830 and 1877 there had been thirty-three cases in which foreign titles were authorised. In the twentieth century there was only one:

President Charles de Gaulle in 1961 authorised the Spanish title of duc de San Fernando Luis held by the marquis de Lévis-Mirepoix, who was then president of the Association d'entraide de la Noblesse Française.[29] Although Béarn was merely seeking recognition of his rights to the Chalais title, the changing legislation, combined with the likelihood of confusion over subtle distinctions in terminology within nobiliary law, did not make the encounter with bureaucracy any easier. At least as a French citizen Béarn did not face the same dilemma that confronted nobles of other nationalities living in France. After the decree of 14 December 1906 any foreign-born noble who wished to be naturalised lost the right to bear their *titre étranger*. Some chose to forfeit French citizenship, and retain their title, which they could do with letters patent.[30]

Was the mentality that prompted Béarn's initial approach to Révérend exceptional for the time? Did other nobles in the France of the Third Republic share the prince's dogmatic mindset in relation to inherited and inalienable titles? To examine the evidence let us first go back to 1890, the year in which Henri's father, the prince Gaston de Béarn, corresponded with Émile Éhret about the inscription of the Chalais title in an edition of *La Société et le High-Life* which Éhret was then compiling.

On 12 January 1890 Gaston de Béarn wrote to Éhret explaining that for the years 1884 to 1887 inclusive the duc de Talleyrand had wrongly had the title of prince de Chalais included in his *Almanach de Gotha* notice. 'I protested,' he told Éhret 'and my reclamation was recognised ... The princesse de Béarn [née Talleyrand-Périgord, Henri's mother] in 1888 and subsequent years was in full possession of her rights ... the title of the princesse de Chalais belonged to her alone.' The prince had another objection: 'I cannot allow you to give Mssrs. Hély and Boson de Talleyrand-Périgord, sons of the prince de Sagan, the titles of comtes Hély and Boson de Périgord ... The comte de Périgord, my father-in-law, always carried this name alone and had the sole right to this title.'[31] Alerted to the situation, the prince de Sagan wrote to the prince de Béarn, via Éhret, to state his view and that of his nearest relatives:

> Monsieur, I communicated to my father the problems concerning our families about which you wrote to me. He believes there is nothing more to say ... My father desires to see neither his name nor that of the

duchesse de Talleyrand appear in a publication where names that belong to him as *chef de famille* are attributed to persons who have no right to them. His sister, the widowed marquise de Castellane, [and] his nephews and niece, the marquise de Castellane, the duc de Montmorency, the comte Louis de Périgord, hold the same view. Needless to say I share the same desire in respect to myself and to my two sons, the comtes Hély and Boson de Périgord.[32]

Having transmitted this letter from prince to prince, Éhret's hands were tied. As he explained to Béarn on 15 January, no contested titles (i.e. the prince de Chalais) could be included in *La Société et le High-Life*. 'It has been necessary to impose an absolute rule on this because unfortunately I have encountered a certain number of difficulties similar to your own.'[33] Béarn's reaction was to demand complete suppression of the notice Éhret had prepared on him and his wife, a demand to which Éhret regretfully acceded. The 1891 edition of *La Société et le High-Life*, like d'Hozier's *Armorial*, would remain incomplete.[34]

In comparison with the families of the French *ancienne noblesse*, how important was it to the *noblesse d'Empire* to ensure accuracy in the attribution of titles and honours? Did those who owed their titles to a Corsican who descended from Italian nobles and who became France's first Emperor also engage in aristocratic male posturing on the level of a Béarn or Sagan?

On 31 July 1907 the prince Roland Bonaparte jotted down some notes about an exchange he had had in 1882 with Monsieur Borel d'Hauterive, then director of the *Annuaire de la noblesse de France* and the vicomte Albert Révérend's predecessor. Following Borel d'Hauterive's death, Révérend took over editorial duties and he modified the text agreed by the former director and the prince Roland Bonaparte for the 1905 issue of the *Annuaire*. In respect to the family branch headed by Lucien, who was Roland's grandfather, Révérend inserted a statement 'qualification of Highness by imperial statute of 2 June 1815'. Roland seems to have been perplexed by this for in scribbling his note he mused: 'What is this imperial statute of 2 June 1815? I only know for this date the decree naming members of the Chamber of Peers.'[35] As a descendant of Lucien Bonaparte, the prince Roland was sensitive to any statement regarding the qualification of Highness because Napoleon III had challenged his relatives' right to it under the Second Empire. Family disagreement over the title stemmed from the complicated history of Napoleon I's succession, which had long been a thorny issue among the Bonapartes.

When he was proclaimed Emperor in 1804 Napoleon I looked to two of his brothers, Joseph and Louis, to assure his succession, ignoring the other two, Lucien and Jérôme, with whom he had fallen out. The rules on inheritance of the imperial dignity were set out in a law of 18 May 1804. This law then formed the basis of a referendum on the question of heredity in which only the direct, natural, legitimate and adoptive lines of Napoleon, Joseph, and Louis were mentioned as eligible for the rule of the Empire. A decree issued on 30 March 1806 defined the status of the imperial family and set down many rules on the behaviour of family members particularly with regard to marriage. During the same year, Jérôme agreed to end his first marriage to Élisabeth Patterson and returned to France from America, with Napoleon's blessing, whereupon he remarried. Lucien, meanwhile, became reconciled with the Emperor only in 1814 when he helped to prepare Napoleon's return from Elba. Subsequently he was reintegrated into the imperial family, given the title 'His Imperial Highness the prince Lucien Bonaparte', and on 2 June 1815 entered the Chamber of Peers. Following the Battle of Waterloo, and Napoleon's abdication, all members of the Bonaparte family were exiled and prevented from holding imperial titles. Most took pseudonyms, but Lucien bore the Roman title of the prince de Canino that had been conferred on him by the pope on 18 August 1814. In 1852 when the Second Empire was established, Napoleon III decreed that the male issue of Jérôme and his second wife the princesse Catherine de Wurtemberg would constitute the line of succession. Three years later, in September 1855, the Emperor set out the terms of an eleven-article decision. It stipulated that Napoleon I's nephews and nephews' eldest sons had the right to bear the title of prince with the honorific Highness, but the nephews' younger sons had the right only to the title of prince. Napoleon III's decision effectively 'separated' the Bonapartes back into two groups, an 'imperial' family and a 'civil' family, and was interpreted by Lucien's descendants as interfering arbitrarily with the rights to the hereditary title of 'His Imperial Highness'. Pierre, one of Lucien's sons by his second marriage, protested against Napoleon III's decision, and so did Pierre's son Roland.[36]

In the France of the Third Republic people connected with the Bonapartes kept a close eye on the ways in which the family was represented in official publications, such as annuals, and by the press. On 5 July 1907 the prince Roland's secretary had written to the director of the *Almanach de Gotha*, acknowledging receipt of proofs for the Bonaparte notice, listing the corrections the prince wished to see implemented, and requesting a revised set of proofs before publication. One of the chief desired amendments concerned the way in which the Bonaparte family was represented in the pages of the annual. 'It would be preferable not to separate the [elder and younger] branches of the family [but rather] to put both in the first part [of the annual] as was done in your editions published under the Second Empire.'[37] Since the director persisted in separating the two branches, further letters were sent. In 1922 the director was instructed to make the correction or to remove from the *Almanach de Gotha* all information on the branch represented by His Imperial Highness the prince Roland Bonaparte.[38]

On 18 May 1912 the *Morning Post* in London ran an article entitled 'A Delicate Position'. It described the peculiar situation occupied by the prince Roland Bonaparte as *chef de famille* and the history of male quarrelling over a hereditary title. But was it the brothers and nephews of Napoleon I with which the article was really concerned? There was talk of war, European eyes were drawn to the Balkans, and the *Morning Post*'s readership was reminded that the first Emperor's great-great-grandniece, the princesse Marie Bonaparte, was married to the prince Georges de Grèce. A French translation of the article exists in the Bonaparte archive, so it appears someone who was not a native English speaker wanted to understand the nuances.[39]

Two world wars and the associated economic crises that engulfed Europe during the first half of the twentieth century increased the potential not just for mistakes in the attribution of noble titles but also for the fraudulent use of such titles. Until 1993 Article 259 of the Penal Code declared the usurpation of titles illegal and punishable by a fine of 1,800–6,000 francs. Under the same Article it was also a breach of criminal law to modify one's family name in order to give it an honorific appearance. Offenders risked having a suit brought against them either by a public prosecutor or by the injured party. Yet cases of usurpation were hardly ever brought to court. The archives of the Massa family provide two examples that indicate some of the inconveniences and difficulties that stood in the way of investigation and prosecution.

In the early 1920s the marquise de Biencourt, who was then living in Athens, began receiving letters written in German that seemed to have been sent from Hanover. Each letter was accompanied by the calling card of her cousin, the duc Jean de Massa, giving his Parisian address and bearing what looked to be his signature. The marquise wrote to her cousin Jean:

Are you aware that a German is perhaps using your name? . . . The strange tone of these letters and their date, the day after 1 April, leaves little doubt about the nature of these communications. But in light of the requests for money they contain (from 5,000 to 10,000 francs) I found the joke a bit much and instead of responding I thought it might be useful for us to put our heads together to try and discover the origin and author of an enterprise that has probably not been confined to myself alone.[40]

There is no further information about this attempt at extortion in the archive so it is not clear whether the marquise de Biencourt and the duc de Massa were able to resolve the matter privately. The letter writer had usurped the duc's title and name, but to be found guilty in a criminal court there had to be evidence that the usurpation was public and that the offender had refused to desist when warned. Whilst a nuisance to those targeted, it could be an onerous exercise to put a stop to this form of harassment.

An even more curious case of 'stolen identity' arose in the next generation of the Massa family. On 6 June 1952 the baron Roger wrote to his cousin the duc André de Massa enclosing letters he had received from two people. One letter was from Paul Vialar, president of the Société des Gens de Lettres, with whom the Massa family was already acquainted. In the late 1920s, the *hôtel* de Massa, formerly the family's Parisian residence at the corner of the Champs-Elysées and the rue de la Boëtie, was taken down and rebuilt on the boulevard Berthier in Neuilly. The Champs-Elysées site was wanted for development by a rich investor, and Minister Édouard Herriot, lobbied by Les Amis du Vieux Paris, intervened to ensure that the *hôtel*, which was classified as a historic monument, became the Société's home. Vialar, the Société's president, had contacted the baron Roger regarding the sepulchre of someone 'who is probably one of your ancestors' and the baron Roger, in turn, asked the duc André de Massa, 'Is he a descendant of the Great Judge [the first duc de Massa] or does his title have nothing to do with your own?'[41]

The sepulchre had come to light as a result of some weeding done in a village cemetery. In the second letter, transmitted from the baron Roger to the duc André de Massa, Madame Jeannin-Valtet explained to Paul Vialar:

> Our little cemetery in Mercurey [Saône et Loire] had the honour to receive in 1914 the ashes of the comte Braniki, duc de Massa. This man was ill and had come to spend the summer holidays in Mercurey with his wife and son in 1913 and 1914. Owing to the outbreak of war his body was not

transported back to Poland and his tomb was never maintained. In 1944, when the thirty-year concession expired, it was completely abandoned as you can see from these four photographs [enclosed with the letter in the archive]. I needed to cut back the thorns to reveal what was there: a dented and rusty cross on to which the funerary plate was still stuck with this epitaph: 'Here lies Xavier Constantin Wladimir Augustin, comte Braniki, duc de Massa, who died on the 25 June 1914 at the age of sixty years. De Profundis.' Monsieur le President, do you not find such neglect distressing? Perhaps you know a descendant of the Massa family who, unaware of this state of affairs, might remedy it?[42]

Up until he received the baron Roger's query, the duc André de Massa had most certainly been unaware of this state of affairs. Instead of writing directly to Madame Jeannin-Valtet, he addressed himself to Paul Vialar on 6 July 1952. Apologising that ill health and absence from Paris had delayed his attention to the matter, he went on to express his view succinctly:

> There is no comte Braniki who could be the duc de Massa. I am the last to hold this name and descend directly from Claude Ambroise Régnier, duc de Massa, Minister of Justice for the Emperor Napoleon I and interred at the Pantheon. All the Massas are buried in the family plot in the Père-Lachaise cemetery, apart from my brother, who was killed at the hands of the enemy in 1940 and buried in the ground on which he fell. I don't understand who this comte Braniki can be whose sepulchre is at Mercurey; there has been an error. To prove my assertion, I am willing to provide as evidence the certificate of investiture for my title, made out at my father's death and in my favour by the Garde des Sceaux, Monsieur Robert Lecour.[43]

Perhaps Braniki was a Polish count? Or perhaps he was one of many hundreds of thousands of European migrant workers who came to France in the decades before 1914. The real identity of the so-called 'duc de Massa' remained a mystery. In that sense, it was little different from the mysterious identities of those persons whose descendants bore noble status of 'extraction' dating from 'time immemorial'. No wonder genealogists and French aristocrats liked to believe that 'proof' was in the paperwork.

What conclusions may be drawn then about the ways in which titles and genealogies structured relations among the French nobility and between nobles and people of other class backgrounds? In the France of the Third Republic knowledge about aristocratic genealogies brought individuals like Révérend and Éhret into the social orbit of men like the prince Henri de Béarn. Such knowledge was a form of power, but in nineteenth-century Europe it scarcely matched up to the power of social privilege invested in those of blue-blooded ancestry. Nobles, and particularly noblemen from what we have seen, were acutely aware of those privileges, which historically had belonged to them and to their families. They were prepared to defend their personal rights to a title to the point of seriously, and sometimes irrevocably, damaging relations with their own relatives, as we saw in poor Éhret's troubles with the princes Gaston de Béarn and Sagan. This drive to defend noble privileges and to ensure accuracy in the attribution of titles was not limited to the *ancienne noblesse*, for there is evidence for it as well among the Bonaparte family. Erroneous personal use or attribution of titles could be deliberate and politically motivated; it could provide the basis for an attempt at extortion as the marquise de Biencourt discovered; or it could be as innocent and well meant as Madame Jeannin-Valtet's concern for an unkempt grave.

In addition to *amour-propre*, there were political and social reasons that help to explain why French nobles were concerned to see their titles acknowledged and respected in the France of the Third Republic. Before the First World War when well-educated male bourgeois continued to rise in the ranks of government and civil service, and came to occupy important bureaucratic positions, it was becoming increasingly difficult to attain verification or recognition for an aristocratic title. This was especially the case after the French government's ruling of 1906 that it would no longer confer titles or authorise foreign titles. One consequence of the government decree was to strengthen latent class affiliation among the nobility. Many French nobles were related to nobles elsewhere; their families were linked together in a pan-European aristocracy. At the highest level of French society, in royal and imperial circles, marriages uniting French and non-French individuals were arranged for dynastic and political interests. To many nobles in France, and in other countries, those dynastic and political interests mattered intensely. Their worldview, in which conservative politics were often linked with profound religious beliefs, was challenged in dramatic as well as mundane ways by republican initiatives and by international developments beyond their control. That is not to say all French nobles were monarchists, or actively wished for the restoration of a Bonapartist Empire; there were also a few republicans among them. The aristocratic *mentalité*, however, adhered to the principle that a titled blue-blooded nobleman, far from being a 'nobody', was historically a powerful player on the military, political, or diplomatic stage.

This mindset, held by people who often considered themselves European before French, informed a letter written by His Excellency the prince de Bianchi de Médicis to His Excellency the prince Henri de Béarn, Ambassadorial Counsellor in Paris, on 19 October 1942. The letter was accompanied by a copy of an article, by the prince de Bianchi de Médicis and published in *L'Italie Nouvelle*, on which the author had underlined some especially significant passages for the diplomat Béarn's attention. The article dealt with two Médici princesses, his own female ancestors, and the most important point to note, he explained, was that from the time of Charles V to the time of Leopold I, Emperor of Germany, all the Médici titles had originated from the Holy Roman Empire and carried the quality of 'Serene Highness'. The prince de Bianchi de Médicis was rather put out that the *Almanach de Gotha* refused to recognise his right to be known as Serene Highness because of a new interdiction imposed by the German Reich. Fortunately, in France, where he had lived for most of his life, all his titles were properly recorded 'with even the official quality of Highness on my civil status documents' and 'my rank of Excellence by legal right and not by courtesy' on his personal identity papers.[44]

The prince went on to recount that given his ancestral connections to Italy, Spain, France, and Germany he held 'an exceptional position'. This was a point he had made 'forcefully' to Rheinbaben, former German Minister of State 'who is in direct contact with the Führer Hitler'. He had also informed Her Royal Highness the Infanta Eulalie of Spain who had assured him of her affectionate friendship and expressed the hope that he should marry a young, intelligent and rich woman who would furnish the means to action for a restoration of the Bourbon monarchy in Spain as well as in France. The prince de Bianchi de Médicis was now approaching the prince de Béarn by letter because, out of profound love for France, he wished to serve the country by taking up a diplomatic post in Paris. Would Béarn be able to help? In addition to his ancestry and titles, the prince de Bianchi de Médicis held the honour to have been baptised by the Archbishop of Bordeaux in the chapel of his own family château. He had also received instructions from Rome that as a Knight of the Order of Malta his uniform, which he already possessed, should include a bicorn hat with white feathers, accessories and plaque. 'You have, my dear prince,' he concluded, 'a spirit too noble and too chivalric not to be convinced.'[45]

Who knows what His Excellence the prince Henri de Béarn made of this extraordinary letter composed in October 1942; his archive does not contain a response. Perhaps the prince recognised something of his youthful self in Médicis? Perhaps he recalled the services of Révérend whom, four decades earlier, he had sent chasing after 'proof' of the Chalais title and so many other knightly orders and dignities. Or perhaps he simply folded the letter back into its envelope and placed it away in his desk drawer.

Notes

1 René de La Croix de Castries, *Papiers de famille* (Paris, 1977), p. 15.
2 On the British peerage, see David Cannadine, *The Decline and Fall of the British Aristocracy* (London, 2005), p. 11. The historical basis for nobility in Scotland differed from that in England: see Keith Brown, *Noble Society in Scotland: Wealth, Family and Culture, from Reformation to Revolution* (Edinburgh, 2000), p. 11.
3 Within the three broad types of nobility (*la noblesse d'extraction, la noblesse par charge* and *la noblesse par lettres*) there are variations. On the complex terminology and distinctions, see Alain Texier, *Qu'est-ce que la noblesse?* (Paris, 1988), pp. 530–45. On numbers and types see Guy Chaussinand-Nogaret, *The French Nobility in the Eighteenth Century: From Feudalism to Enlightenment*, trans. William Doyle (Cambridge, 1985), pp. 28–30; Régis Valette, *Catalogue de la noblesse française contemporaine* (Paris, 1977), pp. 4–6; Texier, *Qu'est-ce que la noblesse?*, pp. 16–17, 22–65, 78–9.
4 La Croix de Castries, *Papiers de famille*, p. 16.
5 La Croix de Castries, *Papiers de famille*, p. 15.
6 Texier, *Qu'est-ce que la noblesse?*, pp. 19, 70–3.
7 Elizabeth M. Hallam, *Capetian France 987–1328* (London, 1980), pp. 9–18.
8 According to the Instruction of 1372 in the reign of Charles V. Texier, *Qu'est-ce que la noblesse?*, pp. 211, 345.
9 Texier, *Qu'est-ce que la noblesse?*, pp. 214–20, 376, 380–2.
10 G. Guérin and E. Guérin, *Législation et jurisprudence nobiliaires* 5 ed. (Limoges, 1978), pp. 65, 212; Texier, *Qu'est-ce que la noblesse?*, pp. 128, 190.
11 The particle *de* is not a sign of nobility although it is often mistaken for one. Some ten thousand names in France contain the particle *de*, yet 10 per cent of aristocratic families do not have the particle in their name. Texier, *Qu'est-ce que la noblesse?*, pp. 428–9.
12 Cyril Grange, *Les Gens du Bottin Mondain: y être c'est en être* (Paris, 1996); Elizabeth C. Macknight, 'Entertaining company: the sociability of le

Tout-Paris 1880–1914' (Unpublished PhD thesis, University of Melbourne, 2003).
13 Texier, *Qu'est-ce que la noblesse?*, pp. 135–7, 144–8; Étienne de Séréville and Fernand de Saint-Simon, *Dictionnaire de la noblesse française* 2 vols (Paris, 1975 and 1977); Gérard de Sède, *Aujourd'hui, les nobles* ... (Paris, 1975); Pierre-Marie Dioudonnat, *Encyclopédie de la fausse noblesse et de la noblesse d'apparence* (Paris, 1982); Jacques Descheemaeker, *Les Titres de noblesse en France et dans les pays étrangers* vol. 1 (Paris, 1958).
14 Vicomte Albert Révérend, *Les Familles titrées et anoblies au XIXe siècle* (Paris, 1974). This book brings together in a single edition three of Révérend's works that were first published at the turn of the century: *L'Armorial du Premier Empire* (4 vols, 1894–97); *Les Titres, pairies et anoblissements de la Restauration* (6 vols, 1901–7); and *Titres et confirmations de titres: Monarchie de Juillet, Seconde République, Second Empire, Troisième République* (1 vol., 1908).
15 'Affaire succession Veuve Révérend c/ Monsieur le prince de Béarn' in AP 69/2 Fonds Béarn de Chalais.
16 Clippings from *The Washington Post*: 'French Secretary replies to statements of the marquise de Fontenoy' 3[?] June 1904 and 1905 article by the marquise de Fontenay in AP 69/1 Fonds Béarn de Chalais. On Cécile de Talleyrand-Périgord see Georges Martin, *Histoire et généalogie de la maison de Talleyrand-Périgord* (La Ricamarie, 2009), p. 104. On Spanish grandees see I. A. A. Thompson, 'The nobility in Spain, 1600–1800' in H. M. Scott (ed.), *The European Nobilities in the Seventeenth and Eighteenth Centuries* vol. 1 (London, 1995), pp. 174–236.
17 *Washington Times* clipping [June 1904?] in AP 69/1 Fonds Béarn de Chalais.
18 18 May 1905 cited in 'Affaire succession Veuve Révérend c/ Monsieur le prince de Béarn' in AP Fonds 69/2 Béarn de Chalais.
19 24 June 1905 cited in 'Affaire succession Veuve Révérend c/ Monsieur le prince de Béarn' in AP 69/2 Fonds Béarn de Chalais.
20 'Affaire succession Veuve Révérend c/ Monsieur le prince de Béarn' in AP 69/2 Fonds Béarn de Chalais.
21 10 January 1907 in AP 69/1 Fonds Béarn de Chalais.
22 8 February 1909 in AP 69/1 Fonds Béarn de Chalais.
23 4 July 1910 in AP 69/1 Fonds Béarn de Chalais.
24 Undated letter [late July] 1913 in AP 69/1 Fonds Béarn de Chalais.
25 16 May 1913 in AP 69/1 Fonds Béarn de Chalais.
26 Letters from Mottet, Moreau, David, and the prince de Béarn (1923–26) in AP 69/2 Fonds Béarn de Chalais.
27 'Affaire succession Veuve Révérend c/ Monsieur le prince de Béarn' in AP 69/2 Fonds Béarn de Chalais.
28 'Les grands d'Espagne' clipping from an unidentified newspaper in AP 69/2 Fonds Béarn de Chalais.
29 Texier, *Qu'est-ce que la noblesse?*, pp. 212, 377.

NOBILITY, TITLES, AND GENEALOGY 39

30 Pierre Assouline, *Le Dernier des Camondo* (Paris, 1999), pp. 240, 246.
31 12 January 1890 in AP 69/2 Fonds Béarn de Chalais.
32 Certified copy of undated letter [January 1890] in AP 69/2 Fonds Béarn de Chalais. On the prince de Sagan and his two sons see Martin, *Histoire et généalogie de la maison de Talleyrand-Périgord*, pp. 159–69.
33 15 January 1890 in AP 69/2 Fonds Béarn de Chalais.
34 The couple's address is withheld from the main listing and from the list of addresses by street in Émile Éhret, *La Société et le High Life: Adresses à Paris* (Nancy, 1891), pp. 23, 344. See for comparison the 1890 edition pp. 19 and 358.
35 31 July 1907 in AP 103/44 Fonds Lucien Bonaparte.
36 Handwritten genealogical notes in AP 103/40 Fonds Lucien Bonaparte. Ingres's drawing of the family of Lucien Bonaparte was completed in 1815, the year of Pierre Bonaparte's birth. See Hans Naef, 'Who's who in Ingres's portrait of the family of Lucien Bonaparte?', *The Burlington Magazine* 114 (1972), 787–91. On this branch of the Bonaparte family see 'Lucien Bonaparte', *Le Magasin pittoresque* (Paris, 1841), 25–6; Joseph Valynseele, *Le Sang des Bonaparte* (Paris, 1954), pp. 37, 41, 50, 58, 59.
37 5 July 1907 in AP 103/40 Fonds Lucien Bonaparte.
38 22 June 1922 in AP 103/44 Fonds Lucien Bonaparte.
39 Extract from *Morning Post* 18 May 1912 'A Delicate Position' in AP 103/44 Fonds Lucien Bonaparte.
40 Card in AP 279/34 Fonds Massa.
41 6 June 1952 in AP 279/35 Fonds Massa.
42 20 May 1952 in AP 279/35 Fonds Massa.
43 6 July 1952 in AP 279/35 Fonds Massa.
44 19 October 1942 and article from *L'Italie Nouvelle* in AP 69/2 Fonds Béarn de Chalais.
45 19 October 1942 in AP 69/2 Fonds Béarn de Chalais.

2

Marriage

On 10 May 1884 a wedding took place in the Chapelle de la Nonciature in Paris; twenty-eight-year-old prince Joachim Murat V married sixteen-year-old Cécile Ney d'Elchingen. 'Ney! Murat! What names, what glories and what miseries!' wrote a jubilant friend from Joachim's regiment. Invoking the historic French victories at Marengo and Austerlitz, he predicted that this marriage would give to France 'new defenders, new glories'. Joachim was then a sub-lieutenant in the fourth armoured division stationed at Lyon. By serving in the army he heeded the call of his father, the prince Joachim Murat IV, 'to carry with dignity the name passed down to us by the head of your family'. In time the couple produced eight children, consolidating the fruitful alliance of two imperial aristocratic houses.[1]

This marriage of nobility illustrates the way in which 'the earliest education, reinforced by all subsequent social experiences' tends to orientate individuals when they pair up to form a couple. 'Socially approved love, love predisposed to succeed, is nothing other than that love of one's own social destiny.'[2] Joachim Murat and Cécile Ney d'Elchingen belonged to the same milieu for their families were similarly invested in the military and political heritage of the France of the First Empire. Moreover, in the nineteenth and twentieth centuries it was still expected that the eldest son of an aristocratic family would marry a noblewoman. Class played a very important role in the choice of marriage partner among the nobility. Endogamy for a noble heir was both a legacy of primogeniture and a reflection of aristocratic concern to preserve the quality of the bloodline.[3]

Aristocratic weddings featured reminders of familial heritage that helped observers to feel complicit in the couple's social destiny. In March 1882 the abbé Viallet conducted the marriage ceremony for the marquis de Villeneuve Esclapon-Vence and the princesse Jeanne Bonaparte in the Église de Saint-Thomas d'Aquin, Aix-en-Provence. The groom belonged to an 'illustrious race' from southern France whose noble ancestry dated back to Charlemagne's time and the bride bore 'a name that had dazzled the world'. Sweeping up his congregation in stories of Christian crusading, French exploration, and empire building, the abbé Viallet confidently pronounced that these two nobles would have a happy marriage for they were 'blessed in heaven' and 'surrounded by the prayers and good wishes of this crowd of relatives and friends'.[4] Press reports of aristocratic weddings also carried details of family genealogies, honorific distinctions, and historic achievements. Such attention to the couple's inheritance of accomplishment served to foster the impression that the marriage was 'predisposed to succeed'. Elaborate descriptions of the bridal party indulged a fondness for spectacle that was characteristic of French society at the turn of the century. Families were encouraged to create a lasting souvenir of the event through an entry in the *Annuaire des grands mariages* published by Chéron and Paz.[5]

But what lay behind and beyond all the publicity for these weddings? To what extent did aristocratic marital strategies under the Third Republic resemble the strategies of earlier times? How did noblemen and noblewomen experience courtship and married life?

Marriage has long been a subject of commentary and debate in France. The custom of arranged marriage, whilst broadly supported through the Middle Ages and early modern period, also attracted criticism for placing some men and women into situations of great unhappiness. During the 1789 Revolution French commentators argued for the need to remove corruption from the conjugal bond and replace it with 'freedom of the heart'.[6] Descriptions of marriage offered a rhetorical device for entering into reflection upon the health of the nation. When a divorce law was first introduced to France in 1792 thousands of individuals, wives especially, took advantage of it. But hopes for further improvement in the rights of married women were not fulfilled during the revolutionary period. A set of articles on the duties of wives and husbands was incorporated into the writing of Napoleon's Civil Code of 1804. Far from resolving the problems associated with marriage under the *ancien régime*, the prescriptions of the Civil Code disadvantaged wives in numerous ways and were repeatedly challenged by women and some men across the nineteenth and twentieth centuries. Many of the same issues debated by the revolutionaries – including cohabitation, dowries, separation, adultery, and divorce – were still contentious subjects in the France of the Third Republic. In 1884 the Senate approved Alfred Naquet's proposal to re-establish divorce legislation that had been abolished in 1816 under the Bourbon monarchy. The progress of the new divorce law through the Chamber of Deputies and the Senate in the 1880s was accompanied by a fresh surge in publications on the topic. Clerics, politicians, academics, and playwrights expounded differing interpretations of the marital bond and its social significance.[7]

Nineteenth-century republican conceptions of marriage centred on the notion of gender complementarity. The active male citizen required an accommodating female counterpart, the woman in the home (*la femme au foyer*), to be his companion and helpmeet. Marriage was meant to underpin a stable democratic society that upheld the three great principles of republicanism: liberty, equality and fraternity. Sexual difference, however, formed the basis for different treatment of spouses in many areas of the law. There were republican couples in the nineteenth century who struggled to break through convention and establish intimate relationships based on equality. The ideal was difficult to put into practice for in the republican model of marriage 'subordination and equality uneasily co-existed with each other'.[8]

Class, at least as much as political belief, helped to set the pattern for gender relations within the domestic environment.[9] The republican template for marriage supposed that the husband's salary alone would support his wife and family. Whilst this was the case in some bourgeois households, lower middle-class and working-class couples pieced together income from various work activities conducted inside and outside the home; women's work was especially important to the peasant household economy. Among the upper class, where income was generated primarily through investment, the experiences were different again. Class disparities were often referred to in the political debates on marriage between 1870 and 1940 and nobles were by no means disinterested or unrepresented in those debates. But the notion of gender complementarity, which republicans saw as the basis for harmonious conjugality and a stable society, did not play the principal role in aristocratic thinking about marriages within their own families. What exercised nobles to a far greater degree was the social status and wealth of the spouses. Interest in rank trumped interest in the complementarity of the sexes.

Marriage has served four main strategic purposes for the French nobility over the centuries. First, it has created and structured alliances between families. Those alliances have often been motivated by the aim of exercising greater political and social power at court, in high society, and in local communities. Second, marriage has served as a flexible barrier to membership of the upper class. The practice of endogamy, not in a complete manner but rather within 'limits' that differ for men and for women, has provided aristocratic families with considerable control over who is admitted to their circles. Third, marriage has been a means for consolidating and enhancing the material interests of a family. Nobles have formed marital alliances that promise a level of income that will enable them to keep up an estate and make other public demonstrations of status and prestige. Finally, marriage has facilitated the reproduction of nobility by legitimising procreation between man and woman so that their offspring inherit family property including names and titles.

Each of these four interconnecting functions of aristocratic marriage remained vitally important to nobles in the France of the Third Republic. The marital bond was key to an aristocratic family's ability to consolidate and transmit capital of all forms for the benefit of future generations. For this reason the selection of a spouse was not a matter of individual concern, but rather a process of negotiation managed by senior relatives who had the authority to make a final decision.[10]

Here is how a reporter for *L'Illustration* described marriage in Parisian high society in 1889:

> Marriages in *le grand monde* are not, for the most part, the simple result of a reciprocal inclination and personal suitability. They are a real institution intended to enrich some, ennoble others, build up status, create relationships and solidarities, [and] sanction the character and credibility of certain families or certain names ... In order to set up a splendid marriage ... it is necessary first of all to have a great name, a great fortune – at least from one of the spouses – a status beyond compare ... an extended and highly placed acquaintance; a sumptuous *hôtel* regularly open to the elite of Society, a reputation for magnificence and *bon ton* ... faultless and sufficiently numerous carriage-teams ... [and] a superb livery ... of impeccable correctness.[11]

As the reporter hastened to add, the chances of both spouses meeting all these criteria were rare, 'even in the most elevated and aristocratic spheres', but matrimonial alliance allowed each party to compensate for what the other lacked and to enhance their mutual prestige.

One approach to studying change and continuity in marital strategies is to chart and compare the rates of endogamy versus exogamy over time.[12] Statistical analysis of couples named in high society annuals shows a slight decline in the rate of endogamy among nobles from the second half of the nineteenth century into the first half of the twentieth century. The index method used produces results on a scale of 0 to 1: the closer the result is to 1, the greater the resemblance in spousal social origins, whilst the closer the result is to 0, the greater the dissimilarity. For marriages contracted in the period 1850–1918 the rate of noble endogamy is calculated at 0.86, dropping to 0.75 for marriages contracted in the period 1919–45.[13] There was a very marked resemblance, therefore, in the social backgrounds of husbands and wives. Sex and order of birth within the family influenced nobles' decisions to marry within or outside their own milieu. Among the aristocracy 'a strongly endogamous group, where marriages between relatives are not uncommon, the rule against exogamy allows for exceptions only among men and principally the youngest [of male siblings], while for women the rule applies strictly, especially on the eldest [of female siblings]'.[14] Studies show that just as it was 'unthinkable' for a nobleman's daughter to marry a commoner some eldest sons who made an exogamous match were subsequently disinherited.[15]

The slight decline in aristocratic endogamy reflected some change in cultural attitudes and priorities. In eighteenth-century Paris marriage between first cousins had been a way for nobles to consolidate economic and symbolic capital. Consanguinity represented 'the paradigm of endogamous marriage in which honour and opulence are protected at the same time'.[16] In the early nineteenth century, however, the nobility continued to favour consanguine marriages in order to offset the effects of partible inheritance. It was only later in that century that other concerns meant such marriages were looked on less favourably. For example, some monarchists feared that the law of exile voted in by the republicans on 22 June 1886 would encourage a pattern of consanguine marriage within the House of France that did not bode well for the lineage. Those fears were very nearly realised in 1889 when the pretender's heir, the duc Philippe d'Orléans, came close to marrying his first cousin, Marguerite. The marquise de Breteuil wrote candidly on the subject in her journal for 1885: 'I loathe marriages between first cousins. In sum, it is almost as if one married one's brother. Since these types of crossings are avoided where horses or dogs are concerned, because they are dangerous for the race, why should we be so easy-going where humans are concerned?'[17]

Marriages within the Greffulhe family provide classic examples of the uniting of wealth and birth. In 1878 the immensely rich comte Henri Greffulhe, heir to the château de Bois-Boudran and the family property in rue d'Astorg, married Élisabeth de Caraman-Chimay, descended from an impoverished Belgian aristocratic family with excellent connections. Ten years earlier, in 1868, one of Henri's sisters, Jeanne Greffulhe, had wedded the prince Auguste d'Arenberg, whose mother was a Talleyrand-Périgord and whose father, the prince Pierre, was born into a ducal family of the Rhineland and became a peer of France. Both these marriages continued a chain of profitable alliances that had begun when Louis Greffulhe, a banker, married a Languedoc noble, Mademoiselle Randon de Pully, in 1793. Henri Greffulhe, who, because of his ancestry, was considered 'so common' by Edmond de Goncourt, brought to his marriage some eight million francs; his wife's dowry, by comparison, was a mere 100,000 francs.[18]

In order to sustain a high rate of aristocratic endogamy political and social fissures within the nobility have often had to be played down. During the sixteenth and seventeenth centuries marriages between different types of noble, *la noblesse de robe* ('robe') and *la noblesse d'épée* ('sword'), had been essential for preserving aristocratic bloodlines and prestige. We can see a similar pattern in the nineteenth and twentieth centuries when there were marriages between *l'ancienne noblesse* and *la noblesse d'Empire*. Yet Proust's observations of Parisian high society before the First World War suggest the amalgamation of 'old' and 'new' nobles through marriage was never comfortably achieved, and that members of *l'ancienne noblesse* always held the powerful upper hand in social relations. The obsession with rank and birth that haunts the characters of *À la recherche du temps perdu* indicates how keenly difference was felt. It is manifest, for instance, in the disdain shown by the aristocrat Saint-Loup toward the prince de Borodino, 'a man whose great-grandfather was a small farmer, and who would probably be a small farmer himself if it hadn't been for the Napoleonic wars'.[19]

Evidence of the sense of inferiority experienced by some members of *la noblesse d'Empire* in relation to *l'ancienne noblesse* is found in the marquise de Breteuil's account of Louis d'Harcourt's marriage to Marie-Juliette Lanjuinais in January 1886. The bride's father, the comte Lanjuinais, was the descendant of a *titré*. According to the marquise, Lanjuinais was so 'in awe at the grandeur of the Harcourt' and 'so grovelled before their nobility' that he mortified his own family. Expecting that his own relatives from Brittany would be thinly arrayed in the choir pews, he also invited the relatives of his deceased first wife, Louise de Pillet-Will, from the clan of bankers. On the day of the wedding the church was over crowded and there were no seats left for Lanjuinais's uncle, the vicomte de Janzé, who was married to a Choiseul-Gouffier. These nobles were forced to sit in the nave with the 'ordinary martyrs'. To add insult to injury, when the wedding gifts were displayed at the signing of the contract, it was discovered that Lanjuinais had chosen not to have his own coat of arms engraved on the magnificent set of silver given to his daughter. This was an embarrassment to both noble houses. By not including his own arms Lanjuinais had created the impression that Louis d'Harcourt was marrying a commoner. The marquise de Breteuil deplored the 'complete lack of dignity' on the part of the comte. The Lanjuinais are 'an honourable family' she wrote, and 'since they have arms they should not blush over them'. These remarks suggest some softening of the disdainful attitudes manifest by the aristocracy of the Parisian Faubourg Saint-Germain toward *titrés* earlier in the century. Yet the incident also shows the continued existence of an internal hierarchy among nobles. The marquise de Breteuil was under no illusion about the motivation for the match among the groom's relatives. She described the twenty-year-old bride as unattractive and of delicate health but 'four hundred thousand *livres* of rent will certainly fortify the Harcourts'.[20]

Most of the really big fortunes in France at the end of the nineteenth century belonged to industrial and banking families whose origins were non-French but whose members became French citizens. Schneider and Wendel, who manufactured cars and military equipment; Say and Lebaudy, who owned sugar refineries; Ephrussi and Kann, who were bankers; and Porgès, who ran a diamond company, established a branch of their families in Paris and, within a generation or two, their offspring married into the French nobility.[21]

Some foreign fortunes came from across the Atlantic. The 1915 edition of *Titled Americans*, an annual produced in New York, listed 454 American women who had married European aristocrats; the majority lived in Paris or London although some were as far-flung as Budapest and Warsaw. Among the 'dollar princesses' of Parisian high society was Winnaretta Singer. Her parents were Isabelle Boyer, a French woman, and Isaac Merritt Singer, the sewing-machine manufacturer; in 1893 she married the prince Edmond de Polignac following an unhappy first marriage with the prince Louis de Scey-Montbéliard. In 1891, Marcellite Garner became the young bride of the widowed marquis de Breteuil, whose father had been aide-de-camp to the duc d'Aumale during the

Algerian campaign. In 1895 Anna Gould wed the comte Boni de Castellane whom she divorced eleven years later, only to marry soon afterwards his cousin, Hélie de Talleyrand-Périgord, prince de Sagan.[22]

Intermarriage across class and national lines meant that in some cases spouses did not share the same political views or religion. The unions of *l'ancienne noblesse* with *titrés* 'show that when stakes were high ... traditional political loyalties were extremely malleable'.[23] None the less, there were penalties when a French noble swapped allegiances. The duchesse Élisabeth de Clermont-Tonnerre recalled that her grandfather, the duc de Gramont, was unable to marry within the Legitimist milieu of the Faubourg Saint-Germain when he attached himself to Napoleon III; he found a Scottish bride instead. Difference of religion presented a more rigid barrier, although one that could be overcome. In 1885 Catholic monarchists were appalled that the duc de Chartres allowed his daughter Marie to marry a Protestant, the prince Waldemar of Denmark, without insisting that religious guarantees would be observed. More caution was exercised when the duke of Clarence, Queen Victoria's grandson, wanted to marry Marie's cousin, Hélène d'Aoste. The comte de Paris intervened and forbade Hélène, who was Catholic, from converting to the Anglican Church. Élisabeth de Clermont-Tonnerre describes how her stepmother, Marguerite de Rothschild, when she decided to marry Élisabeth's father, Agénor de Gramont, who was agnostic, had to defeat the opposition of her own father, the baron Charles de Rothschild. The Faubourg was incredulous that Agénor chose a Jew to be his second wife.[24]

Letters about negotiations for a marriage occasionally reveal the rationale for rejecting a particular candidate. In November 1887 the prince Joseph de Caraman-Chimay explained to his eldest daughter Élisabeth why the marriage she envisaged for her twenty-two-year-old sister Ghislaine to the Protestant Hottinguer was out of the question. In Élisabeth's eyes this friend of the family 'with very fine tastes' who was also 'distinguished [and] decorated on the battlefield' showed every sign of devotion to Ghislaine and could offer her financial security and a home on the boulevard Malesherbes not far from her family's Parisian residence. The prince, however, was concerned by the religious implications and concluded after deep reflection that he could never give his daughter away to a Protestant. To do so would be to place Ghislaine 'in a perpetually humiliating position' that would profoundly disturb 'a girl of her race, education, and character, given the memory of her pious mother'.[25] In Chambéry another father, the baron Frédéric d'Alexandry d'Orengiani, sought advice from his friend the Catholic priest Gaspard Mermillod when his son Lucien seemed to have fallen for a young Polish woman, Victoria Tyskiewiez. Mermillod discreetly used his Church contacts to obtain information on the family. Initially he discouraged the match, writing on 15 February 1878: 'This foreign milieu does not seem to me suitable for [Lucien].' Two days later, however, having received 'new details' on the reported aristocratic status and fortune of the Tyskiewiez he was cautiously encouraging. 'You see that I am making every effort to help you in your concerns of fatherhood.'[26]

These examples illustrate resistance to mixing social backgrounds as well as the perpetual drive to enhance familial prosperity and status. On one level, signs of this resistance were not particularly severe. Foreigners, particularly Americans, were ridiculed for social *faux pas* or for linguistic errors if they were not fluent in French. André de Fouquières, a theatre critic who moved in elegant Parisian circles, recalled a 'quite vulgar' American, Mrs Kate Moore, whose efforts to speak French were legendary: '*Le docteur m'a ordonné de suivre mon régiment*,' she said when placed on a diet (*régime*). '*Je suis en état de prostitution*,' for '*prostration*, naturally', joked Fouquières, enjoying the pun.[27]

Beneath such humour, however, lay deep-seated anxiety to preserve the 'purity of blood' and 'pedigree' that underpinned the cherished concepts of dynasty and house. In the eyes of some, blood that was not 'blue' was 'tainted'. Following France's defeat in the Franco-Prussian War, propaganda was unleashed warning that the nobility was degenerating and had lost its military prowess; there was a frantic search for scapegoats. Émmanuel Beau de Loménie wrote four damning volumes about bourgeois insidiousness that he blamed for the decline of the French nation.[28] In 1898 another author pointed to 'the coats of arms that *les misses américaines* bought with their cash', and wrote of aristocrats who married Jews: 'Let them frankly admit that their half-commonness, half-Jewishness, and half-cosmopolitanism henceforth prevents their claiming to be part of *la noblesse française*: that of Agincourt and of Denain.'[29]

The friction caused by uniting, in matrimony, two people of different faiths raised in separate cultures in which religion had very different cultural meanings is illustrated in the marriage of the comte Boni de Castellane and Anna Gould. Boni was raised at the family château, Rochecotte, in the Loire valley in a household dominated by his grandmother, niece of the prince de Talleyrand. This lady, who was related to aristocrats from all over Europe, spent her evenings in conversation with the local abbé as well as friends and relatives bearing historic, often royal, titles who came to stay. In his *Confessions*, Boni describes the château as 'a temple dedicated to ancestor worship'. 'Religion [Catholicism] was the foundation on which the château had been raised.'[30] Anna, meanwhile, came from a Jewish family and grew up under the constant supervision of her eldest sister, Helen, for her mother died when she was very young. The children's father, Jay Gould, had risen from a penniless state to become 'the modern Mephistopheles', a man hated and feared for his power on Wall Street. He adored his six children, spent as much time as he could with them, and inculcated a strict regard for keeping records of expenditure. A Puritan ethic reigned in the household for Helen was deeply religious and interested only in good works. Boni and Anna's wedding ceremony, on 4 March 1895, took place at the Goulds' house on Fifth Avenue and was solemnised by Monsignor Corrigan, Catholic Archbishop of New York. On the couple's return to France it was expected that they would visit each of the family estates. At Rochecotte, Boni's mother had arranged the traditional welcome of a parade and choral performance by school children, and a municipal address at the local railway station that had been decorated with a triumphal arch, wreaths, and bunting. Anna hated it. To be trotted out in front of peasants, servants, nuns, indeed everyone connected with the château, was a rude awakening to the role she would be forced to play in a foreign country dominated by a foreign religion. From her American perspective, it must have seemed that French Catholicism functioned to keep people in the countryside subject to a social hierarchy and a wife subordinate to her husband. Quickly she realised her part was merely to finance a system that was wholly alien to her and in which she was regarded as alien.[31]

Unlike some other brides of Jewish background, Anna had refused to convert to Catholicism because it precluded the possibility of divorce. During their eleven-year marriage Boni made serious inroads into his wife's fortune through reckless spending habits that broke every rule about making economies that Anna's father had taught her. Boni also humiliated his wife by displaying a disrespectful attitude typified by an off-hand remark he made to friends as he was showing off the couple's bedroom: '*Voilà la chapelle expiatoire.*' Anna had her revenge. She left Boni, taking their children with her, and initiated divorce proceedings that enabled her, through the help of hired detectives, to expose in a very public manner her husband's many sexual infidelities. The case became a scandal.[32]

Few marriage break-ups had quite the same profile as this one but they were often just as legally complex. Alfred Naquet, who led the campaign for a new divorce law, cited examples involving nobles before the Senate in May 1884 to highlight discrepancy between French legislation and 'allowances' made in Catholic Church practices. Senators were informed that the prince de Monaco had his eight-year marriage, from which there was one child, annulled by the Pope. This enabled the prince to wed lady Hamilton, which he would have been prevented from doing under French law. The marquis de Groslay de Virville obtained a *séparation de corps* with the help of his lawyer Jules Favre, then had his marriage annulled in Rome so that he could wed a young woman from Florence with whom he had three children. This second marriage meant the marquis was guilty of bigamy under French law so he was obliged to change his nationality to Italian.[33]

One of the arguments brought forward by deputies and senators opposed to divorce was that it was only for the rich. The wages of a working-class man were not sufficient to pay living expenses for an estranged wife and children, plus his own separate expenses. For this reason it was believed unhappily married couples were more likely to stay together than to seek legal separation, although there were also cases of abandonment among the very poor. Aristocratic couples may have had the financial means to go through with divorce proceedings but there were other factors that usually deterred them. Fear of ostracism was very real, especially for women whose social reputation was seen as a measure of personal worth. Gabriel-Louis Pringué described the way in which friendships in Paris were affected by the stigma surrounding divorce at the turn of the century:

> Society chose not to recognise divorce so the unfortunate persons who came into this situation, which was then looked upon very badly, found they were completely locked out. The duchesse de Mouchy maintained a strong affection for one of her dearest female friends who divorced and subsequently remarried. Since the duchesse never wanted to admit to this state of affairs, and yet wanted to keep in touch with her friend, she got a footman to deliver her letters but would never put the address or her friend's new married name on the envelope.[34]

The threat of social rejection was compounded by aristocratic concerns for the preservation of property and adherence to Catholic doctrine. For women especially, conditioned to put other people's needs before their own, it was difficult to contemplate a struggle for individual autonomy. In her unpublished and undated 'Essai sur l'égalité des sexes', the comtesse Élisabeth Greffulhe asked rhetorically, 'Society women are free ... but do they not suffer like other women from the tyranny of marriage?'³⁵ She highlighted the grip of law and religion that instilled notions of 'obedience' and 'perpetuity' and prevented women from liberating themselves with the key that divorce provided.

To what extent, then, were love and sexual compatibility considered necessary for a successful marriage within the aristocracy? Sex for procreation was certainly very important for nobles needed to reproduce to perpetuate the bloodline. Statistics on marital age and fertility provide a useful starting point for investigating this aspect of married life. Margaret Darrow has calculated age at first marriage and number of children per completed marriage using genealogies of dukes and peers of France in 1789 and their descendants. In the 1780s 'the median age of brides in French ducal families was seventeen'. These girls were 'often married right out of the convent' and in many cases returned to the convent for one or more years after marriage before going to live with their husband. Noble men in the same period also married young: between 1750 and 1799 'the mean marriage age of sons of peers was 21.3 [years]'. Couples at this level of society were not having many offspring: for the period 1750 to 1799 the mean number of children in French ducal families was two.³⁶ There was a change beginning in the last decade of the eighteenth century when the marital age for both sexes began to increase, as did the number of children per marriage. 'The post-Revolutionary norm for women was to marry at 20 to 22, while men postponed marriage until their late twenties.' One of the consequences of men marrying later was that the age difference between spouses widened: six to eight years' difference was the norm in the nineteenth century. By the 1840s the mean number of children in French ducal families was four; that is, double the number from the latter half of the eighteenth century.³⁷

This trend towards larger families and later marriage, especially for males, continued among the aristocracy in the France of the Third Republic. From 1880 to 1899 the average age at marriage for a noblewoman of high society was twenty-two, and for a nobleman twenty-nine. This seven-year age gap is more than double that found between bourgeois couples in northern France from 1889 to 1900. The average age at marriage for a bourgeois woman was twenty-three and for a bourgeois man, twenty-six – just three years' difference. Of noble couples in high society married between 1900 and 1914, 57.2 per cent had between two and four children while 28.5 per cent had five or more children. Noble couples who had at least one child who entered the Catholic Church had a consistently higher fertility rate than the noble average. For example, 'practising' Catholic nobles married between 1900 and 1929 had a fertility rate of 4.4 children compared to the noble average of 3.2 children for the same period. Sex before a couple married was rare. In a sample of 499 births before the Second World War there were only three cases found of pre-marital conception.[38]

Beyond the duty to procreate, it remains difficult to draw conclusions about the quality of intimacy and degree of sexual satisfaction within aristocratic marriages. Letters between spouses provide insight into moments of co-operation, compromise, and complicity on a day-to-day level. Yet the deepest secrets pertaining to a marriage were unlikely ever to have been written down. For French nobles, as for Victorian middle-class couples, evidence of conjugal sexuality 'is so patchy and contradictory that a case can be made with equal confidence for fulfilment or frustration as the norm'. Without making definitive claims, which would not accurately represent the finer realities, it is nevertheless possible to explore 'the contradictory conditions which pushed marital sexuality in different directions'. Of course, there was 'considerable variation in this most private of spheres'.[39]

One of the conditions that shaped relations during courtship was the popular notion of romantic love. This is a dominant theme of letters written before and during a couple's engagement. In March 1884, two months before her wedding, sixteen-year-old Cécile Ney d'Elchingen wrote almost every day to her fiancé, Joachim, and took delight in his prompt replies from the barracks. She was impatient for their reunion:

> Your letter, the first that I have received from you, made me so happy. For me it signifies that I have the right to love you with all my heart, which, believe me, is very sweet and easy to do. I miss you greatly. It seems your absence will never end! The more I think about it the longer it seems and I think about it constantly ... I will be very happy to wear the pearls that you wish to give me, my dear Joachim. I love pearls and everything that comes from you will always be infinitely precious to me.[40]

Within a few days of receiving Joachim's first letter, their correspondence had become a passionate preoccupation for the young woman. 'You cannot imagine how happy I am when I sit down to write to you ... All day long I felt happy to have received a letter from you this morning, with the thought of replying to you this evening.'[41] Joachim was no less caught up in their romance. From Lyon on 17 March he wrote to Cécile: 'I received your letter this morning and I cannot tell you what good it did me. Since yesterday I have been waiting impatiently for it and I assure you these twenty-four hours have been longer than all the others.'[42] When he was not engaged in military duties at the barracks Joachim set about finding an appropriate lodging for the couple to move into after their wedding. 'The apartments are too big and the houses are microscopic, so I am going to go out into the countryside today and in my next letter I hope to be able to give you more positive information, for without that we run the strong risk of being left out in the street.'[43] The search, satisfactorily concluded on 18 April with the rental of a house, proved a useful distraction: 'In spite of our separation, I have just one method left to make the time go faster. It is to think of you and of the complete happiness that awaits us.'[44]

Writing and reading letters were equally pleasurable for Élisabeth de Caraman-Chimay during her engagement to the comte Henri Greffulhe. On a summer evening in 1878, aged eighteen, she wrote to her fiancé:

> There is moonlight and I am thinking of you without knowing why. Our moon so full of poetry! ... I have just been re-reading our notes and it seemed to me that certain words still held the *emotion* and the *melody* with which you pronounced them, they *vibrated* quite on their own ... Do you remember this mysterious clavier that resonated at certain moments? I do not know how or why; perhaps you do not know yourself. Today you spoke of it to me in our blue oasis. It is your clavier. I have my own. It is perhaps one and the same.[45]

The erotic undercurrent of such engagement letters written by young nobles would seem a positive indication of the capacity to engage fully in the taking and giving of sexual pleasure. Contemporary advice literature on marriage certainly recommended physical intimacy as a way of creating happiness and harmony in matrimonial union.[46] But romantic love was not the only condition influencing marital sexuality. Education was another. Within the aristocracy, little if any information about sex was given to females, while males were presented with opportunities to lose their virginity before marriage and were expected to know more or less how to proceed with the sexual act. After a sheltered upbringing, the trauma surrounding loss of virginity coloured some noblewomen's attitude toward sex for the rest of their lives. The princesse Marthe Bibesco recalled of her 'honeymoon': 'the physical union of two people is like murder. All at once one is obliterated; no identity remains except pain.'[47] Alain Corbin has suggested that the culture surrounding sexuality that brought suffering to women in the nineteenth century may also be read for 'signs of masculine suffering'. The intense pain described by the princesse Bibesco was both physical and psychological. In Corbin's view 'the emotion of the partner, wife or concubine, cannot be isolated from the forms of expression or inhibition, or the satisfaction or frustration of masculine desire'.[48]

Letters to the abbé Viollet reveal that Catholic teachings about sin had a tendency to exacerbate negative feelings about sex, making it difficult for wives and husbands to communicate on the subject of carnal need. In 1929 an upper-class woman wrote candidly to the abbé of her concerns about marital sexuality:

> We others, young women of high society, come to marriage with a certain ignorance of our future duties and it is our husbands who have the delicate responsibility to teach us them. But alas! Do we find in them model and scrupulous guides in these sensitive matters? Generally before marriage they were far more concerned with their own pleasure, or even rights, than with their duties, and having led a gay bachelor's life, the voice of their conscience has been terribly stifled and they can very often lead their life companion unconsciously away from the right path.[49]

Interestingly the letter seems to suggest a reversal of the Adam and Eve story for it is the husband who is portrayed as having the knowledge to 'lead their life companion unconsciously away from the right path'. There is a hint, in other words, of subverting the biblical typecasting of female sexuality, except that the overall purpose of the letter is to consult the abbé on ways for women to protect themselves against temptation as daughters of Eve.

If the letters to the abbé Viollet were the only evidence available then it would appear frustration, fear, and resentment were depressingly typical. A striking contrast appears, however, when those letters are compared with the letters written by the duchesse Élaine de Guiche (née Greffulhe) to her mother shortly after departing on her honeymoon. On 15 November 1904:

> My dear darling mother, thank you for your letter, which brought me so much pleasure. It was a delicious voyage; we were alone ... An excellent dinner, *in bed* at 9 p.m!!!!! We spoke until midnight but at the end we slept *very* well. All my manias disappeared in one fell swoop! I woke up at 7 a.m. and Armand a little bit later but he fell back to sleep!!!! ... I am doing wonderfully well; I am no longer tired, and feel *delighted* with my new life.[50]

Three days later it appears the newly weds were continuing to spend considerable time enjoying the comforts of their bed. 'We are doing wonderfully and find our marriage a great success ... I slept from 11 p.m. to 9.30 a.m!!!!!'[51]

Élaine's letters probably generated relief, perhaps even some quiet amusement, for the comtesse Greffulhe. Élisabeth's own husband, Henri, had greatly missed her from bed when she was staying at her parents' château in 1883. Sexual yearning leapt off the pages of his letters. On 6 October:

> I cannot sleep in this room and am going to try for this evening in yours ... It is impossible that you are not aware of how I miss you and how all is sad here without this Bébeth ... You personify life, *mon amour*, and for this reason it is death to be parted from you.[52]

On the 8th, Henri wrote twice to his wife. In one letter:

> I have not been able to go to sleep ... I tell myself a hundred times that the night is a long drawn out agony but this does not suffice to prevent me beseeching *mon amour*.[53]

1 Armand de Gramont, duc de Guiche (1900)

2 Élaine Greffulhe (1900)

And in the other:

> Life continues to be more and more stupid without you ... Decidedly I am not made for separations. As La Rochefoucauld put it so well: 'Absence diminishes the mediocre passions and augments the great ones like the wind blows out the candles and fans the fire.'[54]

Sadly, for this couple, their relationship over the years lost much of the lustre Élisabeth had attributed to it on the moonlit night back in 1878. The comte was repeatedly unfaithful and the knowledge of his extra-marital affairs made his wife feel lonely and wretched. 'Fidelity is a need,' she stated unequivocally in 1892.[55] When one of Henri's mistresses became a permanent fixture in his life Élisabeth's nerves almost gave way. Furious, she declared on 9 August 1905:

I have reached a period of my life in which I no longer want to struggle every day. It defeats me. I am no longer myself. I take horror in existence and my character is affected as much as my health ... To hear each day slanderous remarks concerning those who one loves is intolerable; to have odious scenes at any moment is not bearable ... One can stand these things at twenty years of age or when one has a child. Later, one can no longer stand them. I do not know what the future holds for me, but I have decided at least to have the peace to which I have the right.[56]

She never left him.

Compared with the evidence that some husbands engaged in affairs, it is less clear how common the practice of adultery was among wives. Affairs were a frequent topic of conversation as well as a popular theme of contemporary literature and plays; yet first-hand accounts by middle, and upper-class women are scarce.[57] A great deal of correspondence survives which documents relationships but those letters need to be read carefully without supposing that a passionate friendship was necessarily consummated. *Amitié, amitié amoureuse*, and *amour* rarely appear as distinct tones of relating; rather, these terms point to a blurred spectrum of intimacies with emotional, intellectual, and physical dimensions. For a noblewoman the decision on whether or not to consummate a relationship could depend on religious faith, fear of gossip, the response she might expect from her husband if discovered, and the experiences of older relatives and friends. From surviving letters it appears that some noblewomen came very close to consummating a relationship with someone they loved, but never did. Equally, it was sometimes the case that a noblewoman terminated an affair, whilst still very much in love, because geographical separation or the desire of one but not the other to marry made the relationship unsustainable.[58]

Fed up with the infidelities of her husband Georges, who was diagnosed with syphilis, the princesse Marthe Bibesco met the love of her life, the prince Charles-Louis de Beauvau-Craon, in 1909. In this relationship, Marthe realised how social pressure could strangle the expression of love. The princesse was moving in her spiritual life toward conversion to Catholicism but her continuing extra-marital affair with Beauvau-Craon was a sticking point about which she sought counsel from her close friend and confessor, the abbé Mugnier. The prince Antoine Bibesco observed, 'I don't know how much spiritual discipline [the conversion] will give you, but it certainly will make your life much more complicated, my dear cousin.' The prospect of divorce from Georges Bibesco placed Marthe in much the same position around 1910 that her mother-in-law, the princesse Valentine Bibesco, had been in when separating from her husband in 1874. Valentine had been condemned by Parisian high society for annulling her marriage to the prince Paul de Bauffremont, then changing her religion and nationality to marry the prince Bibesco; the couple settled in the family palace in Bucharest. On breaking the marital bond, Parisian high society had not relaxed its view by the First World War, even after three decades of legalised divorce. Marthe, afraid of the ostracism Valentine had suffered, resisted Beauvau-Craon's proposals that she leave Georges to marry him.[59]

Of course sex was not the direct cause of all marital difficulties, nor was it the only measure of a successful marriage. When problems arose between a couple the influence of the preceding generation should not be discounted, whether or not that influence encouraged a solution or indeed was part of the problem. Husbands and wives carried with them the example of their own parents' marriage. Usually too they had considerable contact with their in-laws. There are some letters that seem to indicate positive in-law relationships but, again, this is an area in which the written evidence tends to be patchy and there are very few oral history interviews that address the topic explicitly.[60] On 5 November 1882 the baronne Mathilde de Mackau wrote to her son-in-law the comte Humbert de Quinsonas:

> I have too good a memory to say to Anne in a learned tone: 'My dear child, it is not reasonable to cry when your husband goes away for eight days; tears should be reserved for things that really matter etc. ... etc. ...' Bear in mind my poor child that your austere mother-in-law would have done just that and dampened her pillow with tears in the same circumstances ... I have the misfortune or the happiness (I think that my grandchildren will find it a happiness) to have forgotten nothing of what my youth was like, and this sometimes keeps me from opening my mouth to moralise to young people ... What I really find most important is the *everyday*. You are entirely right when you say one needs to know how not to be a burden on one's wife, and I think still more that a wife should not be a burden on her husband. I promise to do everything possible so that Anne understands that; I ask you only to let me choose the occasions.[61]

Mathilde de Mackau did in fact do a little bit of moralising – with the best of intentions, naturally. On 4 August 1884 she wrote to Humbert: 'I beseech you not to remain always so closed up. That is your real weak point. The day when in relation to your wife you will have revealed the deepest regions of your heart, the deepest regions of your thoughts, you will have done a lot for the happiness of the two of you.'[62] Although it is not clear what impression this letter made at the time, Humbert kept it as the 'last memory of [his] mother-in-law' who died eighteen months later. Mathilde wished that her son-in-law and Anne would have 'the most happiness possible'. She knew from personal experience that married life did not bring unalloyed bliss and that it was challenging to create and to maintain genuine intimacy, especially with someone who was considerably older or younger. The notes of a nun who watched over and prayed for the baronne de Mackau during the final days of her life provide some insight to Mathilde's reasons for beseeching Humbert not to remain 'so closed up' to his wife:

> [Mathilde] feared her husband a lot in the early days of her marriage and said that she had for a long time been on a polite formal footing with him. She helped him in his writings. When he gave her something to copy there were times when she could not decipher his script. She did not dare to tell him and thought he must regard her knowledge as very slight.[63]

Differences in age, temperament, education, sexual experience, and expectations of intimacy are just some of the internal factors within a marriage that made the lived experiences of conjugality dynamic and unpredictable for aristocratic couples. Enduring the doubts, quarrels, and anxieties that came with being part of a married couple was less frightening, particularly for women, than facing an uncertain and socially anomalous future alone.

During the Third Republic nobles were mindful of the past, as well as immediate circumstances, when considering the suitability of candidates for marriage. The imperative to 'live nobly' meant that marital strategies had to remain flexible enough so that new wealth could be introduced, but in such a way that allowed an aristocratic family to keep the reputation of its blood lineage intact. In a milieu that sought to preserve social hierarchy, marriage was inextricably tied to concern for status. This meant that nobles focused more on prestige and fortune, so were less preoccupied with notions of gender complementarity than republicans. When Boni de Castellane expressed his view of marriages between gentlemen and wealthy young women, he was in no doubt about the nature of exchange between two unequal parties:

> We [the gentlemen] give them, in exchange [for a dowry], that which cannot be bought: in addition to a name, a tradition and a taste that education does not render them fit to achieve for themselves.[64]

Boni, by his comments, intended to correct the view of rich Americans who misunderstood such marriages because they considered themselves social equals who restored ancient coats of arms to glory. Aristocrats believed, to the contrary, that the might of inherited cash could not topple nobility of birth; they would always stand superior.

There was real pressure on noble couples to reproduce not only 'for France' but also to ensure the continuity of the bloodline. The prince Joachim Murat and Cécile Ney d'Elchingen did well in this respect by having eight children. In the eyes of contemporaries theirs had been a match 'predisposed to succeed', and in reproductive terms it certainly did. During the Murats' engagement, in March 1884, Madame Furtado-Heine, the fiancée's grandmother, declared that she was convinced Joachim would make Cécile's 'heart of gold', happy. The sixteen-year-old girl believed it too, writing to her prince: 'I do not have any fears. I know that I will be happy. I will be your wife and that is enough for me. With you I cannot be unhappy.' Thirty years into the marriage, there was another man from her own class who longed to bring joy to the princesse Murat – '*beaucoup*' he always noted discreetly on his notes and cards. The admirer wrote to Cécile: 'It is ridiculous after eight years, to tell you that I love you, it is ridiculous and yet I still want to all the same!'[65]

Notes

1 Letters and documents relating to the marriage in AP 31/68 Fonds Murat.
2 Pierre Bourdieu, *Le Sens pratique* (Paris, 1980), p. 269.
3 Cyril Grange, *Les Gens du Bottin Mondain: y être c'est en être* (Paris, 1996), p. 376; Monique de Saint-Martin, 'Les Stratégies matrimoniales dans l'aristocratie', *Actes de la Recherche en Sciences Sociales* 59 (1985), 74–7; Dominique Merllié and Jean-Yves Cousquer, 'Mariage et relations familiales dans l'aristocratie rurale: deux entretiens', *Actes de la Recherche en Sciences Sociales* 31 (1980), 22–34.
4 *Allocution prononcée par M. l'Abbé Viallet, Chapelain de Saint-Louis des Français à la benediction du mariage de M. le marquis de Villeneuve-Esclapon-Vence avec Son Altesse Mme la princesse Jeanne Bonaparte dans l'Eglise de Saint-Thomas d'Aquin, le 22 mars 1882* (Paris, 1882).
5 Notice for the *Annuaire des grands mariages* and editors' letter to the prince de Wagram, 10 December 1904, in AP 173 bis/437 Fonds Maréchal Berthier. On popular spectacle see Vanessa R. Schwarz, *Spectacular Realities: Early Mass Culture in Fin-de-Siècle Paris* (Los Angeles, 1999).

6 Suzanne Desan, *The Family on Trial in Revolutionary France* (Berkeley, 2004), ch. 1. For case studies of marriage before the 1789 Revolution see Jeffrey Merrick and Suzanne Desan (eds), *Family Gender, and Law in Early Modern France* (University Park, 2009). On second marriages see Stéphane Minvielle, 'Les Remariages nobles à Bordeaux au XVIIIe siècle' in Josette Pontet, Michel Figeac, and Marie Boisson (eds), *La Noblesse de la fin du XVIe au début du XXe siècle: un modèle social?* 2 vols (Anglet, 2002), pp. 109–32.
7 Francis Ronsin, *Les Divorcaires: affrontements politiques et conceptions du mariage dans la France au XIXe siècle* (Paris, 1992); Peter McPhee, *Living the French Revolution, 1789–99* (New York, 2006), pp. 120–1, 154–5.
8 Judith F. Stone, 'The republican brotherhood: gender and ideology' in Elinor A. Accampo, Rachel G. Fuchs, and Mary Lynn Stewart (eds), *Gender and the Politics of Social Reform in France 1870–1914* (Baltimore, 1995), pp. 28–9. For discussion of relationships Whitney Walton, *Eve's Proud Descendants: Four Women Writers and Republican Politics in Nineteenth-Century France* (Stanford, 2000), chs 3, 5, 6.
9 Pierre Bourdieu, *Distinction: A Social Critique of the Judgement of Taste*, trans. Richard Nice (London, 2000), pp. 437–51.
10 On negotiations for marriage in earlier times, see Geneviève Ribordy, 'The two paths to marriage : the preliminaries of noble marriage in late medieval France', *Journal of Family History* 26 (2001), 323–36.
11 *L'Illustration* 21 December 1889.
12 Donna Bohanan, *Crown and Nobility in Early Modern France* (New York, 2001), pp. 8–9, 16; Jonathan Dewald, *The European Nobility 1400–1800* (Cambridge, 1996), pp. 168–9.
13 The method comes from Raymond Boudon, *Mathematical Structures of Social Mobility* (Amsterdam, 1973), pp. 22–6. The results cited are based on data derived from the *Bottin mondain*. Grange, *Les Gens*, p. 104. See also Cyril Grange, 'Fusion des élites aristocratiques et bourgeoises à la belle époque: les mariages à Paris et en Provence' in Claude-Isabelle Brelot (ed.), *Noblesses et villes (1780–1950)* Actes du colloque de Tours 17–19 mars 1994 (Tours, 1995), pp. 247–59.
14 Saint-Martin, 'Les Stratégies matrimoniales', p. 76.
15 Christophe Charle, 'Noblesse et élites en France au début du XXe siècle' in *Les Noblesses européennes au XIXe siècle* (Rome, 1988), pp. 407–33 esp. 421; Merllié and Cousquer, 'Mariage et relations familiales', p. 26; Saint-Martin, 'Les Stratégies matrimoniales', pp. 76–7.
16 Mathieu Marraud, *La Noblesse de Paris au XVIIIe siècle* (Paris, 2000), p. 185.
17 Adeline Daumard, 'Noblesse et aristocratie en France au XIXe siècle' in *Les Noblesses européennes au XIXe siècle* (Rome, 1988), p. 97; Éric Mension-Rigau (ed.), *Journal de Constance de Castelbajac, marquise de Breteuil 1885–1886* (Paris, 2003), pp. 63–4. For anthropological and legal perspectives on

marriage between cousins see Laurent Barry, *La Parenté* (Paris, 2008), pp. 130–43.
18 Anne de Cossé Brissac, *La Comtesse Greffulhe* (Paris, 1991), pp. 13–23; Jean-Yves Tadié, *Marcel Proust: A Biography*, trans. Euan Cameron (New York, 2000), pp. 315–18, 845.
19 Marcel Proust, *In Search of Lost Time* vol. 3 *The Guermantes Way*, trans. C. K. Scott Moncrieff and Terence Kilmartin, revised by D. J. Enright (London, 1996), p. 83.
20 Mension-Rigau, *Journal de Constance de Castelbajac*, pp. 138–9.
21 Cyril Grange, 'Les Alliances entre élites juives et lignées aristocratiques à Paris dans la seconde moitié du XIXe siècle' in Michel Figeac (ed.), *Noblesse en échec? Les aristocraties françaises et européennes et leurs comportements démographiques du XVIIIe au milieu du XIXe siècle* (forthcoming); Gérard Rousset-Charny, *Les Palais parisiens de la belle époque* (Alençon, 1990), pp. 56–7, 92, 102, 120, 124, 221–2.
22 Ruth Brandon, *The Dollar Princesses: The American Invasion of the European Aristocracy 1870–1914* (London, 1980), pp. 1, 33–6, 80–103; Rousset-Charny, *Les Palais*, pp. 70–91, 188–93.
23 David Higgs, *Nobles in Nineteenth Century France: The Practice of Inegalitarianism* (Baltimore, 1987), p. 194; Natalie Petiteau, *Élites et mobilités: la noblesse d'Empire au XIXe siècle (1808–1914)* (Paris, 1997), pp. 222–41.
24 Élisabeth de Clermont-Tonnerre, *Au temps des équipages* (Paris, 1928), pp. 16–23, 43; Sir Denis Brogan, *The Development of Modern France 1870–1939* revised edition (London, 1967), p. 260; Henri, comte de Paris, *Mon album de famille*, texte de Michel de Grèce (Paris, 1996), p. 64.
25 17 November 1887 and 20 November 1887 in AP 101 (II)/38 Fonds Gramont.
26 15 February 1878 and 17 February 1878 in AD Savoie 29F/31 Fonds d'Alexandry d'Orengiani.
27 André de Fouquières, *Cinquante ans de panache* (Paris, 1951), pp. 98–101.
28 Émmanuel Beau de Loménie, *La Responsibilité des dynasties bourgeoises* 4 vols (Paris, 1937).
29 Trans. in Higgs, *Nobles*, p. 28.
30 Boni de Castellane, *Mémoires* (Paris, 1986), pp. 12–13.
31 Brandon, *The Dollar Princesses*, pp. 75–103.
32 André Germain, *Les Fous de 1900* (Paris, 1954), pp. 128–32.
33 Ronsin, *Les Divorcaires*, p. 251.
34 Gabriel Louis Pringué, *Trente ans de dîners en ville* (Paris, 1950), p. 23.
35 AP 101 (II)/150 Fonds Gramont.
36 Margaret H. Darrow, 'French noblewomen and the new domesticity, 1750–1850', *Feminist Studies* 5 (1979), 41–65.
37 Darrow, 'French noblewomen', pp. 50, 60.

38 Grange, *Les Gens*, pp. 154–5, 160–1, 507; Bonnie G. Smith, *Ladies of the Leisure Class: The Bourgeoises of Northern France in the Nineteenth Century* (Princeton, 1981), p. 223.
39 John Tosh, *A Man's Place: Masculinity and the Middle-Class Home in Victorian England* (New Haven, 2007), p. 59.
40 15 March 1884 in AP 31/68 Fonds Murat.
41 19 March 1884 in AP 31/68 Fonds Murat.
42 17 March 1884 in AP 31/70 Fonds Murat.
43 14 March 1884 in AP 31/70 Fonds Murat.
44 30 March 1884 in AP 31/70 Fonds Murat.
45 11 August 1878 in AP 101 (I)/22 Fonds Gramont.
46 James McMillan, *Housewife or Harlot: The Position of Women in French Society* (New York, 1980), pp. 167–9; Mary-Louise Roberts, *Civilization Without Sexes: Reconstructing Gender in Post-War France, 1917–1927* (Chicago, 1994), chs 1–3.
47 Christine Sutherland, *Enchantress: Marthe Bibesco and Her World* (New York, 1996), p. 26. See also Claude Francis and Fernande Gontier, *Mathilde de Morny: la scandaleuse marquise et son temps* (Paris, 2000), pp. 109, 171–6; Celia Bertin, *Marie Bonaparte: A Life* (London, 1982), pp. 94–5, 111–12.
48 Alain Corbin, 'Le "Sexe en deuil" et l'histoire des femmes au XIXe siècle' in Michelle Perrot (ed.), *Une histoire des femmes est-elle possible?* (Paris, 1984), p. 148. Trans. in Robert A. Nye, *Masculinity and Male Codes of Honor in Modern France* (Oxford, 1993), p. 12.
49 Martine Sevegrand, *L'Amour en toutes lettres: questions à l'abbé Viollet sur la sexualité 1924–1943* (Paris, 1996), p. 250.
50 15 November 1904 in AP 101 (II)/33 Fonds Gramont.
51 18 November 1904 in AP 101 (I)/33 Fonds Gramont.
52 6 October 1883 in AP 101 (II)/32 Fonds Gramont.
53 8 October 1883 in AP 101 (II)/32 Fonds Gramont.
54 8 October 1883 in AP 101 (II)/32 Fonds Gramont.
55 25 September 1892 in AP 101 (I)/22 Fonds Gramont.
56 9 August 1905 in AP 101 (I)/22 Fonds Gramont.
57 Michèle Plott, 'The rules of the game: respectability, sexuality, and the *femme mondaine* in late-nineteenth-century Paris', *French Historical Studies* 25 (2002), 531–56.
58 Élisabeth Higgonet-Dugua, *Anna de Noailles, coeur innombrable: biographie-correspondance* (Paris, 1989), pp. 68, 85–6, 125–30; Michael de Cossart, *The Food of Love: Princesse Edmond de Polignac (1865–1953) and Her Salon* (London, 1978), pp. 94–5; Sutherland, *Enchantress*, pp. 69–76.
59 Sutherland, *Enchantress*, pp. 26, 59–66, 78–87; *Affaire de Bauffremont: Séparation de corps* (Paris, 1874) and *Procès Bauffremont: Demande en nullité de naturalisation et de marriage* (Paris, 1876) in AP 229/3 Fonds Durrieu.

60 Merllié and Cousquer, 'Mariage et relations familiales', pp. 26, 28, 30, 32.
61 5 November 1882 in AP 156 (I)/301 Fonds Mackau.
62 4 August 1884 in AP 156 (I)/301 Fonds Mackau.
63 'Notes d'une religieuse' in AP 156 (I)/302 Fonds Mackau.
64 Castellane cited in Rousset-Charny, *Les Palais*, p. 77.
65 Letter [March 1884] from Madame Furtado-Heine and undated letter from Cécile to Joachim in AP 31/68 Fonds Murat. Notes and cards 1903–17 from Roger Luzarche d'Azay to the princesse Murat in AP 31/71 Fonds Murat.

3

Property and inheritance

For nobles, no less than other members of French society, encounters with bureaucracy were an inevitable consequence of owning property. Typically those encounters were occasioned by a transfer in property rights, due to a purchase or sale or partition of property among heirs. During the Third Republic, however, there were also changes in legislation relating to property ownership and transmission, some of which directly impacted upon aristocratic families but did not affect members of other classes in society. From the 1880s proposals were presented to the Chamber of Deputies for a tax on titles, a form of hereditary property. Then, in 1905, Articles 29 to 35 of the law on finances approved the state buyback of *majorats*, a form of entail. Napoleon I had created *majorats* in France to ensure that the men on whom he bestowed a nobiliary title also held property that would generate income appropriate to their rank. A further initiative, of consequence to all French citizens, was the introduction of an income tax. The idea for an income tax had been much debated before the First World War and it was a proposal put forward by the Minister of Finance Joseph Caillaux that was voted in on 15 July 1914. Senate and Chamber debates on the buyback of *majorats* and on taxation were informed by the composition of the parliamentary corps itself that included property-owners from a variety of social backgrounds. The debates were also informed by France's economic climate where the property market fluctuated in response to national and international developments.[1]

In order to secure and manage their investments nobles relied on the services of non-noble male professionals, just as they did for the verification of nobiliary titles. The relationships they formed with solicitors, bankers, accountants, and notaries were sometimes of short duration, for a particular item of business, or they could extend over many years involving the development of trust and credit. Such 'professional' relationships existed alongside nobles' familial relationships upon which the ownership and transmission of property could have significant effects.

The French Revolution had dealt significant blows to the material status of the nobility. Around one-fifth of aristocratic properties were seized and sold; nobles subsequently had to pay a tax on the estimated annual worth of their land; and they were no longer able to levy seigneurial dues. Moreover, like all French citizens, nobles were subject to the law on partible inheritance passed on 8 April 1791. This law followed on from the law of 15 March 1790 abolishing primogeniture, and it precipitated far-reaching social changes in France by giving all siblings, regardless of sex, the right to inherit an equal share of family property. Napoleon I modified the partible inheritance law to allow parents a 'disposable share', which they could bequeath to a child of their choosing. Whilst there were some variations in the way the law was responded to in practice, across different regions and social classes, the principal of equal division remained intact through changes in political regime across the nineteenth and twentieth centuries.[2]

How did partible inheritance affect decision-making about property in aristocratic families? To what extent were nobles able to minimise the undesirable effects of dividing family estates? When a dispute arose among siblings over matters of inheritance how was it resolved and in whose favour? To answer these questions requires investigation of aristocratic attitudes toward assets and investment, which were characterised by continuities across generations as well as by adaptation to broader forces of economic and social change. Nobles held particular views on property because of their upbringing, and the value they ascribed to various items was a reflection of class conditioning as much as it was a matter of personal 'taste'.[3] The practices and preferences arising out of the aristocratic *mentalité* on property were not always especially beneficial to nobles themselves, as some members of families recognised. Since many French nobles had relatives living elsewhere in Europe a number of different taxation systems and currencies were often brought into play when property was divided.

The most important form of property to aristocratic families was land. Rural property ownership was of symbolic significance to the nobility for it underpinned their original separateness from the bourgeoisie or 'town dwellers'. The historical connection between landownership and aristocratic status in France dates back at least as far as the ninth century when the public offices of title-bearing nobility corresponded to administrative units. Rather than pay a salary to his office-holders the king granted them pieces of land, and over time both the office and the land became inheritable. This was in no way a centralised or systematic process, for the property arrangements and inheritance patterns of the *ancien régime* were characterised by a 'jumble of diverse laws and practices'.[4] Written law operated in most of the south and local customary systems in the north; there were different forms of tenure; and practices in some areas were shaped by connections to other kingdoms such as Aragon and Castile.

The estate owned by a noble in the Middle Ages was called a fief.[5] To deter commoners from trying to ennoble themselves by acquisition of a fief the crown imposed a financial penalty on non-nobles for the purchase of such property. This was the same charge, known as *le droit de franc fief*, required of *la noblesse utérine*. Eventually the Edict of Blois in 1579 ruled out ennoblement by fief acquisition across most of France. The fact that it remained possible in the regions of Béarn, Bigorre, Navarre, and Soule astonished at least one commentator on the eve of the French Revolution.[6] In the sixteenth century minimum real estate requirements were established for noble offices and these were ranked so that, for example, a *duché* was more substantial than a *marquisat* and the corresponding title more prestigious. After 1579 the king had the power to ennoble through a process known as the concession or the raising of a *fief de dignité*. This involved the issuing of letters patent that were registered by the court (*parlement*) of the region and the Chambre des Comptes for taxation purposes. When Napoleon became Emperor, he, like the monarchs who had preceded him, also sought to give titles a landed basis by creating grand fiefs of the Empire in 1806 and then introducing the *majorat* system by decree of 1 March 1808.

This historical background on aristocratic landownership helps to explain the deep psychological attachment that nobles manifested toward their family estates. During the nineteenth century land remained the primary investment from which the nobility drew status. For relatively poor nobles, this amounted to one estate with a large residence that was not impressive enough to be called a château, so known as a *maison de maître*, *gentilhommière*, or, in the southwest, a *castel*. Rich nobles meanwhile owned several estates including at least one with a château.[7] The amount of landed property owned by French nobles was relatively small compared with the amounts owned by elites in other parts of Europe. After the 1789 Revolution many émigré nobles returned to their former estates or bought new ones and by the 1830s aristocratic landowners still held perhaps 10 per cent of France's territory, compared with around 25 per cent in 1789. Yet the size of many estates had diminished through forced seizures and sales. Few French nobles in the nineteenth century held as many as 10,000 acres; the average estate was less than 1,000 acres. In Prussia, by comparison, the Junkers owned some 40 per cent of the territory. In England and in Spain the landed elites owned just over 50 per cent of the territory and each of these countries contained over three hundred estates of more than 10,000 acres. It was in Eastern Europe, especially Austria, Hungary, and Romania, that old landowning families held on to vast tracts of 100,000 acres or more. Some of these estates surpassed in size even the largest to be found in Britain.[8]

Evidence of French nobles' attachment to their estates emerges from archives and memoirs where land is often associated with notions of blood and heritage. In the France of the Third Republic, where some noblemen sought to restore their family fortune by marrying a rich commoner from abroad, there was a good deal of aristocratic defensiveness about blood and heritage. This defensiveness was triggered especially easily over the sale of country estates. Châteaux were expensive to maintain, and there was always a pool of speculators waiting for them to be put on the market. A scrawled and undated note from the comtesse Élisabeth Greffulhe, to a journalist who had prepared an article on Parisian high society for *Le Matin*, reveals how protective nobles felt about this symbol of inherited status:

> Mademoiselle! What have you done! You say that the château de La Roche [chief seat of the La Rochefoucauld family] ... will belong to the Porgès, heavens above!! Run quickly to *Le Matin*, the entire [La] Rochefoucauld clan will clamour against this frightful thing, *this sale of the blue blood of the family to a Jew* [my italics] ... M. Porgès has bought the château de Rochefort and not the cradle of the illustrious family, it is only you that have made the gaffe, run quickly to repair it because this will create a real storm at the paper.[9]

Whilst it is not clear from the letter why the comtesse had access to the article before it was published, her panicked response to the journalist's mistake indicates a deep nerve had been hit. As someone who belonged to an 'illustrious family' herself, Élisabeth (née de Caraman-Chimay) recognised that the La Rochefoucauld clan would interpret the error as a bitter insult, probably irrespective of who was cited as the new owner of their château. What mattered was the insinuation that the La Rochefoucauld had given up their land. The news would be received as a slur against family pride.

The integral connection between family property and noble identity is evident in the memoirs of the duchesse Élisabeth de Clermont-Tonnerre. Élisabeth never forgave her father and stepmother, who were trying to save money, for selling the estate of Mangé, which had belonged to her real mother's family and was promised to her when she married. Nor did Élisabeth forgive an American couple, the Mackays, for buying Mangé. Recalling a visit to '[her] old property' she wrote:

> The Mackays had completely distorted the relationship between the château and the land. The costs had been exorbitant, the savings ridiculous. The house itself, stripped of its paintings and Renaissance cabinets that had been its ornament, seemed sordid to me. The drapes were full of holes and dirty, the carpets were worn out.[10]

To the duchesse, the broken link between the château and land (*pays*) was a reflection of how broken she felt at having her mother's family estate removed from her possession. Empty, soiled, and damaged were words to describe what she observed, as well as what she felt inside.

It is possible to read the grudge that the duchesse de Clermont-Tonnerre held against the Mackays into a caricature she made, further on in her memoirs, of the American heiress, Anna Gould:

> I saw this one [Miss Gould] on her first arrival in Paris. It was said that she was ugly, and she was by comparison with the aesthetic of Paris, but perhaps not according to that of her country ... She was small, thin, her face entirely taken up by a large nose and two enormous black eyes, her complexion was yellow; her hair pinned up into wings like an aeroplane made her shorter, and her back was strewn with long black hairs. Boni de Castellane, whom she subsequently married, was to transform her. He had her plucked, shampooed, made-up, [and] styled.[11]

The 'transformation' that Boni performed on Anna, as it is detailed by the duchesse in a description that contains many stereotypes of the Jewish body, functioned in reverse to the changes made at Mangé.[12] Élisabeth aligned her perception of the château interior, after the property's sale, as 'sordid', with the 'ugly' appearance of an American Jewish heiress, a woman with plenty of money. A French aristocrat, Boni, was cast in the role of raising the Jew's external presentation up to the aesthetic of Paris; one racial standard was exchanged for the other. Despite the work to improve Anna's appearance, in the duchesse's eyes this American heiress did not belong to Parisian high society any more than the Mackays belonged on her land.

In addition to rural property, most nobles owned or rented an urban residence, in a provincial town or in Paris, and chose to live part of the year on their country estate and part of the year in an apartment or *hôtel particulier*. They spent winter and spring, the social 'Season', in town, and summer and autumn in the country. The strategies for investing in property were largely determined by income. Nobles of modest wealth in the Somme, for example, sought to build up their estates by acquiring new parcels of land of up to a few hundred hectares that might be dispersed over several communes. They were focused on developing their rural base and often became involved in local agricultural societies whilst also keeping a townhouse in Amiens. By contrast, those with very large fortunes concentrated their investments elsewhere, including the Paris property market. These 'Parisians' still held on to a landed estate, received through inheritance, but they generally did not try to accumulate further land like the nobles who lived year-round in the Somme. At the turn of the century those who could afford to live in the richest neighbourhoods of Paris purchased or commissioned the construction of *hôtels particuliers* that served as luxurious venues for entertaining high society.[13]

One of the ways that nobles sought to generate wealth for the maintenance of property was through marriage; however, this was not the only strategy. During the nineteenth century nobles in France, as well as in other parts of Europe, accrued income from rents, engaged in professional activity, and invested in textiles, metallurgy, mining, glass manufacture, transportation (particularly railways), and insurance. The Murat family is a case in point, although they also did well from marriage; the prince Murat V's wife, Cécile (née Ney d'Elchingen), was the granddaughter by adoption of Madame Furtado-Heine, a very wealthy woman with relatives among the Fould and Heine families involved in banking. The Murats owned shares in French railways, the railways of southern Austria and the Palatinate, the Suez Maritime Canal Company, Robinson Gold Mining, Chinese Engineering and Mining, Silesian Zinc Mines, Discount Share Company of Berlin, the Bank of France, the Bank of Saxony, the Credit Agency of Egypt and De Beers. Their properties included an *hôtel particulier* in the rue de Monceau and the estates of Rocquencourt and Chambly.[14]

The diversification of the sources of income for the nobility had implications for the longstanding connection between property ownership and nobles' occupation of public roles. Whereas in the Middle Ages landownership had been linked with noble office, and the fief system was regulated by the Crown, the Third Republic saw nobles invest more heavily in forms of property that were not land-based. One reason for this was the agricultural crisis that decreased the value of land by one-third between 1880 and 1912. The trend in response to falling rents and reduced agricultural productivity was to move money away from land and into the stock market. Under the July Monarchy 60 per cent of aristocratic wealth was found in real estate compared with only 38.8 per cent in 1911. Increased shareholding meant that noblemen came to occupy new types of public roles as property owners at a time when it was becoming more difficult for them to hold on to their traditional roles in government and diplomacy. In 1902 noblemen made up 30 per cent of the directors of railway companies and 23 per cent of the directors of large banking and steel companies.[15]

At first glance this pattern of nobles becoming more involved, at a high level, in the world of industry and commerce suggests some modification to aristocratic identity. Historically the nobility was required to avoid professional moneymaking activity because it was perceived to compromise aristocratic status, reducing that status to the level of the bourgeois. The laws of *dérogeance* meant that nobles risked certain penalties if they were seen to be engaging in trade. Yet this did not mean that nobles were entirely disinterested in manufacture and financial markets. Management of an estate and the exploitation of resources from the land meant there were business dimensions to the aristocratic lifestyle.[16] Nobles' relationship with industry and commerce was not new in the Third Republic but it did strengthen. If, in terms of holding a public role like company director, a nobleman was prepared to resemble a wealthy bourgeois, then was it the case that a distinctive aristocratic status mattered less to nobles by the late nineteenth century?

Evidence of the continued symbolic importance of landownership and attachment to family estates that characterised the aristocratic *mentalité* indicates that social differentiation did continue to matter. Indeed, precisely because many nobles were struggling financially to maintain their estates, the sense of having a separate experience from wealthy bourgeois property owners was made more acute. The preservation of land became associated with the preservation of 'race'. Whilst nationalist intellectuals like Maurice Barrès are most commonly identified with the development of this association it was by no means exclusive to them. Other writers who elaborated on the theme of land and race at the turn of the century included the comtesse de Martel, under her penname Gyp, and Paul Bourget.[17]

Bourget's 1907 novel *L'Émigré*, set at the end of the nineteenth century, is a tale of secrets and lies over birth and property that bedevil the noble house of Claviers-Grandchamp. The marquis de Claviers, who like his ancestors was passionate about hunting, rode over his estate 'on so many good horses' and knew the forests 'tree by tree, leaf by leaf'. In his eyes, the 1789 Revolution had disrupted the natural social order by promoting the interests of individuals over the interests of the family. The marquis explains to his heir Landri 'the profound social truths' of this natural order: 'Families must put down roots to survive, they must hold on to a territorial seat, they must identify with a piece of land.' During the Third Republic such a conviction posed real challenges for the marquis de Claviers and his only surviving son, Landri:

> We have many costs to bear. If the income from the land was as substantial as it used to be, and perhaps if I had been more strategic in our investments, then we would get by more easily. Just think there have been two generations affected by this monstrous Civil Code with its forced partitions that crush France.[18]

One does not have to look hard to find the sentiments of the fictional marquis de Claviers echoed in other sources by noblemen. Alexis de Tocqueville had earlier devoted great attention to the importance of preserving aristocratic property for descendants: 'The family represents the land and the land the family, perpetuating its name, origin, glory, power and virtue.' The marquis Henri de Breteuil, a contemporary of Bourget, also complained of the effects of 'an inflexible Code' decimating aristocratic estates 'in less than four generations'.[19]

Nobles' sense of difference and efforts to defend their interests on property matters were provoked not only by the declining value of land and partible inheritance but also by specific attempts by the government during the Third Republic to undercut their exercise of economic capital as property owners through legislation. One area in which we can see this tension is in debates on taxation.

Before 1789 taxation was a key factor that contributed to marking out the nobility as different from other members of French society when it came to property ownership. The fact that the Second Estate enjoyed exemption from some forms of taxation was a major cause of social resentment. In this predominantly rural society, where tenants and sharecroppers were required by law to pay seigneurial dues to noble landowners, a redistribution of the fiscal burden along more equitable lines was seen as an essential first step to social reform. In 1787–88 proposals to remove the nobility's fiscal privileges and implement reforms including the introduction of a land tax faltered in the face of aristocratic resistance. But the abolition of the seigneurial system in August 1789 led to complete redesign of the tax system, and the gradual and laborious implementation of new arrangements for tax collection across France.[20]

Paradoxically, it was in the 1880s – when historians consider that the revolutionary changes triggered in 1789 were largely accomplished – that proposals for a tax on titles reopened the issue of specific fiscal treatment for the nobility. What was the basis of the proposals and why was this minority group within the French population (and anyone who wished to identify with it) targeted?

On 26 June 1886 an article appeared in *Le Figaro* written by Hubert-Léon Lavedan, the conservative director of the *Correspondent*, under the name 'Ph. de Grandlieu'. Its publication followed discussion in the Chamber of Deputies of Beauquier's proposal to abolish noble titles (again) and to amend the Penal Code in which usurpation of a title was punishable under Article 259. Grandlieu was opposed to Beauquier's proposal. Instead of the Penal Code provision, imposing a fine for usurpation, Grandlieu argued that it made more sense to allow citizens the 'liberty' of giving their name an aristocratic appearance on the proviso that they would be taxed for doing so.

> The Treasury is worried about the avoidance of many taxes, such as those on alcohol and tobacco. By contrast, here [in the case of a tax on titles] the person to be taxed would himself increase the amount due! The guiding principle of taxation is to feather the hen without making it squawk too much. Under our system, not only would it not squawk, but it would cluck with joy, pride, and gratitude! For the first time since taxes came into existence – and that's a long time ago! – we would witness the tax payer seek out the collector, not to argue for an exemption, but to declare his debts. Imagine a stunned tax collector listening to the most extraordinary protestations: 'What, Sir, I have been overlooked? This is a disgrace! I demand special treatment! I want to pay, and the more the better! Here is my money! I insist on giving it to you! Take it! I will not have it any other way' Wouldn't it be ideal?[21]

Grandlieu's ingenious line of argument inspired proposals for a tax on titles submitted to the tribune of the Chamber of Deputies by Messieurs

Borie and Moreau in 1889 and 1890 respectively. Borie suggested a graded fiscal hierarchy ranging from 5,000 francs payable by princes down to 100 francs payable by those with the particle *de* in their surname. Using statistics that assumed (erroneously) around sixty thousand French aristocratic families he calculated that the implementation of this type of tax would raise nearly 37 million francs in annual revenue, which should be given over to the creation of life pensions for indigent or infirm agricultural workers. Raymond Poincaré, on behalf of the committee that considered the proposal, rejected it on the grounds that, far from reducing criminal abuse relating to usurpation of titles 'in reality, under the guise of being egalitarian and democratic, it would result in the official consecration of the aristocracy and of inequality'.[22]

Moreau went in a different direction with his fifteen-article proposal the following year. Article 1 abolished existing noble titles. Article 2 required that every French citizen wishing to signal nobiliary status through use of a title should include the word '*dit*' beside it on all official and civil documents including electoral rolls. By this measure, not only would the functionaries of the Bureau du Sceau de France be kept busy creating legalised false titles but also the state would generate revenue through an annual tax, applied at differing rates according to the title registered, from 500 francs for a particle through to 250,000 francs for the title of prince. Furthermore, under Article 11 of Moreau's proposal, the hierarchy of noble titles would be mapped on to France's administrative system. Each main centre of a department would be able to hold the title of prince or duc, each main centre of an arrondissement would be able to hold the title of marquis or comte, and so on – all subject to payment of an annual tax. Moreau concluded that the tax 'on vanity' would naturally be of a temporary nature:

> Without doubt the improvement in social customs, the expansion of republican sentiments, the social evolution that is imminent will increasingly tend to eliminate the obsession with the pretentious ornaments of the past. But, in waiting for these positive transformations to occur, there is no harm in a tithe on vanity levied on those vestiges of an odious bygone era to which some would have us return.[23]

That a deputy of the left expressed such ideas in 1890, as part of a serious proposal for generating revenue for the state, does call into question the thesis of a 'triumph' of republicanism at this time. In Moreau's vision of French society 'the expansion of republican sentiments' was yet to come, so, in the meantime, why not capitalise on the inherent vanity of human beings 'that compels some good-for-nothings to deck themselves out in faded old finery'? Given that the number of false nobles in France has been estimated at five hundred thousand by the twentieth century Moreau's scheme might actually have been quite lucrative. But, like Borie's proposal, it was quashed. Article 11, in particular, did not win favour with the commission:

> Would it be proper to put up continuously for public auction the old, respected names of our towns and villages, and to see them used as superficial ornaments by 'beneficiaries' whose ridiculousness or indignity could tarnish the reputation of entire populations! We would participate in a masquerade of titles and sonorous labels, hardly the sort of thing to lend us renown as a serious nation.[24]

Noble titles were, and have remained in France, a form of hereditary property. The proposals put forward by Borie and Moreau had absolutely no basis in nobiliary law; indeed they contradict several fundamental historical principles of aristocratic lineage, not to mention just about every legal regulation governing the transmission of titles in France. Moreover, the calculations of fiscal revenue based on erroneous numbers of individuals holding titles are at odds with what historians now know about the contemporary demographic and economic situation of the nobility. Although the proposals were thrown out at the time, like Beauquier's on the abolition of noble titles, the idea for a tax on titles did not disappear. It was raised again in the Chamber session of 14 December 1906, when the deputy Réville declared that the implementation of such a tax 'would reduce our other fiscal duties'.[25]

Historians' analyses of taxation reform in the context of the Third Republic overlook political discussion of a tax on titles. The focus of analyses for this period tends to be on attempts to introduce an income tax that, like other measures of fiscal reform, were hampered by delays and opposition.[26] Certainly the political and economic arguments for and against a tax on titles differed from the arguments for and against an income tax. Yet there was some similarity between the proposals, which were based on the common principle of using the revenue to support and extend social services in aid of the poor. A proposal for an income tax was put to the Chamber of Deputies during Léon Bourgeois's short-lived ministry from November 1895 to April 1896. Bourgeois was a Radical seeking a compromise between socialism and capitalism that he dubbed 'solidarism'. The solidarist vision, which gained currency in the early Third Republic, was that the rich had a social debt to the poor that they could offset by paying an income tax enabling the state to finance social services. The Chamber of Deputies accepted the proposed law to introduce an income tax to France but the Senate opposed it, leading to Bourgeois's resignation. On 15 July 1914 the law was passed by the Senate and when Poincaré became Prime Minister in July 1926 he sought the confidence of rich investors by reducing their income tax and increasing direct taxes on the poor, the very opposite of what Bourgeois had tried to achieve. Poincaré's term as Prime Minister, during which he also held the Finance portfolio, saw the franc restored to the gold standard at one-fifth of its pre war value bringing stability to the French economy and wiping out state debt to the Bank of France.

Opposition to the introduction of an income tax before the First World War came from deputies and senators who were not noblemen, as well as from those who were and who would have been subject to a tax on titles had one been implemented in the same period. There are many ways of explaining this opposition, including the argument of a 'French' dislike for fiscal inquisition seen to compromise the privacy of the individual. Conservatives displayed a variety of motives, as they did for example in Germany where nobles were against an income tax from the eighteenth century.[27] For titled noblemen in France the combination of the proposed income tax, plus repeated calls for a tax on titles, meant there was the prospect of mounting debt caused by payments to the state to finance a regime that most of them detested. This was not an imaginary prospect. Fiscal duties were increasing for those who owned shares and real estate and who were liable to pay the new inheritance tax introduced from February 1901. Given the contemporaneous decline in the value of land, nobles in France were hardly disposed to tolerate the idea of any further inroads being made on their family fortune. In this respect they shared much the same outlook as aristocratic landowners in Britain where the rise in death duties and quadrupling of taxation between 1890 and 1920 created an atmosphere of financial gloom affecting even the richest peers.[28]

Within this context another pertinent legislative issue that illustrates the clash between republican aims and the interests of aristocratic families was the issue of the *majorat*. In the first few years of the twentieth century the French government took steps to abolish the *majorat* system enabling the state to buy back property for the public domain by paying an indemnity to aristocratic individuals holding this form of entail. A *majorat* consisted of a title of property attached to a title of honour (nobiliary in France) passed down by order of primogeniture. There were two types: the *majorat de propre mouvement* and the slightly less prestigious *majorat sur demande*. The forms such property could take were manifold – for example, farms, forests, meadows, mills, forges, and houses – but the point was that the property could be leased out and hence provide annuities known as *rentes* that were combined in the entail. While the *majorat* system was specifically regulated by French law, similar systems for entail operated elsewhere in Europe under different names.[29] In the Polish-Lithuanian Commonwealth, for example, the equivalent of the *majorat* was known as the *ordynacja*, introduced by King Stefan Batory in the late sixteenth century. The fortunes of wealthy Polish and Lithuanian families such as the Zamoyski and the Radziwill, who had members living in France in the late nineteenth century, were based on *ordynacja*.[30]

The French government's rationale for ending the *majorat* system was formulated from two elements: concern for principle and budgetary considerations. From a republican perspective, the *majorat* contradicted the principle of equality. Incompatible with the law on partible inheritance, the *majorat* system was designed to concentrate a family's resources in the hands of one child to the financial detriment of other offspring. Whilst there would appear to have been a straightforward argument for abolishing the *majorat*, the situation was legally complex because those who held such a title of property also held a title of honour given formal investiture by the sovereign. Any attempt to remove the former created a retroactive decision by the state. In 1835 and 1849 the issue had been given detailed legal and political consideration and no solution was found. It resurfaced during discussion in the Chamber of Deputies over the budget in January 1903 when the deputy Chabert argued that the current budgetary difficulties in France stemmed from continuing demands on the public purse that originated in previous regimes. The Republic was financially supporting through annual payments (*les dotations*) not only those accorded a *majorat* of the First Empire but also those on pensions accorded by Louis XVIII, Charles X, and Louis-Philippe. A resolution was passed inviting a thorough investigation by the Minister of Finance which resulted in two reports. The deputy Rivet led the partisans for complete suppression without indemnity. In the end, however, a more moderate approach was adopted in Articles 29 to 35 of the 1905 law on finances. A Commission comprising representatives of the state and *majoritaires* would determine the price for each title of property subject to buyback. As a consequence of the buyback the *majoritaire* was eligible to receive an indemnity of not more than fifteen times the value of annual revenue received from his *majorat*. In 1905 there were three *majorats sur demande* and thirty-eight *majorats de propre mouvement* remaining in France.[31]

The Massa archive provides one illustration of a family's encounter with the resulting bureaucratic machinery. On 14 April 1921 a lawyer, a notary, a solicitor, and a representative for the duc Jean de Massa met to discuss the duc's wish to reclaim the sum of 79,675 francs paid in error to the Registration Office in relation to the state buyback of his *majorat*. The Massa *majorat* comprised several annuities as well as shares in the Orléans and Loing canals. By virtue of laws passed on 15 May 1818 and 22 April 1905, two of these annuities were deemed reversible to the state domain, and on 9 May 1906 the Minister of Finance ruled that the duc Alfred de Massa was eligible for an indemnity of 318,698.49 francs. This amount was unpaid when Alfred died and in 1913 when his successor, the duc Jean de Massa, sought to claim it he found himself unable to do so because of legal restrictions preventing access to the necessary documents. Worse, he was erroneously charged a fee of 79,675 francs, which he paid to the Registration Office.

In 1921 the duc was hit with a large bill for income tax and the legal team was exploring ways to minimise his financial obligations to the state by offsetting them against the 79,675 francs already paid. The lawyer, Guyot, informed the group that the Registration Office did not pay compensation, except in the case of reparations that did not apply to the Massa *majorat*. The solicitor, Mavré, recalled to the others' attention that the duc de Massa had stated in the presence of Tollu, the notary, a preference for the 'amicable' rather than judiciary route to settle the affair. Gallet, the duc's representative, amended this statement saying that 'in principle' his client 'would always prefer courtesy to force' but that the duc had refused formally to give any personal indication of the route to take, leaving instead the freedom and responsibility of making the decision to his legal team. Guyot took the lead at this point, stating that the judiciary route was essential to obtain a favourable result:

> The Registration Office, as my father rightly says, is a dishonest Administration composed of honest people ... Our only chance of obtaining satisfaction is to use, as you put it, force. In a nutshell, to make the officials there feel that we will not back down. We need to find their weak point ... During the war, the order of the day was 'Pay very quickly what you owe, it is necessary to give confidence'. Currently the order of the day is 'The State's pockets being empty, do whatever you can not to pay'.[32]

Guyot went on to advise the formulation of a document giving justification for the restitution of the sum that had been wrongly paid. It would be necessary in this document to 'cite many well chosen references in order to prove that we know perfectly well what we are on about and that we are strongly armed'. The lawyer then stated his opinion that the duc himself would need to exercise his contacts, status and influence as a nobleman:

> I ask you to insist on this point with Monsieur le duc de Massa; he must apply pressure through a member of parliament. I expect Monsieur le duc knows deputies or senators. This deputy or senator, once the affair is at clinching point, will be able if necessary to enquire in writing to the minister; it is the only way to force the Administration to respond.[33]

Two and a half decades later, in 1947, the *majorat* was still causing complications for the Massa family and was referred to a legal expert, Dr Pierre Ravel. He recommended the reversion of the *majorat* and income from it to the marquis Alexandre de Massa. For this reversion to be achieved, Ravel required a series of documents, including a note on the genealogy of the Massa family and original birth certificates for its male members, that would make up a dossier to be passed to the Ministère de la Finance and then to the Ministère de la Justice. The object of the exercise was to obtain for the marquis de Massa investiture with the title of duc de Massa, since this was the title of honour attached to the title of property. Ravel realised that a new law of 10 January 1942, authorising the Ministère de la Finance to buy back income from the Orléans and Loing canals, would have an impact on the Massa *majorat*. He discovered from the Ministère de la Finance that for a variety of reasons the state still had no systematic procedure in place for converting entail into indemnity capital. The best route was to seek reversion of the *majorat* in the hope the business would be resolved in the next generation.[34]

The archival sources relating to the Massa *majorat* provide insight into the kinds of complex property issues that noble families required the help of non-noble professionals to try to resolve. Sometimes things turned out well for a noble; sometimes they did not. The trickiest cases, from a solicitor's or notary's perspective, tended to be those involving individuals who were related to one another and who had different, competing sets of interests that created divisions within the family. An example is documented in the archives of the comte Xavier de La Rochefoucauld.

On 15 August 1921 the comte wrote in annoyance to his notary, Ader, that he had just received a letter from his nephew, the comte Gaston de

La Rochefoucauld, declaring himself the owner of the Rivarennes schoolhouse. Surprised by this information, Xavier had checked with his brother Jules who confirmed Gaston's ownership of the schoolhouse as the result of an act of property division. 'So,' he complained to Ader, 'despite the very clear expression of my wishes, despite the assurances received on many occasions from yourself, notably two or three days before the signing of the act, that my legitimate and legal wishes would be respected, I discover that they were not in the least bit taken into account.'[35] Ader, returning to Paris on 18 August after a three-day absence, replied immediately to the comte. 'Certainly, like anyone else, I could have made a mistake; but in a delicate arrangement of the type we prepared, with so many difficulties and precautions, it would have been unforgivable of me to translate the intentions of the parties in an inexact fashion.'[36] Ader proceeded to recount the exchanges he had had with Xavier and his nephew in January and February 1921 that had led the Rivarennes schoolhouse to be attributed to Gaston, rather than be kept out of the property division and sold at a later date when Xavier could buy it back. The attribution of the schoolhouse to Gaston had been made, it seems, largely because Xavier grew tired of the wrangling and wanted an end to the business, even if it meant jettisoning the chance to see his own wishes fulfilled. The notary was particularly desirous to convince the comte he had not betrayed his interests, having 'merited your [Xavier's] confidence and sympathy by over twenty years of collaboration'. He received a half-hearted response: 'Was there a misunderstanding in this affair? It's possible, or even probable; what is certain, however, is that we do not agree. One of us is evidently mistaken, but which one?'[37]

Perhaps part of the reason for the comte Xavier de La Rochefoucauld's frustration lay in the fact that there were so many complicated issues of property division to work through. Four years after the Rivarennes business, in February 1925, Xavier finally witnessed the reception of inherited money owing to his wife, mother-in-law, nephews and nieces. The Bonneval inheritance was no simple matter, particularly in 1925, because it involved a large amount of money, accounts opened with a German bank that merged with another German bank, and a sixteen-year period of delay extending over the First World War before the comtesse de La Rochefoucauld and her relatives in France received their respective shares.

On 15 October 1924 a Franco-German Mixed Arbitral Tribunal met at 57 rue de Varenne, Paris, to deliberate. It was established that the baron Fernand von Schickler, a German national and banker in Berlin, had died on 13 October 1909 leaving a will made out on 2 October in which he made his brother, Arthur, sole legatee and left instructions for some particular bequests. One of those bequests was a sum of 1,200,000 deutschmarks payable to his niece, the marquise de Bonneval (née Suchet d'Albuféra) for which the usufruct was not transmissible. The marquise was to receive interest on the capital, whilst the original amount was to be secured in a Gebrüder Schickler bank account and eventually divided equally among the marquise's descendants. Two accounts were subsequently opened: one to receive the sum of 1,200,000 deutschmarks and the other to receive the interest paid on this sum at 3.5 per cent. In 1910, Louis Delbrück and Karl Soerger from the maison Delbrück became associates of the Gebrüder Schickler bank, and the baron Arthur von Schickler became an associate of the maison Delbrück; together they formed Delbrück, Schickler & Co. Under a clause in Fernand's 1909 will, the resulting alteration in the bank's character, from a 'familial' enterprise to one involving 'non-familial' capital and management, would have allowed the 1,200,000 deutschmarks to be withdrawn and divided among the Bonneval inheritors. This was not done in 1910 and the sum remained in the account during the First World War, after which the Bonneval inheritors became the bank's creditors and the case was put before the Tribunal with the following result.[38]

In application of the Articles 296 and 299 of the Treaty of Versailles, and in conformity with the Tribunal's jurisprudence, the creditors' accounts were deemed annulled on 4 August 1914. The balance, plus interest at the rate of 5 per cent from 1914 (a rate established by the Treaty), was to be restored to the creditors. For this to occur, the money had to pass from the German Office of Verification and Compensation to its French equivalent using an exchange rate of 122.76 francs for 100 deutschmarks.[39] The resulting amount of 1,974,972.20 francs went into a Bank of France account in the names of the six inheritors.[40] The amount was then divided and the legal and exchange expenses paid. Paule du Val de Bonneval wrote to her uncle, the comte Xavier de La Rochefoucauld, on 7 October 1925 thanking him for his explanations regarding 'the money from Germany' and asking his advice on what to do with it. 'I am delighted,' she ended 'that *grand'maman* [Xavier's mother-in-law] finally received her inheritance to be able to enjoy a bit of luxury during the final years of her life'.[41]

Thus far we have considered matters of property ownership chiefly relating to land and financial bequest. Let us now turn to cases involving other items of property such as furniture, paintings, decorative objects, jewellery, table services, and linen. Possession of these types of items generated complications, as well as pleasure, within aristocratic families and there were three main reasons for this. First, they were often of substantial monetary value and needed to be insured; second, they were subject to taxation; and third, nobles were brought up to regard them as priceless family heritage.

Aristocratic families were proud of inherited items of furnishing and decoration held in rural and urban residences. This was especially true of family portraits that were generally commissioned by leading artists, making them valuable works of art in monetary terms not to mention the sense of attachment they commanded among relatives. The abbé Mugnier of the Parisian parish of Sainte-Clotilde took the opportunity, on a visit to the prince de Chalais's home, to view and discuss the family portraits. Madame Julia Daudet, wife of the writer Alphonse Daudet, had no choice but to admire the comte Robert de Montesquiou's array of ancestral likenesses; he made a point of showing them off to visitors. Linen and table services, often given as wedding gifts and designed for entertaining on a grand scale, were also significant heirlooms. The baronne Morgan de Belloy's silverware, for example, was estimated at 15,000 francs. François-Charles d'Harcourt recalled that in 1944, when a fire broke out in the family château, hundreds of linen items embroidered with the Harcourt coat of arms were destroyed but a servant managed to save 'a small case containing an admirable Saxon fountain' as well as 'the large gold medal that the pope gave my great-grandfather, the French ambassador to Rome, to thank him for the help he had given him in 1849'.[42]

The preservation of family patrimony had aesthetic as well as financial implications. Research into death inventories has shown that bourgeois home furnishing was characterised by homogeneity and that in the late nineteenth century bourgeois couples did not live surrounded by their parents' furniture but rather purchased their own.[43] By contrast, noble couples felt impelled to live with the belongings of previous generations in addition to items they bought themselves. This produced greater eclecticism in the furnishing of an aristocratic home. For example, in 1879 the baron and baronne Picot d'Aligny inherited family portraits, paintings, and furniture from the baronne's rich uncle Gluflet who had been a collector. These came to the couple's château, Montmirey-la-Ville in Franche-Comté, and over the years new purchases and gifts were added including tapestries in the style of Louis XV, Arab curios sent from Algeria by their cousin Hubert Lyautey, and a Louis XVI iron screen given to them by the baronne's mother. Not all nobles necessarily wanted to live with their parents' furnishings. The comtesse Anna de Noailles, born in 1876, recalled that as a child she did not like her parents' home on the avenue Hoche with its gilt chairs, Oriental carpets, and round divans with puffed-up Turkish gauze cushions. Her ideal space was a leafy garden.[44]

The financial implications of maintaining inherited items often led nobles into negotiation with relatives in an attempt to offset costs. On 23 July 1919 the marquis Pierre de Livron wrote to his cousin, the prince Henri de Béarn, from his estate Bellevue in Dordogne. The marquis had already spoken with another family member concerning a portrait that he and his brother did not have the means to keep after their father's death. Neither brother could afford to pay his share of the 40,000–50,000 francs sum for which the portrait had been insured, but nor did they want to see the item part from family possession.

> It is a maréchal of France, attributed to Largilière, but I don't think it is signed. This painter almost never put his name on his canvases. It is apparently a very handsome painting; the frame is nothing special . . . Roger de Galard would be able to tell you better than I who it was who wanted this Béarn to be preserved for posterity under Largilière's brushstroke.[45]

It is clear from the marquis de Livron's letter that he had not actually met the prince Henri de Béarn. He suggested that the portrait might serve as a pretext for his cousin to visit Bellevue and provide Pierre with 'the very real pleasure of making [his] acquaintance'.

The line between family patrimony and national patrimony was often blurred, and some nobles were more conscious of this than others when ascribing value to items of heritage. On 14 July 1903 Letizia Ruspoli di Castel Delfino wrote to her cousin, the prince Joachim Murat, about two family portraits. Whether this Italian noblewoman purposefully chose Bastille Day on which to write is not certain, but she did try to portray her commitment to the name and historical legacy of the Murat that were of national significance in both Italy and France. Letizia informed her cousin that owing to bad business dealings her husband's fortune was depleted, leaving her and her children in a state of financial difficulty. She had obtained estimates of the market value of the two portraits: one representing her grandmother, the princesse Murat Pepoli, by Gérard, and the other representing the first prince Murat, King of Naples, on horseback wearing his cavalry uniform, by Knoll. Together they were worth between 10,000 and 13,000 francs.

These paintings are worth much more to family members, so I am approaching you to ask if you would like to have them ... Since I am obliged to deprive myself of them, I would be happy to see them pass into your hands, confident that out of respect for our ancestors you would conserve them carefully in the manner that they deserve.[46]

For relatives dispersed within France and across Europe the practice of contacting one another about inheritance matters was common. From archival records it seems that, generally speaking, such matters were easier to sort out between cousins than between siblings. This was perhaps due to the more distant relationship between cousins that facilitated detached formal discussion. The proximity of the sibling experience meant that partition of property and costs of maintenance were more likely to be emotive issues, and there were some very trenchant battles fought over who was the 'rightful' inheritor of particular items.

An example of the type of painful fall-out that could result is contained in the archives of the Berthier family. Alexandre Berthier fought tooth and nail to obtain family portraits that had been bequeathed to his younger sister, the comtesse Marie-Élisabeth de Turenne d'Aynac, by their father, Napoléon-Alexandre, on his death in 1885. There were three children in the family and Alexandre, the only son, was the middle child. The last will and testament of Napoléon-Alexandre, the prince de Wagram, made it abundantly clear – if it had not been already – that Marie-Élisabeth was their father's favourite. Exercising his parental right, introduced by Napoleon I, to allocate a 'disposable share' to a child of his choice, the prince de Wagram left his Parisian apartment at 21 rue Balzac and all its contents including the family portraits to Marie-Élisabeth. In addition, he left her some extremely valuable and rather symbolic pieces, including all his jewels, two blue vases decorated with Boucher's delicate painting, and his deceased wife's lace underwear. All of these items together were estimated at 145,340 francs. Alexandre, furious at this blatant favouritism, also picked some symbolic items to make the focus of a campaign to reassert his 'masculine right' to be principal heir, in contradiction to his father's will. In short, he initiated legal proceedings over the family portraits. On 12 May 1893 a court ruling permitted the comtesse de Turenne d'Aynac to keep the portraits that had been legitimately left to her as part of the contents of the rue Balzac apartment. Alexandre contested the ruling and a year later, when a second court ruling gave his cause as *chef de famille* some backing, the case was annulled because the comtesse chose to renounce her rights to the portraits rather than endure further expensive legal proceedings. Family relations had been strained almost to breaking point for over a decade because of the terms of the will. For Marie-Élisabeth, restoring cohesion mattered.[47]

The Berthier inheritance case illustrates the way in which nobles' understanding of their gendered familial roles produced certain attitudes and behaviours. Alexandre felt emasculated by the terms of his father's will and was determined to assert his status as the principal heir, the *chef de famille*. The aristocratic *mentalité* still adhered to the notion of primogeniture, which Napoleon I had upheld in creating *majorats*, in spite of the law on partible inheritance. Women of this class, although they were accustomed to commanding significant resources, and may have been wealthier than their husbands, were raised to accept that men in their family had superior claims to property because nobility was transmitted through the male bloodline. This way of thinking had very ancient origins, stretching back to the time when the Crown sought to suppress *la noblesse utérine* by imposing *le droit de franc fief* for the purchase of real estate. Where property was concerned, males were seen to hold the prerogative. This meant that, in cases of dispute over property division in an aristocratic family, noblewomen were more likely than their brothers to renounce a strictly equal share of inheritance in order to keep the peace and avoid a legal battle.

Tensions within families often arose over large pieces of furniture such as chests and cupboards, known as *les meubles meublants*, which were typically included with a château and its land in a will. These could be extremely valuable indeed: estimates ranged from 30,000–50,000 francs to well over 100,000 francs. Maxime de Gomer had 117,079 francs worth of furniture at Courcelles-sous-Moyencourt and another 83,244 francs worth at the rue Narine in Amiens. One noblewoman, born in 1924, gave a frank account of the problems of division:

> For people of my generation, all the parents who are not dead are in the process of dying; half my friends have quarrelled with their brothers and sisters owing to matters of inheritance which used to be managed a bit better, whereas now people demand the furniture. I'll admit upfront that, in order not to fight, my sister and I left the two châteaux entirely furnished to our two brothers and we shared the remainder between ourselves, which was the furniture from my parents' Parisian apartment. If we want to get along, there needs to be some who are prepared to relinquish their part of the heritage ... But my sons reproach me for it now and that's the difficulty.[48]

This late twentieth-century account underlines the way in which gender and class-based conditioning shaped decision-making about property in aristocratic families. The archival evidence for the nineteenth century strongly indicates that a golden age where 'matters of inheritance ... used to be managed a bit better' never existed.

Moreover, in the France of the Third Republic, when taxes and duties were steadily increasing, nobles' attachment to familial property could be financially crippling. At an extreme, the effort to keep inherited items in the family rather than sell them could result in a sense of 'privation'. As a noblewoman put it:

> I think that it is all this education we received, my husband and I – happily the same education – and all this past we hold on to, that makes us cling to our property. We are deprived – that's the word – because of this property.[49]

The idea of nobles, historically among the richest people in France, being at a pecuniary disadvantage seems paradoxical. Statistical study of successions shows, however, that those with the largest amounts of patrimony experienced proportionally greater losses than those with more modest amounts especially during the interwar decades. Moreover, partly as a result of rising taxation, fewer and fewer nobles featured within the top category of wealth in the twentieth century.[50]

The extent of debt, a persistent problem for many a noble under the *ancien régime*, is not easily calculated for nobles in the nineteenth and twentieth centuries. Many, but certainly not all, families who experienced material losses of property during the 1789 Revolution had managed to reconsolidate their fortunes before the 1825 law on indemnity to reimburse émigrés. Debt appeared in less than four per cent of Parisian nobles' successions declared in 1911. Nevertheless there were cases under the Third Republic where indebtedness could lead to complete financial ruin and even imprisonment as it did for Charles-Guillaume de France d'Hézecques. More often than not, it seems, relatives pulled together either to provide discreet support for a family member living on meagre resources or to ensure that the extravagances of an over-spender were curtailed.[51]

Nobles, like other members of society, complained about but also had to accept the rising costs of living in the late nineteenth and twentieth centuries. While the experience of wealth could certainly encourage extravagance, it did not mean nobles were incapable of adopting a cautious attitude to expenditure and finding ways to make savings. In 1882, when Jean de Montebello lost part of his capital owing to the collapse of the Banque de l'Union Financière, he and his wife

Emma sold their property Blosseville and cut 'superfluous expenses'. Gowns made at home replaced expensive *toilettes* from the couturier Worth and a brisk walk was favoured (one said for health benefits) over carriage rides in the Bois de Boulogne.[52] Concern to monitor spending and avoid indebtedness necessarily featured more prominently in nobles' thinking during the nineteenth and twentieth centuries. The 'inflexible Code' required great pragmatism over finance, property, and investments.

Understanding the ways in which aristocratic families wrestled internally with property matters helps to shed light on nobles' contributions to public debates about wealth distribution in society. By the beginning of the twentieth century very few people imagined that French society might in some way resume the structural characteristics of the *ancien régime*. Yet the aristocratic perspective in France was still informed by faith in social hierarchy and nobles continued to practise the charitable work that derived from estate ownership in much the same way as their ancestors had done before 1789.[53]

The notion of *noblesse oblige* that underpinned such charity is a central theme in Bourget's novel *L'Émigré* published just two years after the republican government passed its 1905 law on finances. When the heir to the house of Claviers-Grandchamp, Landri, pays a visit to the marquis to discuss his marital intentions, the two men call upon the aged gardener Mauchaussée and his family. Upon taking their leave – to the family's salutations 'Vive Monsieur le comte!' 'Et vive Monsieur le marquis!' – Claviers turns to Landri and reminds him that, as the heir, Landri is not at liberty to marry the woman he loves because she is a bourgeoise with an insignificant dowry: 'That is why the marriage about which you have just spoken cannot go ahead. It is because of the Mauchaussée and all the many people like them who depend on us, on the house of Claviers-Grandchamp, for a living.'[54] Mauchaussée's son has just suffered an accident that has rendered him no longer fit for work and the marquis guarantees the family that he will continue to pay the wages on which they rely. It is a private commitment that reflects his thinking on contemporary political debates. A man of Claviers-Grandchamps's background had little patience for the kind of solidarist proposals put forward by politicians like the Radical Léon Bourgeois. 'You know that I am an old-style socialist,' he says to Landri. 'What distinguishes us from the new style of socialist is that we would have the poor receive money directly from the wealthy whereas today the politicians keep all of it.'[55]

Notes

1 Maurice Lévy-Leboyer, Michel Lescure, and Alain Plessis (eds), *L'Impôt en France aux XIXe et XXe siècles* (Paris, 2006); Thomas Picketty, *Les Hauts revenus en France au XXe siècle: inégalités et redistributions 1901–1998* (Paris, 2001); P. Frain de La Gaulayrie, *Les Majorats depuis le premier Empire jusqu'à nos jours: thèse pour le doctorat* (Rennes, 1909), pp. 77–8; Adeline Daumard, *Les Fortunes françaises au XIXe siècle* (Paris, 1973), pp. 3–40.
2 Peter McPhee, *Living the French Revolution, 1789–99* (New York, 2006), pp. 75–6, 121, 154, 225; Suzanne Desan, '"War between brothers and sisters": inheritance law and gender politics in revolutionary France', *French Historical Studies* 20 (1997), 597–634.
3 Pierre Bourdieu, *Distinction: A Social Critique of the Judgement of Taste*, trans. Richard Nice (London, 2000).
4 Suzanne Desan, *The Family on Trial in Revolutionary France* (Berkeley, 2004), pp. 144–5; Janet L. Nelson, 'Nobility in the ninth century' and Régine Le Jan, 'Continuity and change in the tenth-century nobility' in Anne J. Duggan (ed.), *Nobles and Nobility in Medieval Europe: Concepts, Origins, Transformations* (Woodbridge, 2000), pp. 43–51, 53–68.
5 On the fief see Alain Texier, *Qu'est-ce que la noblesse?* (Paris, 1988), pp. 17–21.
6 L. N. H. Chérin, *Abrégé chronologique d'Edits ... concernant le fait de noblesse* (1788) cited in Texier, *Qu'est-ce que la noblesse?*, p. 18.
7 David Higgs, *Nobles in Nineteenth Century France: The Practice of Inegalitarianism* (Baltimore, 1987), pp. 41–8.
8 Peter McPhee, *A Social History of France 1789–1914* 2 ed. (New York, 2004), p. 115; Robert Forster, *The Nobility of Toulouse in the Eighteenth Century* (Baltimore, 1960), pp. 47–119; Robert Forster, 'The survival of the nobility during the French Revolution', *Past and Present* 37 (1967), 71–86; David Spring (ed.), *European Landed Elites in the Nineteenth Century* (Baltimore, 1977), pp. 3–6, 129; David Cannadine, *The Decline and Fall of the British Aristocracy* (London, 2005), pp. 103–12.
9 Undated letter in AP 101 (II)/119 Fonds Gramont. On the La Rochefoucauld property see Michel Hamard, *La Famille La Rochefoucauld et le duché-pairie de la Roche-Guyon au XVIIIe siècle: reconnaissance royale et puissance locale* (Paris, 2008).
10 Élisabeth de Clermont-Tonnerre, *Au temps des équipages* (Paris, 1928), p. 81.
11 Clermont-Tonnerre, *Au temps*, p. 151.
12 The stereotypes have been applied to a Jewish female body but some derive from stereotypes of the Jewish male body. The way gender operates in the passage is significant because the process Anna undergoes is designed to make her look beautiful or feminine. See Sander Gilman, *The Jew's Body* (New York, 1991), pp. 5, 172–3, 179–93, 203, 205; Kathleen Adler, 'John Singer

PROPERTY AND INHERITANCE 89

Sargent's portraits of the Wertheimer family' and Sander L. Gilman, 'Salome, syphilis, Sarah Bernhardt, and the modern Jewess' in Linda Nochlin and Tamar Garb (eds), *The Jew in the Text: Modernity and the Construction of Identity* (London, 1995), pp. 83–96, 97–120.

13 Jean-Marie Wiscart, *La Noblesse de la Somme au XIXe siècle* (Amiens, 1994), pp. 141–4; Gérard Rousset-Charny, *Les Palais parisiens de la belle époque* (Paris, 1990).

14 For the account books and succession of Mme Furtado-Heine, see AP 31/72–6, 423–30 Fonds Murat. On the Murats' property see AP 31/195 Fonds Murat. On sources of income see Wiscart, *La Noblesse de la Somme*, pp. 148–51; Higgs, *Nobles*, pp. 105–29; Spring, *European Landed Elites*, p. 13.

15 Christophe Charle, 'Noblesse et élites en France au début du XXe siècle' in *Les Noblesses européennes au XIXe siècle* (Rome, 1988), pp. 407–33; Daumard, *Les Fortunes françaises*, pp. 257–67.

16 H. M. Scott (ed.), *The European Nobilities in the Seventeenth and Eighteenth Centuries* vol. 1 (Harlow, 1995), pp. 18, 118, 150–1, 156–7; George V. Taylor, 'Noncapitalist wealth and the origins of the French Revolution', *American Historical Review* 72 (1967), 469–96.

17 On Gyp's writings and her relations with nationalist intellectuals see Willa Z. Silverman, 'Gyp et l'Affaire Dreyfus', *Modern and Contemporary France* 43 (1990), 5–16; Willa Z. Silverman, *The Notorious Life of Gyp: Right-wing Anarchist in Fin-de-Siècle France* (Oxford, 1995).

18 Paul Bourget, *L'Émigré* (Paris, 1907), pp. 69–70, 74, 84.

19 Alexis de Tocqueville, *Democracy in America* ed. J. P. Mayer (New York, 1969), pp. 52–3; Marquis de Breteuil, *La Haute société. Journal secret 1886–1889* (Paris, 2007). On historical connections between family names and places see Tiphaine Barthelemy, 'Patronymic names and noms de terre in the French nobility in the eighteenth and the nineteenth centuries', *The History of the Family* 5 (2000), 181–97.

20 McPhee, *Living the French Revolution*, pp. 12–19.

21 Georges Maurevert, *Fisc et blason ou l'impôt sur la vanité* (Paris, 1923), p. 141; *Journal officiel* (1886) chambre, session extraordinaire, 26 November 1885, annexe 128. On tax avoidance see Daumard, *Les Fortunes françaises*, pp. 34–9; Lévy-Leboyer, Lescure, and Plessis, *L'Impôt en France*, pp. 84–5.

22 Maurevert, *Fisc et blason*, p. 145.

23 Maurevert, *Fisc et blason*, p. 147.

24 Maurevert, *Fisc et blason*, pp. 146, 151; *Journal officiel* (1890) chambre, session extraordinaire, 23 October 1890, annexe 943.

25 Maurevert, *Fisc et blason*, p. 138.

26 Lévy-Leboyer, Lescure, and Plessis, *L'Impôt en France*, pp. 38–9, 69–71.

27 Lévy-Leboyer, Lescure, and Plessis, *L'Impôt en France*, pp. 39, 71, 379.

28 Thomas Piketty 'Fiscalité et redistribution sociale dans la France du XXe siècle' in Lévy-Leboyer, Lescure, and Plessis, *L'Impôt en France*, pp. 109–16; Cannadine, *The Decline and Fall*, pp. 97–8.

29 The Spanish word *mayorazgo* meaning entailment of possessions upon the heir by primogeniture dates back to the fourteenth century. In the seventeenth and eighteenth centuries variations appear in Italian (*maggiorasco*), Russian (*maiorat*), Latin (*maioratus*), and German (*Majorat*). In England entail was commonly known as the strict family settlement. Spring, *European Landed Elites*, pp. 6–10; Scott, *The European Nobilities*, vol. 1, pp. 31–5; Taylor, 'Noncapitalist wealth', p. 472.

30 Robert Frost, 'The nobility in Poland-Lithuania, 1569–1795' in Scott, *The European Nobilities* vol. 2, pp. 183–222; Szymon Konarski, *Armorial de la noblesse polonaise titrée* (Paris, 1958).

31 Frain de La Gaulayrie, *Les Majorats*, pp. 77–8, 105–26; Jacques Descheemaeker, *Les Titres de noblesse en France et dans les pays étrangers* vol. 1 (Paris, 1958), pp. 13–15, 26–7.

32 'Compte rendu' 14 April 1921 in AP 279/35 Fonds Massa.

33 'Compte rendu' 14 April 1921 in AP 279/35 Fonds Massa.

34 24 October 1947 in AP 279/35 Fonds Massa.

35 15 August 1921 in AP 142/13 Fonds Xavier de La Rochefoucauld.

36 18 August 1921 in AP 142/13 Fonds Xavier de La Rochefoucauld.

37 Undated note [August 1921] in AP 142/13 Fonds Xavier de La Rochefoucauld.

38 Tribunal Arbitral Mixte Franco-Allemand Affaire: Consorts de Bonneval in AP 142/13 Fonds Xavier de La Rochefoucauld.

39 17 February 1925 in AP 142/13 Fonds Xavier de La Rochefoucauld.

40 25 February 1925 in AP 142/13 Fonds Xavier de La Rochefoucauld.

41 7 October 1925 in AP 142/13 Fonds Xavier de La Rochefoucauld.

42 François-Charles d'Harcourt, *Regards sur un passé* (Paris, 1989), pp. 47–8; 21 May 1880, 25 September 1881, and 10 April 1883 in AP 238/1 Fonds Chanoine Mugnier; Julia Daudet, *Souvenirs autour d'un groupe littéraire* (Paris, 1910), pp. 190–4.

43 Adeline Daumard, *Les Bourgeois et la bourgeoisie en France depuis 1815* (Paris, 1987), pp. 22–7, 73–4.

44 Mark Girouard, *Life in the French Country House* (London, 2000), p. 328; Anna de Noailles, *Le Livre de ma vie* (Paris, 1976), pp. 12–15.

45 23 July 1919 in AP 69/2 Fonds Béarn de Chalais.

46 14 July 1903 in AP 31/69 Fonds Murat.

47 AP 173 bis/420 and 422 Fonds Maréchal Berthier.

48 Éric Mension-Rigau, *Aristocrates et grands bourgeois: éducation, traditions, valeurs* (Paris, 1994), p. 115; Wiscart, *La Noblesse de la Somme*, p. 148.

49 Mension-Rigau, *Aristocrates*, p. 110.

50 Piketty 'Fiscalité et redistribution sociale', pp. 115–16; Daumard, *Les Fortunes françaises*, pp. 115–77, 264–7.

51 Adeline Daumard, 'Noblesses parisiennes et civilisation bourgeoise au XIXe siècle' in Claude-Isabelle Brelot (ed.), *Noblesses et villes (1780–1950)* Actes du colloque de Tours 17–19 mars 1994 (Tours, 1995), p. 113; Wiscart, *La Noblesse*

de la Somme, p. 145. On the diversity of émigré experiences see McPhee, *Living the French Revolution*, pp. 100, 209–10.
52 Duchesse de Sabran-Pontevès, *Bon sang ne peut mentir* (Paris, 1987), p. 127.
53 Elizabeth C. Macknight, 'Faiths, fortunes, and feminine duty: charity in Parisian high society, 1880–1914', *Journal of Ecclesiastical History* 58 (2007), 482–506; Mension-Rigau, *Aristocrates*, pp. 463–6.
54 Bourget, *L'Émigré*, p. 78.
55 Bourget, *L'Émigré*, p. 70.

4

Serving the household

Five liveries with yellow pants, eleven liveries with sleeved waistcoats and yellow collars, seven blue frock coats, thirteen toques, one red hunting jacket with black pants ... These colourful items that sound like costumes for a baroque opera are usually associated with an era before 1789 when aristocrats used dress to signal their position at the top of the social hierarchy.[1] Noblemen and women wore splendid attire. They also fitted out their servants in rich liveries showing the family colours to present a public image of wealth, privilege, and prestige. Cissie Fairchilds observes that in the France of the *ancien régime* long trains of servants helped to create what E. P. Thompson, writing on eighteenth-century England, described as a 'theatre of rule'. Their dress, and the great numbers of them attached to one household, showed how servants embodied 'the obedience and deference they – and, by implication, everyone else – owed to their masters'.[2]

Between 1750 and 1789 patterns of servant employment in France altered. Wages increased, the numbers of female servants surpassed that of males, and the middle classes began to employ one servant per household.[3] In these decades, according to Fairchilds, domestic service lost two of its former characteristics: 'it ceased to be public and it ceased to be patriarchal'. From the late eighteenth century, she argues, a husband 'abdicated his traditional authority over household and servants in favour of his wife, the mistress of the house, *la ménagère*'. Domestic manuals produced for the bourgeoisie conveyed the notion that household management was a feminine responsibility, a notion later interpreted by historians as a sign of 'separate spheres'. 'Man's role was to go out in the world and work for the sustenance of his family; woman's was to remain at home and organise their daily existence.' For the nineteenth-century middle classes, a servant was merely 'someone hired to do housework or personal service in return for a wage'.[4]

Domestic service in aristocratic households was organised along different lines, retaining particular features that distinguished these households from those of the bourgeoisie. Rather than employing one maid (*la bonne à tout faire*), nobles employed up to thirty servants including a *maître d'hôtel*, chef, cooks, valets, maids, kitchen hands, drivers, and grooms. The master of the household had a *valet de chambre* who was at his personal service. The mistress had a *femme de chambre* who was at her personal service. A wet nurse, nanny, governess, and *précepteur* cared for and educated aristocratic children.

Aristocratic households varied in size because of the diversity of status and fortune among the nobility. By the late nineteenth century these households were smaller than they had been in the seventeenth century when a great noble employed around one hundred servants.[5] The most splendid *grandes maisons* in turn-of-the-century Paris had a permanent staff of about thirty people. The prince and princesse Murat, for example, employed thirty-five servants at their *hôtel* in the rue de Monceau in 1906. There were also slightly less opulent *grandes maisons* that had a permanent staff of around eighteen servants. The marquis and marquise d'Harcourt employed some fifteen servants during the 1870s. Outside Paris, household size was partly determined by the family's wealth but also by patterns of residency. At some properties the number of staff fluctuated during the year, so that in the hunting season, for example, permanent caretakers were supplemented with maids, valets, and additional hands in the kitchens and stables. Nobles who lived year-round in the Somme typically employed between four and eight servants. At Rocquencourt (Seine-et-Oise) the Murats employed a total of forty-five people in 1913.[6]

Certainly *les grandes maisons* formed a tiny minority of households within France as a whole. Only a few thousand employers could afford over a dozen staff. A bourgeois family of solid income employed no more than three servants at the turn of the century. In 1870 there were 60,800 middle-class households with solid incomes of 20,000 to 100,000 francs. Below them were 417,000 lower middle-class households with incomes of 5,000 to 20,000 francs. Families in the latter category could afford to hire a single maid.[7] The greater numbers of servants employed by nobles led to structural and operational differences in domestic service too. In aristocratic households male servants outnumbered females and they dominated the top ranks of the servant hierarchy. By contrast, in bourgeois households male servants were virtually never employed. It was not uncommon for a servant to be employed by the same aristocratic family for the duration of his or her working life. By contrast, in bourgeois households there was often a high turnover of maids.[8]

To understand the motive for nobles' distinctive arrangements for domestic service we may look to Thompson's argument about class relations in eighteenth-century England. For Thompson, the control exercised by the ruling class over the working class was founded less on the expression of economic or military power than on the maintenance of 'cultural hegemony'. This was achieved in part by fulfilment of public functions especially in the administration of the law. Even more important, Thompson argued, was engagement in rituals of conspicuous display through which the upper class manifested a theatrical hegemonic style. 'This social lubricant of gestures could only too easily make the mechanisms of power and exploitation revolve more sweetly.' The aristocracy and gentry judged with precision the modes of conspicuous display appropriate to each rank and station: 'what coach, how many footmen, what table, even what proper reputation for "liberality"'. Among workers, Thompson argued, the performance of cultural hegemony by the upper class 'induces a state of mind in which the established structures of authority and even modes of exploitation appear to be in the course of nature. This does not preclude resentment or even surreptitious acts of protest or revenge; it does preclude affirmative rebellion.'[9]

In the France of the Third Republic the conspicuous display afforded by a bevy of servants was key to nobles' creation of a convincing 'show'. Nobles knew that in compensation for the financial sacrifice of paying staff wages there was symbolic and strategic value in preserving those rituals and attitudes embedded in the culture of domestic service within their homes. This was a longstanding aristocratic technique for reinforcing social hierarchy and perpetuating nobles' dominant position.

The items of clothing listed at the start of this chapter were not a bundle of props. They figure in a clothing inventory made on 5 June 1912 at 15 avenue d'Alma, now 13–15 avenue Georges V, the Parisian address of Alexandre Berthier, prince de Wagram. Whoever made the inventory observed that these garments, for *valets de pied*, drivers, and guards, were 'very worn' and 'stored in the linen cupboards'.[10] They were probably not among the liveries then worn by servants employed by the prince. In 1882

Alexandre Berthier had married Berthe de Rothschild. The couple's wealth derived from their respective personal fortunes including Berthe's inheritance from the baron Carl de Rothschild. With annual income of several million francs, and inclinations to renovate properties and surround themselves with *objets d'art*, the Wagrams are unlikely to have tolerated faded or tatty clothing on their servants.[11]

Contemporaries understood that despite the titles of prince and princesse this couple did not belong to the *gratin* of Parisian high society. Alexandre Berthier's family were of recent ennoblement; his grandfather served as Minister of War and Major General under Napoleon I. Although Berthe had converted to Catholicism for the purposes of marriage, her parents were devout practising Jews. For reasons of ancestry and religion, therefore, the Wagrams were looked down upon by the superior-minded Catholic *ancienne noblesse* of the Faubourg Saint-Germain.[12] Nevertheless, a princely title, property, and wealth gave this couple a substantial foothold in the more expansive high society that had developed under the July Monarchy.

Like all members of Parisian high society, the Wagrams owned properties in Paris and the countryside; their country address was the château de Grosbois at Boissy-Saint-Léger (Seine-et-Oise). Servants' lives and routines were geared to the seasonal migration of their noble employers between urban and rural residences. In June, at the close of the social 'Season' in Paris, an aristocratic household typically moved *en masse* from the *hôtel particulier* to the family estate.

The role of servants in the cultivation of public image by aristocratic families is best appreciated within the Parisian context, although there is evidence of it in the countryside as well. Proust captured the culture of servanthood brilliantly in *The Guermantes Way*, where he describes how a valet in the Guermantes household entertains Françoise, maid to the Narrator's bourgeois family, with gossip from his vicarious social life:

> We go now and again to the Opéra, usually on the evenings when the Princesse de Parme has her box, that's once a week. It seems a fine show they give there, plays, operas, everything. Madame refused to rent a box herself, but we go all the same to the boxes Madame's friends take, now one, now another, often the Princesse de Guermantes, the Duke's cousin's lady. She's sister to the Duke of Bavaria ...[13]

Françoise's attitude shows she is not privileged to see this world from inside but she picks up on the signals of family prestige: '"Ay, they're a great family, the Guermantes!" she added, in a tone of respect, founding the greatness of the family at once on the number of its branches and the brilliance of its connexions.'[14]

Servants in aristocratic households were appointed to different gendered roles geared to facilitate their employers' engagement in social duties. A noblewoman had a male secretary to keep her address book up to date and to manage some of her correspondence. She had a male driver to transport her around Paris for shopping, to attend functions, and to make her round of afternoon calls (*la tournée des cartes*). She had a *femme de chambre* to assist with changes of toilette throughout the day. She had a nurse and governess to take care of her children. She had a *maître d'hôtel* to manage arrangements for luncheons and dinner parties, and she had *valets de pied*, maids, a cook, and kitchen hands to tidy, light fires, carry, scrub, polish, and prepare.

The other side of domestic labour 'behind the scenes' in an aristocratic home was the contribution that servants made to the public performance of what Thorstein Veblen called 'conspicuous leisure' that reinforced the employers' social and economic standing. For instance, following the death of her husband and two sons, the widow Doudeauville continued to live in the family's *hôtel particulier* in rue de Varenne. François-Charles d'Harcourt recalled that when he and his cousins visited their great-aunt in the decade before 1914 they were received in the vestibule of the *hôtel* by no fewer than three *valets de pied*. 'One of the valets relieved us of our coats, the second opened the doors, and the third led us through several salons towards the room where our great-aunt sat . . . surrounded by one or two *femmes de chambre* who arranged her hair or shawls.'[15] Veblen argued that men had an advantage in the performance of conspicuous leisure. Since male servants were 'obviously more powerful and more expensive than women', their symbolic function in the home of an aristocratic employer was to show 'a larger waste of time and of human energy'.[16] Footmen stationed in the vestibule of a *hôtel*, and in the dining room to help guests into their seats at the commencement of a grand dinner party, performed this function.

Servants dressed according to their role and the task at hand. Men and women wore generic items for menial tasks, such as white aprons for dusting or making beds, and blue aprons for dirtier heavy labour. When assisting at receptions or accompanying their employers outdoors servants dressed in expensive liveries. The livery, in family colours trimmed with family emblems, allowed for immediate identification in a crowd, and was a form of 'conspicuous consumption' that benefited their employers; servants did not have any choice in what they wore.[17] For instance, livery was worn for the annual coach race (*le jour de drags*) around the streets of Paris. This was a spectacular event not only because of the excitement of the race but also because of the brilliant display of family colours on coaches and clothing. Knowledgeable witnesses were able to match these colours to names: the dark red of the La Rochefoucaulds, the blue and yellow of the Potocki.[18]

A sumptuary practice that symbolised more profoundly how servants were considered part of the aristocratic family or 'house' was the wearing of black mourning clothes when an employer or one of their employer's relatives died. The dramatic visual statement of an entire household in mourning was a powerful way to get the message of family unity, and strength of faith, across to others.[19] When Jean Chabot was accepted into the service of the marquis and marquise d'Harcourt, the household was just emerging from a period of mourning following the death of an aunt. One day Jean was taken by the *maître d'hôtel*, Monsieur Félix, to a store where a tailor took his measurements for a brand-new *tenue*; he had previously worn a hand-me-down from an old servant. After a second visit for the fitting, Jean wore with pride his trousers and a waistcoat crossed with dark green and fastened with four buttons embossed with the family coat of arms. His uniform fitted like a glove and cost a small fortune.[20]

The position of third driver at which Jean Chabot entered the service of the Harcourts was a modest one within the gendered servant hierarchy of an aristocratic household. In its basic structure this hierarchy looked much the same in the nineteenth century as it had in the eighteenth. Most of our information about the servant hierarchy comes from wage records.[21] Although they are uneven and incomplete, such records can be used to analyse changing rates of pay and fluctuations in numbers and types of staff. Wage records, however, offer only a partial indication of the way hierarchical relationships operated; they do not reveal the subtleties of human competition for privileges and preferment.

François Lalliard observes that under Napoléon-Alexandre Berthier annual wages remained on the whole quite static in this household.[22] His summary of those annual wage figures for the period 1830 to 1886 is represented in the left-hand columns of Table 1. The right-hand columns contain annual wage figures for 1904 from the archives of the prince Joachim Murat V and his wife Cécile who lived at 28 rue de Monceau.[23] The table is divided horizontally with male staff listed in the top rows and female staff beneath.

98 ARISTOCRATIC FAMILIES IN REPUBLICAN FRANCE

Wagram		Murat	
Position	Annual wage (francs) 1830–1886	Position	Annual wage (francs) 1904
Men			
l'intendant	4,000–6,000		
le cocher	1,600	les mécaniciens (2)	3,000–3,600
le maître d'hôtel	1,400	le maître d'hôtel	2,400
le concierge	1,200–1,600	le concierge	2,400
les jardiniers (2–3)	1,300	le jardinier	2,400
le régisseur	1,200	les hommes	480–3,000
le garde-portier	1,200		
le menuisier	1,200		
le frotteur	1,200		
le palefrenier (1–3)	not specified		
le cuisinier principal	not specified	le chef de cuisine	1,800
le cuisinier second	not specified	1e aide	960
		2e aide	840
		3e aide	600
le valet de chambre	1000	le valet de chambre	1,200
l'argentier	800	l'argentier	1,200
les valets de pied (2)	540–720	les valets de pied (4)	960–1,200
		les garçons d'office (2)	720–840
Women			
		la cuisinière	1,440
		la femme de charge	1,200
la bonne	700 (in 1836)	la bonne d'enfants	960
la lingère	700	la lingère	840
la femme de chambre	600	les femmes de chambre (4)	530–1,200
		la fille de cuisine	600
la fille d'office	420–480	la fille d'office	480
la couturière	300–360	la gouvernante	420
			(half-yearly)

The financial resources needed to employ twenty to thirty staff and own a sumptuous *hôtel* in the eighth *arrondissement* of Paris signal that the Wagrams and Murats, who were linked by marriage, belonged to the wealthiest bracket of the French nobility. Lalliard calculates that between 1831 and 1872 the proportion of the Wagram household budget spent on domestic service was 8.39 per cent; between 1891 and 1902 that figure declined to 5.14 per cent. In the nineteenth-century bourgeois families analysed by Marguerite Perrot such fluctuations were tied to the presence and ages of children in the household. In the case of the Wagrams, however, the lower percentage for domestic service in the 1890s must be seen in conjunction with a doubling of the family's patrimonial expenditure caused by the injection of Rothschild capital. Alexandre and Berthe raised three children in the 1880s–90s as Napoléon-Alexandre and his wife Zénaïde did in the 1830s–50s. Changes in the distribution of the household budget reflected the improved financial situation and somewhat different spending priorities of the younger, wealthier generation.[24]

The ranking of male and female servants was determined by the nature of their specialist skills, responsibility for managing others, and physical proximity to their employers. As the table shows, the most senior and highly paid servants in nineteenth-century aristocratic households were men: the *intendant*, driver (*le cocher* or *le mécanicien*), and *maître d'hôtel*. On a lower rung were skilled male servants such as the gardeners (*les jardiniers*), joiner (*le menuisier*), and chef. These were followed in descending order by the head valet (*le valet de chambre*), silversmith (*l'argentier*), and footmen (*les valets de pied*). Among the female servants, the head maid (*la femme de charge*), cook (*la cuisinière*), and laundry woman (*la lingère*) held seniority, with lower ranks filled by additional maids, the butlery girl (*la fille d'office*), and seamstress (*la couturière*). The mistress's personal maid (*la femme de chambre*) and the children's nanny and governess occupied special positions based on investment of trust.[25]

Servants were categorised by their area of labour (stables, personal apartments, or kitchen) and this produced internal subdivisions within the gendered hierarchy. It was not uncommon for a married couple to be employed in the same household; often they worked in the same area of labour, at the same or similar grade, with the husband receiving higher wages than his wife. For instance, within the Murat household in 1906, the butlery girl, Madame Parain, was married to the butlery boy; the laundry woman, Madame Cornet, was married to the silversmith; and the head maid, Madame Dubois, was married to the *maître d'hôtel*.[26]

There were blood ties between some servants. The comtesse de Pange recalled that in the household of her parents, the Broglies: 'All the servants were more or less related to each other. My mother's *femme de chambre* was the sister of the *maître d'hôtel*, my father's *valet de chambre* was the nephew of the coachman, and so on.'[27]

Of course, there were aristocratic families who had smaller incomes than the Murats or Wagrams and for them the employment of servants represented a greater financial burden. The importance to nobles of reproducing what Thompson called 'a theatrical hegemonic style' can be seen from the way families bore the costs of a large household over the decades, maintaining a commitment to the lifestyle that distinguished them from classes below. The comtesse Marie d'Armaillé, youngest daughter of the général de Ségur, recalled the attitude within her Parisian milieu during the 1850s:

> Far from being embarrassed by the lack of fortune, by the need to live economically, to dress modestly, to be content with old servants with country manners, of using antique carriages and of observing the abstinences and religious and charitable practices of the past, the heads of family and the mistresses of the houses showed in all this a very justifiable pride and thus succeeded in again displaying some dignity. It was in that manner that it was known how to live in the houses of Gontaut, de la Rochefoucauld, de Périgord, etc., the families of Montesquiou, de Biencourt, d'Orglandès, de Vogüé, Champagne, many others, and finally ourselves.[28]

Recognition of 'the need to live economically' without compromising standards that justified 'pride' and 'dignity' informed some nobles' thinking well beyond the 1850s. In March 1890 the comtesse Élisabeth Greffulhe wrote to her husband, Henri, from the family estate of Bois-Boudran with instructions for reducing their household expenditure, a subject he had raised in conversation with her. The comte Greffulhe was personally very rich and loved to spend money. By contrast, his wife came from a very old and distinguished family that was virtually impoverished.[29] The comtesse Greffulhe's background made her acutely aware of what it meant to protect aristocratic family image on a restricted budget. The extravagant spending habits of her rich husband (from which his mistresses, among others, benefited) appear to have exacerbated her sense of 'moral responsibility' within the marriage to guard against the dissipation of wealth.

> I think that with a great fortune like your own it is sufficient not to make large outlays during the course of the year in order to save easily two or three hundred thousand francs in receipts... The monthly household

expenses must not exceed 25,000 francs – instead of 35. It is easy to do the sums: 10,000 francs per month makes *120,000 francs per year* . . . This year you are going to leave 35 horses here [at Bois-Boudran]!! . . . You must: sell two pairs of carriage horses. Sell two pairs of delivery horses. Sell my five ponies. There's a reduction of 13 horses. The carriage horses are done for; we must get rid of them without making replacements this year. Barrot [a servant] can ride your horse – it will only do him good – that makes a reduction of at least 16 horses here . . . The cook is horribly expensive – I put him in charge of the kitchen ordering, I don't even see the accounts . . . I also plan to sell all the produce from the garden and to keep for ourselves only the new season's crop and the indoor plants so we won't have the gardener's bill in Paris . . . Then you must reduce your hunting a little. In any case, do not borrow . . . Each month I will see the receipts and expenses . . . There you are, my dear Henri, a business letter that you surely won't read amid the distractions of the capital.[30]

It is not clear from the archive whether the comte Greffulhe obeyed any of his wife's instructions for saving money in 1890. The issue of reducing household expenditure evidently came up again within the marriage for in 1923 she wrote a note demanding that he stick to the budget laid down for that year.[31] Élisabeth's letter of 1890 obviously represents her personal view of where savings could be made, but Henri was unlikely to have sold horses willingly or to have curtailed hunting given his passion for the sport. Interestingly, Élisabeth complained about the cook's expensive ordering but she did not propose a way to resolve the problem. This may have been because she had actually given instructions to the cook to order some expensive items. The comtesse portrayed her own resolve to make savings through the plan to sell off garden produce and thus eliminate the cost of hiring a gardener.

While the letter makes no reference to the wages of staff at Bois-Boudran, these were part of the monthly household expenses and a reduction in the number of horses would have meant fewer men were needed to work in the stables. The agricultural crisis in France from the 1880s made cutting the number of men employed casually on an estate necessary for some nobles. Of course this only boosted the reputation of those who could afford to keep plenty of men on the books. At the turn of the century the prince and princesse Murat had a small permanent caretaking staff at their Rocquencourt estate and hired some forty additional staff on a daily or monthly basis during their summer residency. At the Murats' other estate, Chambly (Oise), where there was a stud and hunting establishment, the outdoor staff of thirty-nine included four

3 Stables at the prince de Radziwill's Parisian residence (1884)

grooms, nine gamekeepers, eight men at the home farm, three men in the infirmary dispensary, and two mechanics.[32]

Responsibility for estate management lay with one of the most senior men of an aristocratic household, the *intendant* or *régisseur*. This man fulfilled a host of duties that made his role a conglomerate of personal assistant, secretary, accountant, pay administrator, and public relations officer. Under the *ancien régime* he was sometimes of petty noble status and referred to as *un homme de confiance*.

Two men successively held the position of *intendant* in the Wagram household between 1850 and 1935. First was Alexandre Gaut, who commenced service for Napoléon-Alexandre Berthier at the age of twenty. His father was the mayor's secretary in the village Sucy-en-Brie, not far from the château de Grosbois, and the young man trained as a rural notary. Gaut retired to the village in 1896 (he died in 1898) and his successor was René Maîche. Like Gaut, Maîche was less than thirty years of age when he entered the Wagram household, and he served until his retirement in 1935. Unlike his predecessor, however, Maîche received his training in the Rothschilds' offices. Born in Mans in 1869, he 'came from the Bank'.³³ The appointment of Maîche as *intendant* had much to do with his employers' marriage. The skills he brought to the position were vital for the family given that Berthe's investments and revenue significantly amplified the scope of financial management required for the Wagram estate.

Longevity of service is often mentioned in nobles' memoirs along with descriptions of servants' loyalty to the family.³⁴ There were numerous cases in which a servant, male or female, entered the service of a noble family in their youth and remained with the same family until retirement. Some servants were buried alongside their master or mistress in the noble family's cemetery plot. In the late nineteenth century, like under the *ancien régime*, nobles often stipulated in their wills that a pension and items of clothing were to be left to a favourite servant. On 15 January 1890, when the duchesse Pozzo di Borgo wrote her last will and testament, she bequeathed to servants who had served her for more than four years a sum of 1,500 francs on top of what was owed to them in wages. The duchesse left to her personal maid 'all the clothing from my wardrobe, except for my cashmere shawls, lace and furs, plus a sum of 4,000 francs'.³⁵

Of course, it is necessary to approach the information in memoirs with caution. These are the writings of the literate elite, and unfortunately we are rarely able to compare them with accounts from the working class. Memoirs may well paint a rather glossy picture of employer–servant relationships in the nineteenth century, and the individuals who served longest are likely to have been remembered best by the authors. Bearing these points in mind, evidence that some servants spent years, decades, or even a lifetime serving one family (like Gaut and Maîche) contrasts with the high turnover of maids typical in middle-class homes during the nineteenth century. A common complaint of bourgeoises, often satirised in cartoons, was the difficulty of finding reliable help.³⁶

What was it about working for nobles that encouraged longevity of service? Surely one factor was that young servants could, and often did, rise up the ladder as they gained experience and expertise. There were no such opportunities for promotion within a middle- or lower-middle-class household where a single maid had the 'superhuman task' of juggling multiple tasks from the outset.³⁷ A second factor was prestige. Historians have argued that as domestic service became 'feminised', because increasing numbers of the petty bourgeoisie employed a maid, the profession itself became 'proletarian' and lost some of its former association with elites.³⁸ In this context, servants drew symbolic benefit from being employed by nobles. As we saw earlier in the extract from

Proust, the valet of the Guermantes took pride in his employers' 'great name'; it was a form of social capital that marked him out from his peers. A third factor, and probably the one that mattered most to servants, was the facility mentioned earlier for married couples to work in the same household and thus be lodged under the one roof. Not all employers were amenable to their servants' wishes in this respect. Following his marriage to Yvonne Yven, maid to a bourgeois family, Jean Chabot left the service of the Harcourts when the petulant marquise refused to allow Jean the 'privilege' of living with his wife. In France in 1906, 62 per cent of female domestic servants were unmarried and 13.4 per cent were divorced or widows. The situation was different for male servants; 57 per cent were married.[39]

Discerning the extent to which loyalty and sentimental attachment figured in employer–servant relationships is very difficult for the historian. Nevertheless, it is possible to advance some speculative comments about the nature of emotional bonds, taking into account gender and age differences. Most female servants entering domestic service in well-to-do Parisian households were young women in their late teens or early twenties from rural towns and villages. On their arrival in Paris, if they had not been recommended to a particular employer, they faced the daunting prospect of finding a placement through agencies, whilst living on their wits in precarious circumstances. No doubt, for many, obtaining a maid's post alleviated loneliness and hardship, encouraging a view of the employer as benefactor. Anne Martin-Fugier describes the bond between a mistress and her maid as 'suffocating love'.[40]

Equally, sexual rivalry probably featured in some of these relationships. The physical labour of servants – including washing dirty clothes and dishes, preparing meals, sweeping floors, disposing of garbage – involved dealing with household waste. Well-to-do men and women were repulsed by the physicality of servants' work, yet also fascinated because they associated it with all that was taboo, especially illicit sexuality. 'To speak of servants, is to come in contact with filth, desire, sex.'[41] A common stereotype of the maid in nineteenth-century French fiction was *la souillon*, or slut, a woman whose personal appearance and morals were soiled (*souillée*). Invoking this stereotype gave a spicy edge to dinner conversation:

> My aunt had a *femme de chambre* who was filthy, but whose service was excellent; so she tried to persuade her to wash herself... One day, from the next room, I heard her say: 'Let's imagine, my girl, suppose the house

4 The princesse de Radziwill's *cabinet de toilette* (1884)

catches fire ... you are obliged to leave as you are ... without putting shoes on, among all the tenants, the concierge, the firemen, the crowd ... what do you expect all those people to think if you don't have clean feet?'[42]

Behind the fictional stereotyping of the maid as *la souillon* lay grim realities for maids made prey to sexual advances by upper-class men, or more commonly by male servants with whom they shared cramped living spaces. Typically a maid who fell pregnant had to choose between abortion and the abandonment of her baby. At the end of the nineteenth century almost one-third of mothers who abandoned their child were in domestic service. Most were single women; their average age was twenty-two years.[43] In cases where a female servant experienced rape and/or unwanted pregnancy, a noblewoman's responses may have been influenced by rage and sexual jealousy, by the longstanding emphasis on 'moralisation of the masses' that informed their charitable practices, or by the continuing notion of a severe God who administered punishment for sinful behaviour.[44] Some nineteenth-century novels depict solidarity between maid and mistress but whether it actually existed or not remains far from clear.[45]

The social milieu in which nobles cultivated their public image required attention to etiquette, like in the court society analysed by Norbert Elias. Men and women of high society were accustomed to observing others in public, and this in turn required the internalisation of self-control mechanisms or 'self-observation'.[46] Servants, who accompanied their aristocratic employers on public outings, and served at mealtimes and receptions, also engaged in observation and self-observation. What kinds of conditioning resulted from the daily proximity of servants and their employers?

The first point to note is that the employment of servants required the master and mistress of an aristocratic household to be able to give orders. This capacity can be understood as a prerequisite for what Thompson described as the 'theatrical role in which the great were schooled in infancy and which they maintained until death'.[47] Language and gesture were mediums to convey power and the ability to use them effectively required training and experience. For nobles this was a lifelong process: from childhood, when they observed their parents and senior relatives give orders; through the early days of married life when they took charge of their own household; to old age when it was crucial that respect not be compromised by physical frailty. François-Charles d'Harcourt recalled the trepidation he once felt, as a young boy, when his mother or grandmother asked him to transmit a message to the *maître d'hôtel* after lunch. Descending by a staircase to the long corridor on the ground floor of the *hôtel particulier*, where the laundry, scullery, and kitchen were located, he eventually reached the servants' dining room. Seated around the table were twenty servants who greeted the small boy with smiles at once 'benevolent and slightly sarcastic'. François-Charles stammered over the message and galloped off.[48] In aristocratic households the management of servants was not considered a feminine responsibility. The master gave orders to his *valet de chambre* and the mistress gave orders to her *femme de chambre*. Orders for other servants within the household were transmitted via the *maître d'hôtel* who received instructions from one of his employers during the morning. Alexandre Berthier seems to have been a pugnacious employer who expressed dissatisfaction readily and did not mince words. Rebukes punctuate his remarks in a book of orders for 1900: 'If you continue to perform your service in the manner you do now, you will not remain in my service because everything is done poorly.'[49]

Second, employers were conditioned to exercise discretion when speaking to others within earshot of servants. Since the eighteenth century in France novelists had portrayed servants as intruders and spies.[50] Sensitive matters could all too easily become fodder for gossip. In an undated note to his wife, Élisabeth, from the late nineteenth century, the comte Henri Greffulhe made his concern for discretion plain, although not the subject on which he believed it necessary: 'These days every wall has enormous ears, surpassed first by tongues and then newspapers. Our best safety lies in silence ... Beware always to the Butler' (last phrase in English in original).[51]

Servants who worked in the personal apartments of noble spouses knew some very intimate details about their employers. For instance, a nobleman retired to his personal apartment on nights when he or his wife wanted to sleep alone, or when he returned late from his club and did not wish to disturb her. The marquis d'Harcourt spent most nights with his wife in her apartment and in the morning his *valet de chambre* Narcisse usually asked whether Monsieur and Madame had spent a good night. When the marquis had slept in his own bed Narcisse asked, 'I trust Monsieur slept well?'[52]

Whereas nobles tailored their behaviour and language to exercise authority, servants had to behave and use language in respectful ways. One example of this was the use of the third person to address an employer: 'As Madame wishes'. Another was the rule that servants should stand in the presence of their employer, just as nineteenth-century shop assistants were required to do before customers.[53] In some aristocratic households old court customs to signal deference were maintained. Boni de Castellane recalled that an elderly woman, Madame Mencion, who waited on his grandmother at the château de Rochecotte, always performed a curtsy on approaching her mistress. 'Do I have permission, my queen?' she would ask, and only when assent was given did she take a seat.[54] We cannot be sure of the degree to which guides like the pocket-sized *Manuel du valet du chambre* were used to 'instruct' servants in behaviour and use of language, especially at a junior level.[55] Perhaps more effective was the culture of learning aurally and through observation of the whims and expectations of 'Monsieur le comte' or 'Madame la comtesse'. One of the responsibilities of a *maître d'hôtel*, for instance, was to teach novice footmen the art of table service; that is, to serve dishes to family members and guests in correct order, to pour wine without splashing it, and to remove the plates and cutlery for each course once it was concluded.[56]

Years or even a lifetime of experience intuiting and meeting the needs of employers made senior servants' 'knowledge' of appropriate behaviour so engrained in the psyche that to implement that behaviour was 'effortless'. The effects were only startling to the uninitiated. For example, in an account of the first meeting between Jean Chabot and the Harcourts' *maître d'hôtel*, Monsieur Félix, there is more than a hint that Jean was taken aback, not to say flummoxed, by the encounter.[57] His limited prior experience of service, as a young lackey in a rural château, had not prepared him for the polished graces of a gentleman in white gloves bearing a silver tray to whom the marquise deferred for an opinion on whether Jean should be hired! The driver of the Briet de Rainvillers family was so accustomed to intuiting the needs of his employer that he liked to declare: 'Monsieur le baron and I are the most intelligent ones at Boismont.'[58]

The physical appearance and disposition of servants mattered to their employers. Male servants were not to grow a moustache, symbol of manhood, because a clean-shaven face signalled they were under another man's authority.[59] In the nineteenth century, like under the *ancien régime*, male servants stood a better chance of gaining employment in aristocratic households if they were tall and had a robust physique.[60] Once a post had been obtained, staying in it no doubt required an even temperament, or at least the ability to 'mask' anger, frustration, or glee. This was a hard-won lesson for the unfortunate footman in *The Guermantes Way* who was desperate for a chance to spend time with his betrothed. Thinking he had been awarded an evening off by the duc, his face 'glowed with happiness'. Oriane de Guermantes, perceiving this joy, guessing the reason, and, feeling irritated by it, insisted the footman remain in the house all night. As Veblen observed, 'the leisure of the servant is not his own leisure'.[61]

Nobles' capacity to maintain cultural hegemony in the France of the Third Republic must also be looked at from the perspective of what Thompson described as the 'countertheatre' of the working class. 'There is a sense,' he wrote of eighteenth-century England, 'in which rulers and crowd needed each other, watched each other, performed theatre and countertheatre in each other's auditorium, moderated each other's political behaviour.'[62] Thompson discussed countertheatre primarily in terms of crowd action but it encompassed interventions from individuals as well. To consider the evidence for countertheatre in the France of the Third Republic let us return to the Wagrams' estate, Grosbois, at Boissy-Saint-Léger.

Napoléon-Alexandre Berthier was mayor of Boissy-Saint-Léger under the Second Empire. His son Alexandre stood as a Bonapartist candidate in the canton elections of 1889 but was defeated by the republican candidate Savary.[63] Nevertheless, Alexandre and his wife Berthe were high-profile figures in Boissy-Saint-Léger and the surrounding district. In 1892 the couple founded a home for the elderly poor, the Asile Charles-Louis run by the Filles de la Sagesse, as well as a crèche at Villecresnes. Berthe was patron of several charities and sat on the board of the Boissy-Saint-Léger library for which she nominated books for purchase. In late July each year the prince gave his permission to the mayor for the town square to be used for the communal *fête*. The Wagrams donated the square to the commune in 1906.[64]

Alongside these public acts of good will, which served to reinforce nobles' cultural hegemony, one longstanding feature of the aristocratic lifestyle caused particular tension in the Wagrams' relationship with locals. Since the forests of Grosbois were within easy travelling distance of Paris, the estate was a popular destination for hunting parties. Alexandre Berthier was an avid sportsman. His *livres de chasse*, in which the names of party companions and their 'trophies' were recorded, contain thumbnail sketches of pheasants, hares, squirrels, deer, dogs, hunting bags, horns, guns, and the Wagram coat of arms.[65] Of course, hunting and game shooting were among the privileges of aristocratic landowners criticised by peasants in the *cahiers de doléances* before the 1789 Revolution. Nobles' continuing practice of these sports in the nineteenth century was anathema to the rural working class since the damage to crops caused by animals and birds of a hunting establishment could have dire consequences for peasants' family economy.[66]

The prince de Wagram's archive contains letters of complaint from owners or tenants of small farms near Grosbois demanding compensation for damage to fields planted with wheat and beet. It fell to the *intendant* to deal with this correspondence and in Maîche's time compensation was often sent tardily, a fact that irritated recipients and probably did not do his employers' public image any good.[67] The *intendant*, however, had many balls to juggle. He also had to keep track of payments for hunting rights, allowing well-to-do visitors to access sections of the estate, and he had to plan for a steady supply of game in the forests, a task made difficult by the heavy demand imposed by the prince as well as by illegal poaching. To help control the latter problem, a head guard was employed to serve as part-game-keeper, part-forester. His duties included a nightly round of the estate to ensure the other guards were at their correct posts keeping watch for poachers. Like the *intendants* Gaut and Maîche, the head guard Roux gave long service to the Wagrams. The guard books documenting Roux's service date from 27 March 1872 to 5 May 1896: a period of just over twenty-four years.[68]

Relations between the head guard and the men employed casually to work on the estate were vulnerable to strain because the former enjoyed comparative security while the latter lacked the working conditions that might otherwise have encouraged loyalty. Written remarks on twenty-two guard contracts in the family archive reveal some of the reasons given for dismissal. They also suggest that some guards left their employer voluntarily. Four contracts contain no mention of service having ended. Three indicate the guard had died. Four contain the single word 'dismissed'. One indicates dismissal 'for dishonesty (sale of wood)' and another 'for absences without permission'. Four indicate dismissal 'for drunkenness', another for 'drunkenness and laziness', and another 'for inadequacy as pheasant-keeper'. Two indicate the servant 'left service' without citing the reason, and another 'left service following illness'.[69]

Illegal poaching, letters of complaint about damaged crops, and guards' misbehaviour illustrate Thompson's notion of 'countertheatre' operating on and around the Wagram estate in the France of the Third Republic. Each was symptomatic of underlying strain in the Wagrams' relationship with the local community. Peter McPhee has shown that in rural French society of the 1820s the very ancient dynamics of deference operated no longer on the basis of peasants' belief in the nobility's mystique but rather on the basis of economic inequality and dependence.[70] By the turn of the century, farmers' letters to 'Monsieur le prince de Wagram' indicate 'that deference could be very brittle indeed'.[71]

Senior male servants such as the *intendant* and head guard were important characters in the theatre and countertheatre of rural French society because they worked at the interface between château residents and the wider community. Their roles were especially demanding in the sense that they rarely fitted into either world; even Gaut who grew up and trained as a notary in Sucy-en-Brie was 'distanced' from the village by some four decades' work for the prince de Wagram, which probably made his two years of retirement back in the village community not entirely straightforward and easy. The loyalty of the *intendant* and head guard was crucial to nobles because these men carried a responsibility to monitor and react to the 'countertheatre' of the poor. The comtesse Greffulhe was in no doubt about the value of a reliable *intendant* when she wrote to her husband: 'You are fortunate to have a man like [Levasseur] in charge of Bois-Boudran.'[72]

At the outbreak of the First World War many of the men employed by nobles as servants or outdoor labourers left these positions. Some women in domestic service or working as governesses were fearful of the effects the war would have on their own continuing employment or ability to find an alternative post. This was the case for a German woman, Mademoiselle Klein, who gave lessons to a number of children in aristocratic families including Solange de La Rochefoucauld. She wrote to the comte Xavier de La Rochefoucauld from Préty (Saône et Loire) on 14 December 1914, thanking him for his letter:

> I know too well that in present circumstances I cannot hope to secure a position as I would like to; everyone is cutting back. But I would willingly accept the terms offered to me, even to be *au pair* or similar during the war, especially if it led to a future position ... Above all I do not want to be expatriated ... I would also accept something provisional ... The longer I wait the more I shall fall into debt, and at present it is too difficult to find anything in Paris for me to dare staying there without any means. Living expenses are going up.[73]

Although the First World War certainly had a disruptive effect on male and female servants' employment, the continuing viability of aristocratic households seems to have been more threatened by economic and social developments in the interwar period. Servants' wages increasingly fluctuated from the 1920s. A journalist for *Le Temps* reported in January 1922 that a female servant's monthly wage had risen from 120 francs to 150 francs. In the same year Marie Delille sought employment as the princesse Murat's second *femme de chambre* at the rate of 140 francs per month. When the princesse refused she accepted 100 francs per month.[74] Servants increasingly began to join trade unions. Paul Chabot claimed his father Jean 'never knew what *le syndicat* was' during his years as driver to the Harcourts, since everything was subject to 'arrangement with the boss'. The formation of unions, following on from labour laws passed in the 1890s, altered class relations in many fields of employment including domestic service.[75] The rising costs of living, combined with financial pressures sustained from the late nineteenth-century fall in land values and new taxation, meant that aristocratic families further reduced the numbers of household staff they employed.

Changes in domestic service were neither sudden nor evenly spread among the nobility. By the mid-twentieth century the trend was towards hiring a cleaner (*la femme de ménage*) and many regretted the decline of 'familial-style' bonds with live-in servants.[76] Through a series of lavish costume balls hosted in the 1920s and 1930s nobles and *haut bourgeois* turned the 'theatre of rule' on its head by parodying a 'lost' world of public and patriarchal privileges. In 1927, as a marvellous homage to the author who had died four years earlier, the Faucingy-Lucinges received guests costumed *à la Proust*. The princesse de Polignac arrived rather cheekily disguised as Jupien, the tailor. In 1928 the duchesse de Doudeauville (née Radziwill) staged a Regency Ball. '*Valets de pied* in knee breeches and powdered wigs wore the livery of former times with the arms and colours of the House of La Rochefoucauld-Doudeauville.' Here was a nostalgic and flamboyant farewell to court etiquette and customs. As one guest remarked wistfully: 'Our vision of what France used to be could barely be sustained.'[77]

Notes

1 Philippe Perrot, *Fashioning the Bourgeoisie: A History of Clothing in the Nineteenth Century*, trans. Richard Bienvenu (Princeton, 1994), pp. 15–20.

2 Cissie Fairchilds, *Domestic Enemies: Servants and their Masters in Old Regime France* (Baltimore, 1984), pp. 12–13; Jean-Pierre Gutton, *Domestiques et serviteurs dans la France de l'ancien régime* (Paris, 1981), p. 7. On servant characters in pre-revolutionary French comic opera and plays, see Sarah Maza, *Servants and Masters in Eighteenth-Century France: The Uses of Loyalty* (Princeton, 1983), pp. 227–37. The phrase 'theatre of rule' comes from E. P. Thompson, 'Patrician society, plebeian culture', *Journal of Social History* 7 (1974), 382–405.

3 Fairchilds, *Domestic Enemies*, pp. 14–15; Maza, *Servants*, pp. 270–80.

4 Fairchilds, *Domestic Enemies*, pp. 16–17, 152. Sarah Maza argues that wages had been 'a crucial factor in the relationship' of servant and master as early as the sixteenth century, see Maza, *Servants*, pp. 14–15. In Bonnie Smith's account the reciprocal relationship between servant and mistress also perpetuated a 'moral economy' in bourgeois households of northern France, see Bonnie G. Smith, *Ladies of the Leisure Class: The Bourgeoises of Northern France in the Nineteenth Century* (Princeton, 1981), p. 75.

5 Gutton, *Domestiques*, p. 23; Sharon Kettering, *Patrons, Brokers, and Clients in Seventeenth-Century France* (Oxford, 1986), pp. 34–5, 214–21.

6 Anne Martin-Fugier, *La Place des bonnes: la domesticité féminine à Paris en 1900* (Paris, 1979), pp. 72–5; Michel Chabot, *Histoire de Jean et Yvonne*

domestiques en 1900, racontée par Paul, leur fils, à Michel, son petit-fils (Paris, 1988), pp. 64–6; Jean-Marie Wiscart, *La Noblesse de la Somme au XIXe siècle* (Amiens, 1994), p. 158.

7 Martin-Fugier, *La Place des bonnes*, p. 72; Charles Sowerwine, *France since 1870: Culture, Politics and Society* (New York, 2001), p. 8.

8 There were long-serving and long-suffering maids in some bourgeois homes: Mme Céleste, Proust's housekeeper, is a notable example. See Céleste Albaret, *Monsieur Proust*, ed. Georges Belmont, trans. Barbara Bray (New York, 1976).

9 Thompson, 'Patrician society', 388–90.

10 Inventory 5 June 1912 in AP 173 bis/408 Fonds Maréchal Berthier.

11 For statistical breakdown of the Wagram income and investments at the turn of the century see François Lalliard, *La Fortune des Wagram de Napoleon à Proust* (Paris, 2002), pp. 315–17.

12 Marquis de Breteuil, *Journal secret*, 1886–1889 (Paris, 2007), pp. 268–9.

13 Marcel Proust, *In Search of Lost Time*, trans. C. K. Scott Moncrieff and Terence Kilmartin revised by D. J. Enright, vol. 3 *The Guermantes Way* (London, 1993), p. 31.

14 Proust, *The Guermantes Way*, p. 17.

15 François-Charles d'Harcourt, *Regards sur un passé* (Paris, 1989), pp. 13–14; Thorstein Veblen, *The Theory of the Leisure Class: An Economic History of Institutions* (New York, 1934), pp. 57–65.

16 Veblen, *Theory of the Leisure Class*, p. 57.

17 A new lambskin coat to protect a driver against the winter cold cost 300 francs or nearly six months wages, see Chabot, *Histoire de Jean et Yvonne*, p. 32. On servants' liveries as 'conspicuous consumption', see Veblen, *Theory of the Leisure Class*, pp. 79–80.

18 Gabriel-Louis Pringué, *Trente ans de dîners en ville* (Paris, 1950), pp. 76–7. The colours of the Broglie family were also blue and yellow, see Comtesse Jean de Pange, *Comment j'ai vu 1900* (Paris, 1999), p. 21.

19 Anne d'Uzès, *Souvenirs de la duchesse d'Uzès née Mortemart: préface de son petit-fils le comte de Cossé Brissac* (Paris, 1939), pp. 26–8; Anna de Noailles, *Le Livre de ma vie* (Paris, 1976), pp. 119–35. On the stages of mourning, see Baronne d'Orval, *Usages mondains. Guide du savoir-vivre moderne dans toutes les circonstances de la vie* (Paris, 1901), pp. 362–87.

20 Chabot, *Histoire de Jean et Yvonne*, pp. 31–2.

21 Gutton, *Domestiques*, p. 23; Lalliard, *La Fortune*, pp. 229, 250; Martin-Fugier, *La Place des bonnes*, ch. 2.

22 Lalliard, *La Fortune*, p. 250. The wages of a maid in a bourgeois home also remained relatively stable throughout the nineteenth century. Martin-Fugier, *La Place des bonnes*, p. 87.

23 Lalliard, *La Fortune*, p. 250; AP 31/292 Fonds Murat. The Murat annual wage figures have been calculated by multiplying the monthly figures for November 1904 by twelve.

24 Lalliard, *La Fortune*, pp. 315–18, 450; Marguerite Perrot, *Le Mode de vie des familles bourgeoises* (Paris, 1961), p. 10.
25 Lalliard, *La Fortune*, p. 250; Martin-Fugier, *La Place des bonnes*, p. 80.
26 Martin-Fugier, *La Place des bonnes*, p. 77.
27 Pange, *Comment j'ai vu*, pp. 16–17.
28 Marie d'Armaillé, *Quand on savait vivre heureux (1830–1860)* trans. in David Higgs, *Nobles in Nineteenth-Century France: The Practice of Inegalitarianism* (Baltimore, 1987), pp. 212–13.
29 Jean-Yves Tadié, *Marcel Proust: A Life*, trans. Euan Cameron (New York, 2000), pp. 315–16.
30 March 1890 in AP 101 (II)/22 Fonds Gramont.
31 Undated note (1923) AP 101 (II)/22 Fonds Gramont.
32 AP Fonds Murat 31/292 and 465–6.
33 Lalliard, *La Fortune*, pp. 195–7, 291–3.
34 Boni de Castellane, *Mémoires* (Paris, 1986), pp. 37–8; René de La Croix de Castries, *Papiers de famille* (Paris, 1977), p. 237; Harcourt, *Regards*, pp. 18–20, 47–8.
35 15 January 1890 in AP 399/324 Fonds Chartrier de Malesherbes.
36 Susan K. Foley, *Women in France since 1789* (Basingstoke, 2004), pp. 67–8.
37 Chabot, *Histoire de Jean et Yvonne*, pp. 145–6.
38 Between 1851 and the turn of the century the proportion of servants who were female rose from 69 per cent to more than 80 per cent. Foley, *Women in France*, p. 66; Fairchilds, *Domestic Enemies*, p. 15.
39 Chabot, *Histoire de Jean et Yvonne*, pp. 134–5, 172–3, 241; Christophe Charle, *A Social History of France in the Nineteenth Century,* trans. Miriam Kochan (Oxford, 1994), pp. 252–3.
40 Martin-Fugier, *La Place des bonnes*, pp. 42–71, 171–7.
41 Martin-Fugier, *La Place des bonnes*, p. 198.
42 'Article de Paris' *La Vie Parisienne* 23 November 1901; Yates, *Maid and Mistress*, pp. 11, 76, 101–2, 128–9. Octave Mirbeau's novel *Journal d'une femme de chambre* (1900) exploited the potent mix of power, physicality, and sensuality in relations between a maid and mistress. Considered pornographic by some critics, the novel was intended primarily as a comment upon corruption and anti-Semitism in French society in the wake of the Dreyfus Affair. The novel was adapted to film by Jean Renoir and Luis Buñuel. See Richard Ings's introduction in Octave Mirbeau, *The Diary of a Chambermaid*, trans. Douglas Jarman (Cambridge, 1991).
43 Rachel G. Fuchs, *Abandoned Children: Foundlings and Child Welfare in Nineteenth-Century France* (Albany, 1983); Rachel G. Fuchs, 'Morality and poverty: public welfare for mothers in Paris, 1870–1900', *French History* 1–2 (1988), 288–311; Rachel G. Fuchs, *Poor and Pregnant in Paris* (New Brunswick, 1992).
44 On 'moralization of the masses' see Peter McPhee, *A Social History of France*, 1789–1914 2 ed. (New York, 2004), ch. 12. On Catholic perceptions of God in

nineteenth-century France see Ralph Gibson, *A Social History of French Catholicism, 1789–1914* (London, 1989), pp. 241–8, 251–4.
45 Susan Yates, *Maid and Mistress: Feminine Solidarity and Class Difference in Five Nineteenth-Century French Texts* (New York, 1991).
46 Norbert Elias, *The Court Society*, trans. Edmund Jephcott (Oxford, 1983), pp. 104–5.
47 Thompson, 'Patrician society', p. 389.
48 Harcourt, *Regards*, pp. 23–4.
49 18 April 1900 'Livres des ordres 1900' AP 173 bis/447 Fonds Maréchal Berthier.
50 Maza, *Servants*, p. 259.
51 Undated note (Sunday evening) in AP 101 (II)/31 Fonds Gramont.
52 Chabot, *Histoire de Jean et Yvonne*, p. 43. One nobleman, born in 1910, who completed Mension-Rigau's questionnaire in the 1980s, was very specific about the moral capacities required of servants employed to do the laundry in an aristocratic household: '*discrétion, honnêteté, propreté*'. Mension-Rigau, *Aristocrates*, p. 34.
53 Orval, *Usages mondains*, pp. 307–8.
54 Castellane, *Mémoires*, p. 37.
55 *Manuel du valet de chambre* (2 ed., n.d.).
56 Chabot, *Histoire de Jean et Yvonne*, p. 82.
57 Chabot, *Histoire de Jean et Yvonne*, p. 27.
58 Wiscart, *La Noblesse de la Somme*, p. 161.
59 According to Mension-Rigau, the moustache, as well as being a sign of virility in the nineteenth century, was also a sign of a male autonomy; he notes that in the France of the Third Republic many a politician kept a moustache. Mension-Rigau, *Aristocrates*, p. 36.
60 Chabot, *Histoire de Jean et Yvonne*, p. 27; Maza, *Servants*, pp. 206, 208; Veblen, *Theory*, p. 57.
61 Proust, *The Guermantes Way*, pp. 679–80; Veblen, *Theory of the Leisure Class*, p. 60.
62 Thompson, 'Patrician society', p. 402.
63 Lalliard, *La Fortune*, pp. 189–95, 303.
64 On the Asile Charles-Louis and crèche: AP 173 bis/416–17 Fonds Maréchal Berthier; on the princesse's charitable patronage and work for the library: AP 173 bis/426–7 Fonds Maréchal Berthier; for the mayor's letters (1892–1906) regarding the village square: AP 173 bis/365 Fonds Maréchal Berthier.
65 AP 173 bis/405 Fonds Maréchal Berthier.
66 On seigneurial control, the fragility of peasants' family economy, and deference in the 1780s and 1820s: McPhee, *A Social History*, pp. 17, 155–6.
67 When she did not receive a response to her letters, the widow Carronget enlisted her son to write on her behalf. AP 173 bis/388 Fonds Maréchal Berthier.
68 AP 173 bis/398 Fonds Maréchal Berthier.
69 AP 173 bis/405 Fonds Maréchal Berthier.

70 McPhee, *A Social History*, pp. 155–6.
71 Thompson, 'Patrician society', pp. 399–400.
72 March 1890 in AP 101 (II)/22 Fonds Gramont.
73 14 December 1914 in AP 142/13 Fonds Xavier de La Rochefoucauld.
74 Martin-Fugier, *La Place*, pp. 87–8.
75 Chabot, *Histoire de Jean et Yvonne*, p. 75; Theresa McBride, *The Domestic Revolution: The Modernization of Household Service in England and France, 1820–1920* (London, 1976), pp. 57–60. The issue of maternity leave loomed large in debates about the regulation of labour. See Anne Cova, *Maternité et droits des femmes en France (XIXe–XXe siècles)* (Paris, 1997), pp. 49–61.
76 Mension-Rigau, *Aristocrates*, p. 40.
77 André de Fouquières, *Cinquante ans de panache* (Paris, 1951), pp. 168–9, 172. Proust died on 22 November 1922.

5

Paternity and politics

Every politician knows the power of words. In nineteenth-century France political news and opinions were communicated very commonly through social gatherings, the press, and meetings of all kinds. Parliamentary records contain the words of men alone in an age when electoral candidacy was restricted to the male sex. Letters, diaries, and memoirs, however, show that women and men discussed politics with one another and both sexes acted as generators, recipients, and promoters of political messages. Noblemen's participation in the political debates about paternity during the Third Republic was closely bound up with their experiences of family life. One of the central issues of contention raised by the Ferry laws of the early 1880s was the power of the state versus paternal authority (*la puissance paternelle*) in determining the content and direction of children's education. By instituting free, obligatory, and secular schooling in 1882 republicans effectively limited a father's right to choose a form of education in which religious instruction was maintained at the core of the curriculum. Following on from this was the law of 13 July 1889 to create state protection for delinquent children; Henri Taudière, Professor of Law in Paris, described it as 'the most serious blow to paternal authority'.[1]

How did noblemen respond to these republican initiatives? What were the lived experiences of fatherhood for French noblemen in the late nineteenth and early twentieth centuries? This investigation of aristocratic paternity contributes to a growing historical literature on fathers and more broadly on masculinity.[2] The letters of noblemen provide unique perspectives on fatherhood, and in using them two key matters will be addressed.

The first matter is the transmission of political heritage. To what extent did aristocratic fathers communicate to their sons and daughters the nature of their political beliefs? How much did children know about their father's political views and activities? To answer these questions is to probe into the educative strategies of the nobility. By this I mean to investigate 'education' in the broad sense, intended by Bourdieu, which encompasses not only scholastic activity but also the influence of family and milieu.[3] Among the French aristocracy there exists a long tradition, dating back to the Middle Ages, of men and women writing educative texts for their offspring. By the late nineteenth century, education in France looked quite different from the way it had appeared to medieval court circles. Processes of secularisation, democratisation and *francisation*, begun in 1789, were steadily transforming the substance and style of learning. The teaching role of clerics and religious orders was scrutinised and then heavily curtailed. Within these broad currents of social change, aristocratic families retained certain longstanding educative strategies and one of those was the role of fathers in the transmission of political heritage.

The second matter concerns the emotional dynamics of the father–child relationship that evolved over time as parents and their offspring grew older. There is of course a limit to which a historian is able to read those dynamics accurately, for reasons ranging from the practical difficulties of deciphering handwriting to the fact that both sides of a correspondence are not always preserved in *archives privées*. Yet the richness of the sources that have been kept amply warrants the effort to overcome the challenges to their interpretation.

Within the context of the Third Republic the subject of paternity requires us not to treat the male sex in isolation but rather to consider the interrelationship of gendered roles. That interrelationship was core to republican understandings of the political threat to the regime represented by conservative opponents. In a speech made on 10 April 1870 the republican minister Jules Ferry made the following observation:

> There is going on today a silent but persistent struggle between the society of the past ... with its edifice of regrets, beliefs, and institutions that do not accept modern democracy, and the society which emerged from the French Revolution. There remains within our midst an 'old regime' that still persists, and when this struggle, which is the very foundation of modern anarchy, when this intimate struggle ends, the political struggle will be over in one stroke.[4]

Like Jules Michelet before him, Ferry argued that the 'society of the past' relied on 'the secret and continuous help' of women who, influenced by the priest, spread their religious convictions to other family members. A wife and mother had the power to compromise the republic's secularising, democratic aims – especially in the formation of citizens – because hers was such an effective voice in matters of education.

Historians have written about the republican government's ambitious reforms to education led by Ferry, and their works address the impact of those reforms on girls and women. There has also been important scholarship on the role of the mother, and of the Catholic Church in girls' education.[5] Considerably less attention has been paid to the role of the father and to what monarchist and Bonapartist families were doing in their homes around the time that the republican government was devising and implementing its educational reforms. Filling this gap in the historiography is made possible here through an analysis of noblemen's letters. *Archives privées* provide some insight into what was going on behind the 'edifice of regrets, beliefs, and institutions that do not accept modern democracy'. From the inside Ferry's 'society of the past' looks rather more progressive, in certain areas, than the republican minister might have believed. Crucially they show that aristocratic fathers, ably supported by 'the secret and continuous help of women', rendered a powerful influence upon their children by shaping their views on politics, faith, and the social order.

Noblemen participated in regional and national politics as elected representatives, and most who sat in the Chamber of Deputies and Senate in the early Third Republic were Legitimists; they belonged to the right or extreme right. A small minority were Orléanists (centre right) or centre left.[6] To some extent ideology reflected place of origin for these men. France before 1877 may roughly be divided into two zones each with its own distinct electoral patterns: the western side of the country, from the department of Côtes-du-Nord to the Pyrénées centrales, was politically oriented towards the right, with a high proportion of conservatives holding electoral office, while the eastern side of the country was politically oriented towards the left. There was a gradual shift away from the right in the southwest as voters there became more favourable to the Republic. After 1877 electoral patterns in the regions of Aquitaine, the north of the Massif central, the north of Paris, and the Mediterranean made the former west–east divide less marked; Aquitaine, notably, became 'a terrain of conflict between the left and the right'.[7] Various detailed studies on political representation in particular regions and departments contain breakdowns by class of those holding office during the Third Republic. These studies, like research on mid-nineteenth-century notables, confirm that the aristocracy dominated in areas traditionally oriented towards the right. The Côtes-du-Nord, for example, had a high proportion of nobles. Of its ninety-two deputies and senators elected during the Third Republic, thirty (or approximately one-third) were titled nobility; they included a duke, four marquis, nineteen comtes, four vicomtes, and two barons. Similarly in the Sarthe thirteen out of a total of forty-nine political representatives (more than one-quarter) were noble.[8]

The concept of heredity makes a useful heuristic tool for analysing the longevity of aristocratic dominance in such areas. It also reveals a startling paradox within the French democratic system. As Claude Patriat writes:

> To discuss heredity in politics, or more precisely here the transmission of electoral mandates between relatives, jars with democratic common sense ... Kinship upsets the ideal of individuality and equality; the maintenance of electoral mandates within a lineage over a long period contradicts the idea of the rotation of office that one associates with the idea of election.[9]

Aware of the paradox of heredity continuing to play a part in an electoral system, the revolutionaries of 1789 had sought to dissolve it by introducing legislation to prevent relatives from holding mandates simultaneously or in close succession at the municipal level. Under the terms of Article 12 of the law of 14 December 1789: 'the conditions of eligibility for municipal administrations will be the same as for department and district administrations; however, relatives by blood or marriage who are father and son, father-in-law and son-in-law, brother and brother-in-law, uncle and nephew, may not be members of the municipal body at the same time'. Similar wording found its way into Article 176 of the Constitution of Year III: 'Parents and direct descendants, brothers, uncles and nephews, and relatives by marriage of the same type, may not at the same time be members of the same administration, nor follow each other in office with an interval of less than two years.'[10] There is little sign, however, of the effectiveness of such legislation in preventing the formation of powerful political dynasties especially on the right during the nineteenth century. On the basis of evidence provided by regional prosopographies, heredity remained 'strong within the aristocracy' during the Third Republic. It was not at all uncommon for a local mandate to be transmitted from father (or father-in-law) to son or from uncle to nephew. This then served as a stepping-stone for a nobleman to move into national politics via election to the Chamber of Deputies or the Senate.[11]

Historians have adopted three main explanations to account for the 'permanence of dynasties' in the Third Republic. The first of these is the power and prestige associated with the family name. Especially in the west, where traditions of counter-revolution, Catholicism, and royalism hold such historical significance, and were joined to collective memories of suffering in the Vendée during 1793–9, certain families exercised 'a quasi-feudal influence' so that names such as La Rochette and Rohan Chabot become symbolic reference points for a territory's political and cultural affiliation.[12] The second explanation is public visibility, manifest through the holding of multiple offices (administrative, political, socio-professional) and through the ownership of prominent residences that signified the reality of economic and political power. In the Loire-Inférieure, for example, certain families were well known for 'the *longue durée* of their presence in deliberating assemblies', and the sense of mastery over social time that this conveyed was symbolised in the improvement of existing châteaux or the construction of new and imposing homes.[13] The third explanation is familial strategies that included marital alliances to consolidate political power as well as the preparation of males for political candidature. Building self-perception as a candidate and conviction of the ability to hold power was at least as important to nobles as encouraging public perceptions of masculine ambition and taste for office.[14]

While each of these explanations helps to account for the 'permanence of dynasties', we need to remember that they also point to why in some regions of France voters rejected conservative candidates. Republicans cannily used the message of 'quasi-feudal influence' on the right to scare voters away from their opponents whom they depicted as returning France in the direction of the *ancien régime*. Election results and campaign propaganda have been deployed in the writing of political histories to reveal the tactics of different parties as well as the personalities and factionalism involved.[15]

Letters from the *archives privées* of aristocratic families enhance these explanatory frameworks for interpreting heredity in politics by revealing the cross-generational affective bonds between noblemen and younger relatives. The emotional gravitas with which fathers explained to their children, and to their children's children, the nature of and reasons for their political beliefs is striking, as we shall see presently from the documents. It is impossible to measure in a precise way the impact such explanations had on those who were related by birth or marriage. Some indication, however, may be derived by tracking the passage of younger male relatives into politics via exactly the sort of prosopographical research that has been carried out at local and regional levels. For example, between 1885 and 1940, excepting the years of 1894 and 1917–19, the Loire-Inférieure always had a member of the Le Cour Grandmaison family among its parliamentary representatives. Charles Le Cour Grandmaison sat in the Chamber of Deputies from 1885 to 1893 then in the Senate from 1895 to 1901. Succeeding Charles in office were his brother Henri, then Charles', eldest son Jean, and finally Jean's maternal uncle who was a senator from 1920 to 1940. There were similar patterns in the Sarthe, exemplified in the d'Aillières family commencing with Alfred, then Bernard, and finally Michel d'Aillières who was deputy from 1958 to 1977 then senator from 1977 to 1995.[16] Of course, there are some drawbacks to prosopography, some elements of history that cannot be recovered through this methodology alone. We need also to seek to understand the affective bonds that united relatives and which made the sharing of ideas and opinions part of the dynamic of family life.

Some three weeks after news of the French army's defeat at Sedan reached Paris, triggering the fall of the Second Empire and the declaration of the Third Republic on 4 September 1870, the prince Murat IV wrote to his son Joachim who was then fourteen years of age. Murat senior was a general and a descendant of one of Napoleon's key military men, the prince Murat I. In the immediate aftermath of France's shameful capitulation to Bismarck's forces his own legacy as much as the legacy of his ancestor weighed on his thoughts.

> My dear son,
>
> Your mother tells me you have grown up and are now a man; I am delighted by that for in my absence it is up to you to protect your mother and your sisters in all circumstances. God has willed that at your age you should have the strength and size of a man, it is also necessary to grow in wisdom so that I should be confident that in my absence you would be able to stand in for me. Children quickly grow into men in times of crisis such as those we are passing through. But one must not neglect work for one is truly a man only when one can say to oneself that one is independent and that one can meet one's needs through one's own intelligence. You must understand that you have a name that is very heavy to bear and that what might be considered very good for another will only be counted as passable for you; so you must act accordingly. You see that I consider you as a man, I am not writing to you as a child. Our misfortunes are so much the greater

that they came suddenly and at a moment when we were far from expecting them. Our poor country will take a long time to recover. I do not think I shall live to see France's fine military days again. At any rate I would no longer be in a fit state to take part in its glory, but I am convinced that you will play your part in this glory and I want you to be ready to carry with dignity the name that was passed down to us by the head of your family. Remember that what brought us undone was the lack of principles of all types, political as much as religious, which meant that in the army we no longer had even a shadow of discipline, no longer the sentiment of duty nor of fidelity to that which we all held in common ... Of principal import for a nobleman [*un homme de coeur*] is never to deviate from the straight path, so in your case you must be, and you will be, I am certain, completely devoted to the Prince Impérial, who is the head of your generation, as his father is the head of ours and, whatever the circumstances, you must not waver in the matter of politics between your own interest and his. My dear son, it is the first time that I am speaking seriously to you, but you have reached an age at which the terrible events that are happening engrave themselves in the memory and are no longer forgotten. Ask your mother to read you my letter and to explain to you what you do not understand.

I kiss you and ask God to bless you,

your father, Joachim.[17]

The prince's references to the family name in this letter ('you have a name that is very heavy to bear ... the name that was bequeathed to us by the head of your family') reminds us that the power and prestige associated with an aristocratic family name, which historians have argued impressed others and influenced voting patterns in some areas of France, placed a heavy weight of expectation upon noblemen themselves. There is not a sliver of ambiguity to the father's expectations of his son in the matter of politics: 'you must be, and you will be, I am certain, completely devoted to the Prince Impérial, who is the head of your generation, as his father is the head of ours and, whatever the circumstances, you must not waver in the matter of politics between your own interest and his.'

In the wake of a battle, thoughts inevitably turn to the dead as Murat's did. Yet even in less troubled and troubling times than France found itself in September 1870 the dead featured in noblemen's expressions of political duty. The sense of 'inheriting' a political mantle from the deceased was put candidly by the duc Francis d'Harcourt who made reference to his late father-in-law, the baron Gérard, when standing for election in 1929: 'His last wish, as well as my own resolution to uphold the political and social tradition of the deputies of Bayeux, compel me to offer myself to you as candidate.'[18]

Contemporaries paid interest to the maintenance of political sentiments from father to son. The archives of the Gouvello family from Brittany contain a testimonial from 1908 signed 'd'Ormesson' on the character of Paul de Gouvello. It is very interesting to see the way in which the letter-writer privileges the influence of Paul's father, Amédée de Gouvello, especially with respect to politics:

> I hasten, my dear friend, to respond to the confidential questions that you put to me ... The principles of Paul de Gouvello have never ceased to be perfect, even beyond perfect. His father, a good man if ever there was one, organiser of the agricultural orphanages, combined with the highest moral worth an excess of rigidity in his opinions. It was he who founded the Light-Horse faction [*les chevau-légers*], quite well known at the time, in the Assemblée Nationale at Versailles. Paul has somewhat inherited it, which is, moreover, a rather natural phenomenon.[19]

So far we have been concentrating on noblemen, but the transmission of political heritage from generation to generation was not restricted to male lines of descent. This is an important point because the political 'education' of females has not been especially well studied despite the emphasis historians have placed on marital alliances for bolstering and consolidating political dynasties. To investigate the transmission process further let us now turn to a set of letters written by Armand de Maillé de La Tour-Landry, comte de Maillé, to his daughter Blanche. They cover the period from 1869 to 1903, the year in which Maillé died.[20]

Maillé was deeply involved in, and felt passionately about, the political drama of his time. Over the period of his letter writing to Blanche, he lived through the Paris Commune, the death of the comte de Chambord, the rise and fall of Boulangism, and the passing of the Law on Associations. His letters are a powerful testimony to the range of emotions provoked by these and other events in the heart and mind of a Catholic Legitimist. Maillé identified with the moderate right, a group of monarchist deputies who in the wake of the White Flag Manifesto sought to be loyal to the comte de Chambord but rejected the uncompromising line taken by far right deputies known as the *chevau-légers*.[21] He was personally involved in the fruitless negotiations with the Bourbon heir over the issue of the flag, advocating for acceptance of the tricolour.[22]

From the 1870s to the turn of the century Maillé wrote several times per week to his daughter, and the tone in which he discussed political matters reveals a vivid spectrum of emotional responses. Profound frustration expressed on one day leads to sober reflection on the next and a sense of urgency on the next, and so on. The two strongest sentiments about politics that emerge from the letters are commitment, on the one hand, and reluctance, on the other. Maillé undertook his duties as a politician with great seriousness and endeavour, even though he regularly expressed distaste for and boredom with some of those duties to Blanche. He travelled constantly, read copiously, and wrote unstintingly. The demands of office included meetings with electors, preparation of budgets, consultation with colleagues, and of course his presence and contributions through Chamber and Senate proceedings. Concurrent with these activities, the letters show that Maillé also enjoyed a very full and fruitful family life, visited different countries, regularly attended the Opera and theatres of Paris, paid calls, joined hunting parties, and revelled in spending time at his country estate, La Jumellière (Maine-et-Loire).

Here is an excerpt from Maillé's letter of 21 June 1871, written on Assemblée Nationale notepaper, in which he explains to Blanche what he understood to be the basis of Legitimism:

> Legitimism is a great principle of the social conservative; it is not a divine right ... it is nothing other than the return to the old national law, the succession to the throne by order of primogeniture. It is not a right that the country gives to a family. It is a duty that one imposes upon it and a right that belongs to the nation to preserve it from the dangers of competition for sovereign power. It is the head of the House of France [*le chef de la Maison de France*] who personifies this national law.[23]

A fortnight after Maillé wrote this letter the comte de Chambord's White Flag Manifesto appeared in the national press. Maillé was among the delegation of three Legitimists who visited the pretender at the château de Chambord in the first week of July 1871. Like La Rochefoucauld-Bisaccia and Gontaut-Biron, he was chosen because his name and family heritage signalled commitment to the Legitimist cause.[24] At the time of composing the letter Maillé was no doubt preoccupied by Chambord's imminent trip to France. His reference to 'the dangers of competition for sovereign power' is a general point but perhaps also reflects his dismay at the outcome of the June elections. The republicans had just won ninety-nine seats in the Assembly against the monarchists' twelve, of which only three went to the Legitimists.

From the letter, however, it is clear that another reason Maillé entered into an explanation of Legitimism was to correct what he saw as a weakness in his seventeen-year-old daughter's approach to politics. Just over a month earlier he had written to Blanche praising the pretender's letter about the treaty with the Prussians, promising to send her a portrait of Chambord, and enclosing a publisher's notice for the book *Henri V et la monarchie traditionelle*.[25] Now he wrote:

> the political sentiments that you possess are worthy of quite long explanations from me ... those sentiments must be carefully thought out and represent something other than a vague love for a form of government ... Political opinions generally, and the Legitimist opinion particularly, are bound up with principles, memories and passions. To a certain extent, memories and passions can and should play a part in each person's political opinion and especially in that of women who are more impressionable than reflective; however, they should not form the basis and even less so the whole of the political opinion.[26]

Acknowledging that Blanche was 'very young for [him] to enter into all these details with [her]' Maillé does respect and express confidence in her judgement. He clearly admired 'her political passion', which he wished to nurture, whilst also seeking to cultivate an intellectual basis for that passion so that she would be guided 'not only by [her] heart and [her] imagination but also by [her] reason'. Only then would she be appropriately able to judge her political adversaries 'who also have their passion, their ideal and their legitimate goal'.

Evidently Maillé wanted Blanche to understand his own position and intellectual development, for he went on to describe the historical reasons for division in the monarchist camp between the Legitimists and the Orléanists.[27] His concerns over the consequences of that division had led him to become, as he put it, 'one of the most active agents for re-establishing the union'.[28] Maillé knew all too well the ongoing difficulties of achieving meaningful dialogue between Legitimists and Orleánists, let alone their respective leaders. In June 1871 the Orléanist princes, the duc de Joinville and the duc d'Aumale, were elected to the Assembly and the laws of exile were overturned with the help of the Legitimist vote. Yet there remained a distinct lack of enthusiasm on the part of the royal cousins for bringing about the fusion of the House of France. Chambord's note to the comte de Paris on 3 July, designed to delay their reunion until he had let France know 'his whole thought', cancelled any tentative optimism among monarchists.[29]

Even before that fateful first week of July, Maillé recognised that the cause of restoration was headed for disaster due to Chambord's obstinacy:

The princes [d'Orléans] are coming but they do not put in the zeal and ardour that I would have liked to see from them and that our confidence towards them merited. On the other hand, Monsieur le comte de Chambord, alas I must say, has not demonstrated the intelligence that the situation warranted nor shown his friends the respect that their efforts deserved. The refusal that was made to us ... at this time is a great mistake that seems to indicate a breakdown in communication between the comte de Chambord's ideas and the liberal reaction of the Legitimist party of which I am one of the representatives. Leaving aside the personal dimension, it indicates on [his] part a set of ideas that the country will not easily accept ... It is clear that this revolutionary country deplores our ideas because of their conservative and religious obsessions; if therefore the comte de Chambord distances himself from us, he distances himself still further from the country.[30]

In 1871 Maillé was all too accurate in his analysis and predictions. There is evidence in the letters, however, that Blanche, having received her father's explanations, was prepared to challenge his views occasionally. In December 1874 Maillé observed: 'You make fun a bit of your dear papa in speaking of the calm and moderation of his opinions ... One is not perfect in this world, one tries to get there and one achieves it more or less.' By this stage the eighty deputies known as the *chevau-légers* had split decisively with the moderate right. Maillé went on to stress the self-control required in dealing with the attitudes of those on the extreme right:

> They do not want to do anything and do not want to see the ruin into which they are going to plunge us. It hardly matters to them. It would seem that this is a storm that will pass against which everyone will be able to take cover. The admissions made by the right to the extreme right are not lost but they are not succeeding and will not succeed. It is very sad because that has been and will remain our sole experience.[31]

During 1874 the monarchists had once again fared badly in by-elections, gaining only one seat against six to the Bonapartists and sixteen to the republicans. It was in this context that moderates including Maillé formed an alliance with conservative republicans to establish the Constitution of 1875. The institutions of republican government, a Chamber of Deputies and Senate, were created and the election system of single member constituencies with two rounds of voting was introduced.[32] At the end of the following year, when elections to the Senate were held, it became clear that the alliance that had produced the new Constitution had benefited the republicans and been a disaster for the monarchists.

Of the seventy-five life senators elected by the Assembly, fifty-seven were republicans. Maillé wrote to Blanche, asking her to show the letter to her mother as well:

> We are in a dire political situation. Everything is collapsing around us; we are being directly attacked by the Bonapartists and by the die-hards of the extreme right; our friends are providing only half-hearted support; we are given a pounding by some of our own who are not on the list of senators; in short we are doomed and we cannot yet see the way out of this destruction ... Can you imagine that fourteen deputies of the extreme right and one of the right ... have cast their lot in with the senators of the left? Among them is Monsieur de La Rochejacquelin. *It is a disgrace for the son as well as for the father* [my italics].[33]

Maillé was correct that this 'most serious' situation would have 'an immense influence' on the elections for the new Chamber of Deputies held on 27 February and 5 March 1876. Republicans won 360 out of the 535 seats in the Chamber – a clear signal that most French men believed the republican regime offered the best outcomes for the country. Publicly Maillé was trying hard to convince his colleagues not to weaken their resolve or become demoralised, but privately he confessed to Blanche: 'I feel terribly wretched.'[34]

Most difficult for a man of Maillé's background to accept was the shame attached to the monarchists' political defeat, which he likened to a military defeat. His letter to Blanche on 16 December 1875 reveals the extent to which the binary of 'honour' and 'shame' coloured his perception of events and of the roles that different groups played in *la politique du pire*:

> Thank you for your charming letter in which you seek to console my poor heart from the disasters of our sad political battle. We are beaten beyond redemption, every day returning very proudly to fight but defeated by the number of traitors who have abandoned us ... Gambetta came up with the words for what has been offered to the extreme right in return for their treason: we house them, we feed them, but we will not pardon their sins [*on ne les blanchit pas*]. All the papers, I think, have repeated such things ... I confess that I cannot summon words to think that all these scoundrels were from the right, the extreme right, but these are still Legitimists. I was so proud of the honour of Legitimists; it has vanished like the rest.[35]

The letters discussed above show the ways in which Maillé communicated to Blanche the nature of his political beliefs. They also indicate how important it was to him to inform her and other members of the family about his activities and the evolution of the political situation in France. But there is another equally significant dimension to these letters.

There was more to life than politics for Maillé. In the autumn of 1875 the comte and comtesse were preoccupied by the matter of finding a husband for Blanche. She had turned twenty-one, the average age at which a noblewoman of her generation got married. A letter Maillé wrote on 11 November 1875 indicates that Blanche had discussed the question of matrimony with her parents and was willing to consider candidates from outside her known circle. Maillé agreed with her thoughts but stressed that any approach to or enquiry about a potential candidate was 'the business of parents and not of young people'.[36] There was little delay in finding a suitable husband. The following spring, on 22 May 1876, Blanche married Bertrand de Caumont La Force, marquis (later duc) de La Force. In customary fashion news of the aristocratic wedding was widely publicised in newspaper social columns. With pride, Maillé wrote: 'Your marriage is spoken about here [in Paris] with interest and all those who I think know you sing your praises in a manner that pleases me.'[37] One week after the wedding Maillé reported on a dinner he had enjoyed at the home of Blanche's in-laws where 'I found as always a very warm welcome and naturally we spoke much of Blanche and Bertrand'.[38]

Whilst Blanche's marriage in no way diminished the bond of love and affection between her and her father, it was nevertheless a turning point in their relationship. Henceforward Blanche became legally and financially linked with her husband and carried his family's name. Maillé's letters from the early summer of 1876 indicate a healthy respect and fondness for his son-in-law that seems to have deepened over subsequent years. To mark the occasion of the marriage, Bertrand made gifts of money to the poor who lived on and around his father-in-law's estate. Maillé wrote to Blanche: 'Do thank [Bertrand] for his good grace shown to the inhabitants of La Jumellière, I am very touched by it! It is for you that he goes to this expense of giving to people whom he does not know and whose tributes would certainly bore him.'[39] To help make his son-in-law feel welcome on the estate, Maillé gave orders for an apartment at La Jumellière to be redecorated specially for the young couple to stay in when they visited. When Blanche and Bertrand departed on their honeymoon to Holland, he wrote enthusiastically about the country he had visited three decades earlier. 'There are immense riches in artwork of all kinds, in Chinese porcelain, in ivories, [and] bronzes. Enjoy and make the most of seeing the beauty of all these human creations.'[40]

Entering a new stage of life, as a married woman, was exciting but not without sadness for Blanche. She seems to have had a bout of melancholy after the honeymoon, at the moment of her parents' departure from Paris to return to La Jumellière. Movingly, her father wrote to reassure her:

> Your thoughts matched our own at this time and you understand all that is bitter in separating from a past full of charms and illusions ... There is profound sadness in it for everyone, I hope that it will only be painful for us and that you will find in the core of your being that which will make you not forget, I hope, but cherish the days gone by that have prepared you for the happiness of the relationship. We suffer the fate of parents who have lived happily with their children and who see them pull away little by little without ever breaking the precious ties of childhood. Our duty is not to seem too affected by it and our hope is to see you return from afar as often as possible with your husband and with all that love may bring you.[41]

Twelve months later Blanche gave birth to a daughter, named Élisabeth, and the following year to a son, named Auguste. The arrival of these grandchildren inspired immense joy in Maillé. On 14 September 1878, as Blanche recovered from the labour of her son's delivery, he wrote: 'Your mother told me you are strong and well which gives me pleasure. Auguste is also very vigorous and will soon be a little devil. As for Élisabeth she is always charming and I am profoundly touched to see her holding out her arms to come to me.'[42]

The blessings of becoming a grandfather were mixed with ongoing concern for the state of his daughter's health, especially in the wake of a miscarriage Blanche suffered in April 1879, just seven months after the birth of her second child. Heavily occupied in preparing for the upcoming canton elections at La Jumellière, Maillé relied on news from his wife who went to care for Blanche and to supervise her recovery. The gravity of his concern, expressed in a series of letters from late April through to early May, reflects the very real dangers that pregnancy and childbirth posed in the nineteenth century for women who were vulnerable not only to miscarriage but also to post-partum infections.

Interestingly what emerges from the unfortunate episode of the miscarriage is that Maillé had equipped his daughter with some degree of knowledge about sex. On 29 April 1879 he wrote:

> The accident [Blanche's miscarriage] is over and we must accept it ... it seems you are doing well. I beg you my dear child to care for yourself properly, conscientiously, but even more so intelligently and then when

you are fully recovered remain at ease for a while and remember the excellent education that I gave you and say Monsieur, Monsieur, Monsieur!!![43]

This discreet reference to how his daughter might exert control over sexual relations in the marriage, by demanding a period of abstinence, is significant. For Maillé to have given Blanche even the most elementary education on the subject made him an unusually responsible father for his time. Was this education intended to prepare her for her wedding night? Or did he wait until Blanche had experienced conjugal sex before imparting advice? Whatever the case, there was a modest two-year gap before Blanche again found herself pregnant in May 1881. Two more boys, Armand and Jacques, completed the family that she raised with Bertrand. With three sons and one daughter, the continuation of the Caumont La Force bloodline was reasonably secure.

The births of these grandchildren coincided with republican efforts to pass new laws on education that horrified Catholics like Maillé and Blanche. A trenchant national debate ensued producing social effects that rippled out across the following decades. Within this context the letters of nobles provide fascinating evidence of reactions among politically engaged and committed individuals on the Catholic side. In March 1879 Jules Ferry introduced two education bills to the Chamber of Deputies, designed to remove clergy from positions of influence within state education and to weaken the private system of education controlled by the Church. Especially controversial was Article 7 of the second bill stating that no one belonging to a non-authorised religious congregation was to be allowed to teach in state or private schools, or to direct a teaching establishment of any kind. Although passed by the Chamber in July 1879, the bill did not come before the Senate until February 1880 by which point a well orchestrated opposition campaign led to its rejection by 149 votes to 132. Retaliation from the republican camp was swift. On 29 March 1880 the *Journal officiel* published two executive decrees based on laws passed in the late eighteenth century. The decrees required that all unauthorised orders, except the Society of Jesus, had within three months to seek government authorisation or face the possibility of dissolution, and that the Jesuit order was to be dissolved within three months, except its colleges which were granted a special extension until the end of the school year in August.[44]

Maillé's letter to Blanche dated 12 April 1880 reveals how the news of these decrees was received outside Paris and the tactical manoeuvring that resulted at the local political level. Maillé was at this point a member of the Conseil Général for Maine-et-Loire. Although he had not yet assumed the council's presidency, which he would do in 1884, the letter gives some indication of his influence and standing among other councillors.

> You have not heard from our Conseil Général because we have said nothing about the famous decrees. I am partly responsible because Monsieur de Mackau, who is the secretary of the senatorial gathering and of the deputies who are busying themselves with the resistance to come, told me that the committee wished the councils not to concern themselves with the 29 March decrees ... We have had some quite serious discussions and we have found within the Conseil Général a very good arrangement for resistance to the Prefect.[45]

Resistance to the republican crackdown on religious orders took many forms. There was lobbying by way of letters, pamphlets, and petitions; questioning and debate in the Chamber of Deputies; resignations from some four hundred magistrates and civil servants who refused responsibility for implementing the measures; and the occupation of chapels by priests, monks, laymen, and noblewomen until the gendarmes evicted them. Maillé's letter, on the other hand, paints a portrait of less sensational but no less significant activity. Maillé was closely involved in complex deliberation among his fellow councillors whose opinions on the issues at stake must have varied but who, in his account, reached an understanding. Ultimately they were the ones who would need to handle the local consequences of the government's decrees.

The issue of the Church's role in education had been debated on and off in France for decades, both publicly and in private. Brought back under the spotlight by the Ferry laws, it aggravated sensitivities that stemmed right back to 1789 when the revolutionaries had sought to destroy the Church's material power. A letter written in 1871 by the vicomte Emmanuel d'Harcourt to the comte Albert de Mun provides insight into one nobleman's reflections. Albert de Mun had lent Harcourt a copy of Keller's *L'Encyclique sur les principes de '89*.[46] Keller was a deputy and staunch Catholic; Jules Ferry referred to his book several times in the Chamber's debates on education and anticlericalism during June 1876. After reading it Harcourt was moved to commit his thoughts to paper:

> On the great question of education Keller sees things the same way that I do today. Religion must have its place in education, the priest must keep or rather reclaim his authority in the school. One does not make citizens

capable of voting or soldiers capable of winning wars merely by teaching children to read, write and count ... what we need are men who understand our moral duties ... I am therefore very much in favour of obligatory education ... religious as opposed to the theory of obligatory secular instruction whose only aim is to rebuild through the exclusion of all positive belief a sort of state religion that would be atheism ... But can one believe in the necessity of religious teaching without attacking the principle of the freedom of conscience? Is this principle true and necessary? ... Note that I do not call for the separation of Church and State. No matter what people say, France is and must remain Catholic. Catholicism, in some form, under whatever name, will always be and should always be our religion of State. Napoleon agreed to define it as the religion of the majority of Frenchmen.[47]

For Emmanuel d'Harcourt in 1871, the issue of the Church's role in education figured within his broader concern for the political direction of France in the immediate aftermath of *l'année terrible*. Not only had the country been shamefully defeated by its external enemy, Prussia, it had also been torn apart internally by the actions of the Parisian *communards*. In the eyes of conservatives, there were parallels between 1789 and 1871, which probably helps to explain why Albert de Mun had lent Keller's book to his friend at that particular point in time. Emmanuel d'Harcourt continued:

In between these points that are irreproachable in their clarity the Syllabus contains certain proposals that by their vague drafting lend themselves to very diverse interpretations. This one for example: 'The Roman Pontiff can and should be reconciled with progress, liberalism and modern civilisation.' What is meant by 'to be reconciled'? What is meant by 'progress'? What is meant by 'civilisation'? ... Following mature and often painful reflection, I am convinced today that it is necessary to separate oneself sharply from a certain progress, from a certain liberalism, from a certain modern civilisation that is profoundly wrong and dangerous: the *progress* that consists of substituting reason for faith and human passions for God's laws; the *liberalism* that allows for anything to be said, to be hoped for and to be taken, beginning with the property of one's neighbours; the *civilisation* that is only the perfected art of revolution. These words, these theories which it is necessary to break from completely, are justly condemned by the Church ... I am convinced that the moment has come to fight resolutely against this democratic, rationalist, revolutionary movement that is sweeping our country and towards which, I admit, my inexperience and the charm of some sweet-sounding phrases led me for a moment.[48]

The vicomte d'Harcourt, not unlike Maillé, was adamant about the need to fight 'this democratic, rationalist, revolutionary movement'. He also displayed the same sense of monarchist rectitude in the face of opposition: 'I do not believe all my social and political ideas are false.' Nevertheless the vicomte recognised, as Maillé did, that it was 'a great mistake and a great danger' to take an extreme line and to reject everything that had been introduced to France as a result of the 1789 Revolution. 'That is a utopia that Pius IX and the comte de Chambord each pursue in their own way. They do not want to distinguish in the tide of modern ideas what is just from what is unjust, what is viable from what is impossible.'[49]

By the early 1880s it was clear that the republicans were out not only to attack the Church but also, in the eyes of the opposition, to place the state's authority above that of the father. Jules Ferry, for his part, sought to quell the alarm of conservatives by explaining that the aim of the March 1882 law on obligatory primary schooling was to ensure compliance with the state's goals among the working class, not to remove *la liberté des pères de famille* among the middle and upper classes. 'You should understand,' he declared to the Senate 'that the legal weapon that we aim to secure will never be directed against *l'éducation des châteaux* or bourgeois families ... We do not aim to intervene between you and your children; we want, however, to make sure that a supposed "family" education does not become a last resort for those who resist primary schooling.'[50] The duc de Broglie, an Orléanist senator, was among those who did not believe Ferry's rhetoric that a father's rights remained 'intact' and that republicans would honour those rights by allowing a father to give 'to his children the system of education that matches his ideas, that corresponds to his beliefs'.[51] In 1883 Broglie, with support from the senator Chesnelong, interrogated Ferry in the Senate on the matter of textbooks and respect for the commitment to neutrality of instruction. This matter was taken up again in the first decade of the twentieth century by clerics when the Catholic newspaper *La Croix* became a mouthpiece for conservatives within the public debate. The mobilisation of Catholics saw the growth of a movement of *pères de famille* that by 1914 had 659 local branches, twenty-two regional federations and 55,000 supporters.[52]

Letters to the baron d'Alexandry d'Orengiani, senator for Savoy, illustrate the way in which friendly relations between clerics and aristocratic families bolstered political resistance at local and national levels. On 5 June 1881 François de Sales-Albert Leuillieux, a priest in Carcassonne, sent apologies for the delay in taking up his new position in Chambéry due to continuing grave difficulties in Paris 'which you have had the goodness to help me resolve'.[53] Unity of purpose in confronting 'the enemies of Religion and Society' meant that on 27 July Leuillieux promised to welcome to Chambéry 'the delegation of *pères de famille* that you have told me about' and assured the baron of his full support for their project. The warm rapport between the two men is also apparent in a letter from November 1883 when the priest sent congratulations for 'the brilliant success of your son Humbert' and assurances that he never forgot Madame d'Alexandry in his prayers. 'I thank you for your gracious attention; it corresponds to the affection that I feel for you in particular, and for that reason it is especially precious to me.'[54]

In 1907 another proposal was brought forward to deal with the problem of pupils' absenteeism by reorganising school funds to assist very poor families and giving Justices of the Peace a role in controlling absence. The initiative was not welcomed by the comte Henri Greffulhe who saw it as an underhand measure to divert attention away from issues raised by the 1905 Separation of Church and State. The socialist Aristide Briand, Minister for Religious Affairs, was then engaged in complicated negotiations with the Church hierarchy and the Conseil d'État to resolve problems of public and private law that were arising out of the Separation, including the permission for clergy to use church buildings for religious services.[55] In a letter to his wife, written on the occasion of the Catholic celebration of All Saints Day, Greffulhe fulminated against the political manoeuvring that threatened a further inroad to be made on paternal authority:

> I tell myself that all the great saints of heaven must have a 'serene' pity for the petty politics of our France. How wretched these little men are and how petty and malicious!! Selfishness, vanity, factionalism and self-interest – no grandeur, no goodness. They speculate on the naivety of opponents in disarray who continue to give their all in playing at bridge by the rules of piquet. But in the end are they not of the same country, the same race? They do not understand, poor things, that their politics makes for hatred, for reprisals – cutting, separating, dividing into two almost equal parts the most beautiful country in the world. Ah well! Those who make use of these processes cannot benefit from them much longer ... The Separation has placed our ministers in a deadlock. The Conseil d'État want a standard law. So, feeling themselves out on a limb, they look for distractions and have found one, the most abominable of all. To throw a bone to gnaw among the most progressive socialists, Monsieur Briand declares that he will get rid of the last vestiges of the freedom of education. Henceforth, it will formally be forbidden for a father to remove his children from a course of

instruction that revolts his conscience and attacks his most sacred rights. The father will no longer even be able to raise the child himself. As an idealist, he will be constrained to entrust [the child] to the official materialism. As a liberal, he will be obliged by law to impregnate his child with Jacobin instruction. From the top to the bottom of the university ladder, from the first lessons in the alphabet to higher studies, Freemasonry is going to monopolise French youth!! And one calls that governing!![56]

While the political debates raged over education, attracting press coverage, galvanising lobbyists to action, and prompting interventions from the Roman papacy, the nobility steadily continued to give financial support to the Church. Bequests and donations provide clear evidence of aristocratic families' commitment to preserving private educational traditions, based on religion, in the face of republican efforts to build a stronger secular state system. A study of wills made by the Faubourg Saint-Germain nobility shows that this set of Parisian nobles retained a strong attachment to Catholicism that went beyond shallow conformism. The prevalence of invocations to God (slightly more pronounced in the second half of the nineteenth century) and the high proportion of nobles who left a portion of their estate to benefit the work of the Church indicate sustained religious conviction. 'In the second half of the century nobles continue to remember the poor in their wills, but more and more they support institutions for education or assistance maintained by members of religious congregations.'[57]

Nobles' financial support for the work of the Church was significant not only in terms of the new educational laws but also in the way opposition was expressed to the proposal for a law to create state protection for delinquent children. Under Napoleon's Civil Code fathers had been allowed to imprison delinquent children. When the text of the new law reached the Senate in 1883, Waldeck-Rousseau, then Minister for the Interior, explained that he had some reservations because it pointed toward a decline in paternal authority and would impose a substantial new burden on the state that interfered with the natural and legitimate rights of the family. Waldeck-Rousseau's concerns highlighted weaknesses in the proposed law that the outspoken monarchist senator for Landes, Henri de Gavardie, exploited in his opposition to it. For Gavardie there were three problems: the law would encroach on the right to private charitable initiative, there would be no religious provision in the state's protection, and it would undermine paternal authority. Of these three consequences the most detrimental in Gavardie's eyes was the attack on the 'natural and divine' right of fathers, which he feared would destabilise families. The monarchist senator submitted fifteen amendments to the text in order to slow down the Senate vote. In 1883 the debate on the law split the Senate. Partisans for it were found among the republicans and centre left, while adversaries were found among the centre right, right and extreme right. It was not until 1889 with the weakening of conservative representation in parliament that the law came back on to the agenda and was voted through the Senate on the eve of the Bastille Day celebrations, one of many symbolic markers of the centenary of the 1789 Revolution.[58]

Waldeck-Rousseau's concerns about a new burden on the state were legitimate. To meet the demand for assistance it was critical for private benefactors to work in tandem with state authorities and during the three decades before the First World War nobles were heavily involved in charitable initiatives, including those directed toward minors. As estate owners and company directors, upper-class males often exhibited a paternalistic approach to the problems of poverty and perceived moral decline among workers. They believed, as the Legitimist deputy Lucien-Brun put it in 1887, that the 'law of a Christian social order was charity at work in a respected hierarchy'.[59] Upper-class men's charitable activities were directed towards both urban and rural working-class populations, but there was a tendency especially among aristocratic landowners to see agricultural workers in a more positive light. From the mid-nineteenth century such men were active in helping to set up a farm school programme to teach agricultural day labourers practical techniques in farming. Although the scheme was criticised for exploiting cheap labour, and Napoleon III reduced the number of *fermes écoles* under the Second Empire, the idea of developing and promoting agricultural education persisted into the Third Republic.[60]

It is evident for example in the agricultural orphanages established by Amédée de Gouvello, mentioned in the testimonial on his son Paul above. At these institutions the orphans worked under the supervision of a priest assisted by two brothers of the Order of Saint Joseph; they received primary instruction as well as lessons in agriculture and were encouraged 'to love rural life and customs'.[61] To support the work of the orphanages, Gouvello established the Société des Orphelinats Agricoles and attracted as presidents of the patronage committee the duc and duchesse de Vendôme who visited the Gouvello estate of Kerlevenan on 29 July 1897. Gouvello also managed to attain blessing for the Société from Pope Leo XIII. One of Amédée's sons, Gaston de Gouvello, observed that encouragement from such high levels boded well for the extension of the

Société's work and congratulated his father on this testimony to his 'devotion to the orphans'. The government, however, did not share the Gouvello enthusiasm for this type of initiative. In 1882 Paul Bert introduced a bill to remove members of religious congregations from elementary education and to deprive priests of their membership of school committees. Gaston's letter of March 1886, written just six months before this bill became law, has a defiant ring to it: '[The Société] will continue to bring together clerics and truly Christian members of society. I knew that the government had suppressed large numbers of curates' salaries, but I was not aware that Sarzeau [the Breton town in which the orphanage headquarters were located] had been so privileged by the minister's anger.'[62]

Beyond the symbolic paternalism of their charitable initiatives, it is difficult to determine the degree to which aristocratic male benefactors felt parental-type concern toward minors requiring assistance, or indeed how much direct contact they had with them. There was considerable diversity in nobles' motivations for charity work, and social and economic forces contributed to changing relations between benefactors and orphans over time.[63] Alongside the emotional dynamics of biological fatherhood lay the rich diversity of men's parental-type activities not underpinned by blood ties.

Evidence of the interplay between politics and paternity among the male aristocracy shows that class and family background closely informed noblemen's political viewpoints and electoral representation. Like their ancestors, noblemen who entered politics in the late nineteenth and early twentieth centuries benefited from social, material, and cultural advantages. Faced with the rising tide of support for the Third Republic, conservatives deployed those advantages in ways that sometimes helped them to maintain their mandates in particular regions. It was easier to have a brilliant political career when heredity facilitated the conditions and created the assumptions to support it.

The expectations of aristocratic forefathers created pressures for these men in their personal and professional lives. At the turn of the century Maillé, by then in his eighties, was still pursuing a punishing schedule of political activity. His duties as a senator kept him permanently on the move between Paris and La Jumellière. Family responsibilities still had to be juggled with political and social ones. Mourning the death of his sister-in-law, who 'bound me to the memory of my brother who I dearly loved', he returned from her funeral depressed by the capacity of death to destroy 'so many ties of which one does not appreciate the value until they are no longer there'.[64] In the face of continuing pressing claims on his time the comte confided to Blanche: 'the job I am doing is always tiring and monotonous.'[65] Writing from Angers on 23 August 1901 he apologised and shared his worries:

> I would have written yesterday but I had too much to do and it was simply impossible. We are overwhelmed with work of all kinds and I am overwhelmed with requests for visits. Our Conseil Général will not conclude its business before next Thursday ... The political events are unreal for us after the Law on Associations ... The Conseil Général is occupied with the concerns of the department, which are considerable.[66]

Old age had caught up with a man who still felt there was so much he had to do to protect Catholic conservative interests in a decidedly hostile political environment. On 24 April 1903 he reported: 'The situation is getting complicated by the socialist demonstrations ... which tend to get us mixed up in their anti-Catholic sentiment.'[67] The department's schools were in difficulty. The death of the councillor, who had beaten the conservatives for the post less than a month before, meant that new elections would be needed. 'I will be very busy', he wrote. This is the last of Maillé's letters to Blanche preserved in the collection. He signed his farewell: 'Mille tendresses à tous depuis A jusqu'au Z.'[68]

Letters are not the only sources in which historians can find evidence of the transmission of political heritage. The memoirs of noblewomen also reveal the process and significance of that transmission, for Blanche was by no means the only girl to have learnt about Legitimism from her father.[69] Although in Blanche's generation women were ineligible to vote, or to run for political office, Blanche's brother, Louis de Maillé, did follow in his father's footsteps. He served as deputy for Maine-et-Loire from 1903 to 1907, a political career abruptly terminated when a fatal illness claimed him at the age of forty-six. Of course it was not always the case that the political allegiance of a nobleman determined, finally, the allegiance of his son or daughter. Like other girls in nineteenth-century France, the comtesse Anna de Noailles was enamoured of Napoleon Bonaparte. France's first Emperor was a figure that fitted effortlessly into childhood fantasies whether or not those fantasies later translated into Bonapartism. Quite often they did not.[70] In considering the documentary evidence we need to remember that the transmission of *mentalités*, including political allegiance and, more broadly, political sensibilities, rested fundamentally upon a vibrant oral culture. What appeared in written form was only one version of an ongoing oral narrative. Through stories recounted over the generations, nobles passed on the model for power relations within the family that was the bedrock of a monarchic regime.⁷¹

The profession of politics demanded a lot from noblemen. In a different way, the experience of fatherhood was equally demanding, and for some men at least the rewards were certainly greater. Maillé put it beautifully when he wrote to Blanche:

> You are right to recall our life at La Jumellière to me ... This family life where we were all together, which is so rare for a great number of families, brought me enormous pleasure. It is a happiness that has been ours for a long time but what may we know of the future? So I hold fast to this memory that will remain as the ideal of all that a father may desire on this earth.⁷²

Notes

1 Véronique Antomarchi, *Politique et famille sous la Troisième République 1870–1914* (Paris, 2000), pp. 51–8, 73–9.
2 Rachel G. Fuchs, *Contested Paternity: Constructing Families in Modern France* (Baltimore, 2008); Yvonne Knibiehler, *Les Pères aussi ont une histoire* ... (Paris, 1987); Jean Delumeau and Daniel Roche (eds), *Histoire des pères et de la paternité* (Paris, 1990); Leslie Tuttle, 'Celebrating the *père de famille*: pronatalism and fatherhood in eighteenth-century France', *Journal of Family History* 29 (2004), 366–81; Anne-Marie Sohn, *'Sois un homme!' Construction de la masculinité au XIXe siècle* (Paris, 2009); Judith Surkis, *Sexing the Citizen: Morality and Masculinity in France, 1870–1920* (Ithaca, 2006); Christopher E. Forth, *The Dreyfus Affair and the Crisis of French Manhood* (Baltimore, 2004); Robert A. Nye, *Masculinity and Male Codes of Honor in Modern France* (Oxford, 1993).
3 Pierre Bourdieu, *The State Nobility*, trans L. C. Clough (Stanford, 1996).
4 Jo Burr Margadant, *Madame le Professeur: Women Educators in the Third Republic* (Princeton, 1990), p. 25.
5 Françoise Mayeur, *L'Enseignement secondaire des jeunes filles sous la Troisième République* (Paris, 1977); Linda L. Clark, *Schooling the Daughters of Marianne: Textbooks and the Socialization of Girls in Modern French Primary Schools* (Albany, 1984); Karen Offen, 'The second sex and the baccalauréat in republican France, 1880–1924', *French Historical Studies* 13 (1983), 252–86; Laura S. Strumingher, *What Were Little Girls and Boys Made Of? Primary Education in Rural France, 1830–1880* (Albany, 1983); Phyllis Stock-Martin, *Moral Education for a Secular Society: The Development of Morale Laïque in Nineteenth-Century France* (Albany, 1988); Marie-Françoise Lévy, *De mères en filles: l'éducation des françaises 1850–1880* (Paris, 1984); Caroline Ford, *Divided Houses: Religion and Gender in Modern France* (Ithaca, 2005).

6 Robert R. Locke, *French Legitimists and the Politics of Moral Order in the Early Third Republic* (Princeton, 1974), pp. 70–1.
7 Jean Estèbe, *Les Ministres de la République 1870–1914* (Paris, 1982), pp. 61–4.
8 Patrick Harismendy, 'Les Parlementaires des Côtes-du-Nord: perspective cavalière' and Dominique Parcollet 'Le Personnel parlementaire du département de la Sarthe' in Jean-Marie Mayeur, Jean-Pierre Chaline, and Alain Corbin (eds), *Les Parlementaires de la Troisième République* (Paris, 2003), pp. 97–106, 123–33; André-Jean Tudesq, *Les Grands Notables en France* 2 vols (Paris, 1964), esp. vol. 1.
9 Claude Patriat, 'Perspective cavalière: où il est question de personnes éligibles naturellement et légitimement par voie d'héritage' in Claude Patriat and Jean-Luc Parodi (eds), *L'Hérédité en politique* (Paris, 1992), pp. 1–2.
10 Françoise Fortunet, 'L'Interdit parental. De l'inéligibilité pour cause de parenté: l'exemple des elections municipals à l'époque révolutionnaire' in *L'Hérédité en politique*, pp. 37–44.
11 Sylvie Guillaume and Bernard Lachaise, 'Essai de synthèse régionale' in *Les Parlementaires*, pp. 65–85; François Naud, 'Représentants, deputés, sénateurs de Loire-Inférieure' in *Les Parlementaires*, p. 116.
12 Bernard Ménager, 'La Succession des mandates: une affaire de familles?' in *Les Parlementaires*, pp. 197–210; Annie Laurent, 'La magie du nom' in *L'Hérédité en politique*, pp. 173–235.
13 Naud, 'Représentants', p. 117; Ménager, 'La Succession', pp. 206–7; Anne Beton-Ruget, 'Territoire de famille. De l'office seigneurial au mandat parlementaire de la IIIe République: du bon usage de la parenté dans la transmission du pouvoir chez les notables ruraux bressans' in *L'Hérédité en politique*, pp. 45–63.
14 Christian Le Bart, 'L'Héritage dans la compétition' in *L'Hérédité en politique*, pp. 187–98; Françoise Mayeur, 'Affinités, mariages et alliances' in Jean-Marie Mayeur and Alain Corbin with Arlette Schweitz (eds), *Les Immortels du Sénat 1875–1918: les cent seize inamovibles de la Troisième République* (Paris, 1995), pp. 45–51.
15 Charles Sowerwine, *France since 1870: Culture, Politics and Society* (Basingstoke, 2001); Jean-Marie Mayeur and Madeleine Rebérieux, *The Third Republic from Its Origins to the Great War 1871–1914*, trans. J. R. Foster (Cambridge, 1984); Jean-Marie Mayeur, *La Vie politique sous la Troisième République 1870–1940* (Paris, 1984).
16 Naud, 'Représentants', p. 116; Parcollet, 'Le Personnel parlementaire', pp. 124–6.
17 23 September 1870 in AP 31/69 Fonds Murat.
18 Ménager, 'La Succession', p. 206.
19 19 December 1908 in AD Morbihan 31J/173 Fonds Gouvello.
20 AP 353/30 Fonds Caumont La Force. In the fourteenth century Geoffroy IV de La Tour-Landry wrote a treatise for the education of his daughters that was translated into English, *Book of the Knight of La Tour-Landry*. As far

as I can tell from the archive, Armand de Maillé de La Tour-Landry's letters to his daughter Blanche do not bear any relationship with this earlier work.

21 Marvin L. Brown, Jr, *The Comte de Chambord: The Third Republic's Uncompromising King* (Durham, 1967), p. 93; Samuel M. Osgood, *French Royalism since 1870* (The Hague, 1970), pp. 16–17; Steven D. Kale, *Legitimism and the Reconstruction of French Society, 1852–1883* (Baton Rouge, 1992); Steven D. Kale, 'French Legitimists and the politics of abstention, 1830–1870', *French Historical Studies* 20 (1997), 665–701.

22 For a Legitimist's account with details of Maillé's role: Vicomte de Meaux, *Souvenirs politiques 1871–1877* (Paris, 1905), pp. 104–28. On returning from the château de Chambord, Maillé wrote his own account of the meeting with the pretender that was circulated to members of the right but did not go to press at the time. It was published in the *Correspondant* on 25 September 1902.

23 21 June 1871 in AP 353/30 Fonds Caumont La Force.

24 Meaux, *Souvenirs*, p. 116; Brown, *The Comte de Chambord*, p. 90; Osgood, *French Royalism*, p. 16.

25 15 May 1871 in AP 353/30 Fonds Caumont La Force.

26 21 June 1871 in AP 353/30 Fonds Caumont La Force. For illustration of the way in which Legitimism was 'sustained by collective memories' see Peter McPhee, 'Social change and political conflict in Mediterranean France: Canet in the nineteenth century', *French Historical Studies* 12 (1981), 68–97.

27 For the diversity of Legitimist behaviour and attitudes toward the Orléanists see Marvin R. Cox, 'The liberal Legitimists and the Party of Order under the Second French Republic', *French Historical Studies* 5 (1968), 446–64; Kale, 'French Legitimists', 665–701.

28 21 June 1871 in AP 353/30 Fonds Caumont La Force.

29 Osgood, *French Royalism*, pp. 13–14.

30 21 June 1871 in AP 353/30 Fonds Caumont La Force.

31 7 December 1874 in AP 353/30 Fonds Caumont La Force.

32 Sowerwine, *France since 1870*, pp. 30–1.

33 10 December 1875 in AP 353/30 Fonds Caumont La Force.

34 10 December 1875 in AP 353/30 Fonds Caumont La Force.

35 16 December 1875 in AP 353/30 Fonds Caumont La Force.

36 11 November 1875 in AP 353/30 Fonds Caumont La Force.

37 Undated letter, spring 1876 in AP 353/30 Fonds Caumont La Force.

38 29 May 1876 in AP 353/30 Fonds Caumont La Force.

39 27 May 1876 in AP 353/30 Fonds Caumont La Force.

40 3 July 1876 in AP 353/30 Fonds Caumont La Force.

41 3 August 1876 in AP 353/30 Fonds Caumont La Force.

42 14 September 1878 in AP 353/30 Fonds Caumont La Force.

43 29 April 1879 in AP 353/30 Fonds Caumont La Force.
44 John W. Padberg, *Colleges in Controversy: The Jesuit Schools in France from Revival to Suppression, 1815–1880* (Cambridge, 1969), p. 265; John McManners, *Church and State in France 1870–1914* (London, 1972), pp. 50–2.
45 12 April 1880 in AP 353/30 Fonds Caumont La Force.
46 Jules Ferry, *La République des citoyens*, vol. 1, ed. Odile Rudelle (Paris, 1996), pp. 354, 357, 361.
47 [n.d.] 1871 in AP 378/11 Fonds Albert de Mun.
48 [n.d.] 1871 in AP 378/11 Fonds Albert de Mun. The *Syllabus* was touched upon in the Chamber of Deputy's June 1876 debate when the marquis de Castellane cheekily accused Ferry of not knowing what it was. Ferry, *La République des citoyens*, pp. 357–8, 362.
49 [n.d.] 1871 in AP 378/11 Fonds Albert de Mun.
50 Ferry cited in Surkis, *Sexing the Citizen*, p. 25.
51 Speech on 23 April 1879 in Ferry, *La République des citoyens*, p. 380.
52 Antomarchi, *Politique et famille*, pp. 77–8.
53 5 June 1881 in AD Savoie 29F/31 Fonds d'Alexandry d'Orengiani.
54 27 July 1881 and 5 November 1883 in AD Savoie 29F/31 Fonds d'Alexandry d'Orengiani.
55 Dansette, *Religious History*, pp. 244–6.
56 Undated letter (le soir de la Toussaint) in AP 101 (II)/31 Fonds Gramont.
57 Elizabeth C. Macknight, 'Faiths, fortunes, and feminine duty: charity in Parisian high society, 1880–1914', *Journal of Ecclesiastical History*, 58 (2007), 482–506; Claire Biquard, 'Piété et foi dans le Faubourg Saint-Germain au XIXe siècle', *Histoire, économie et société* 2(1993), 299–318, esp. 310.
58 Antomarchi, *Politique et famille*, pp. 52, 54.
59 Lucien-Brun cited in Locke, *French Legitimists*, p. 153.
60 Locke, *French Legitimists*, pp. 67, 149–55, 169, 215.
61 Statuts de la colonie agricole de Nourray (Loir-et-Cher) in AD Morbihan 31J/167 Fonds Gouvello.
62 24 March 1886 in AD Morbihan 31J/152 Fonds Gouvello.
63 Lenard R. Berlanstein, 'Growing up as workers in nineteenth-century Paris: the case of the orphans of the Prince Imperial', *French Historical Studies* 11 (1980), 551–76; Macknight, 'Faiths', 482–506.
64 28 November 1899 in AP 353/30 Fonds Caumont La Force.
65 28 November 1899 in AP 353/30 Fonds Caumont La Force.
66 23 August 1901 in AP 353/30 Fonds Caumont La Force.
67 23 August 1901 in AP 353/30 Fonds Caumont La Force.
68 24 April 1903 in AP 353/30 Fonds Caumont La Force.
69 See for example Anne d'Uzès, *Souvenirs de la duchesse d'Uzès née Mortemart* Préface de son petit-fils le comte de Cossé-Brissac (Paris, 1939), pp. 11–12.

70 Anna de Noailles, *Le Livre de ma vie* (Paris, 1976), pp. 31–47; Whitney Walton, *Eve's Proud Descendants: Four Women Writers and Republican Politics in Nineteenth-Century France* (Stanford, 2000), pp. 15–17.
71 A. S. Byatt, *On Histories and Stories: Selected Essays* (London, 2000), pp. 123–50, 165–71; David Higgs, *Nobles in Nineteenth-Century France: The Practice of Inegalitarianism* (Baltimore, 1987), pp. 212–13; Judith F. Stone, 'The republican brotherhood: gender and ideology' in Elinor A. Accampo, Rachel G. Fuchs, and Mary Lynn Stewart (eds), *Gender and the Politics of Social Reform in France 1870–1914* (Baltimore, 1995), pp. 28–9.
72 15 November 1879 in AP 353/30 Fonds Caumont La Force.

6

Aristocratic motherhood

In the France of the Third Republic the concept of 'republican motherhood' encompassed three longstanding duties incumbent upon women. The first and most important of these duties was to bear children. Prussia's victory in the war of 1870–71 prompted widespread fear over 'depopulation' in France where the birth rate was in decline. Childbearing in the Third Republic became a mark of patriotism; French women gave birth for the nation. The second duty of republican motherhood was maternal breastfeeding. Scientists and doctors of the time argued that breast milk carried superior health benefits for a baby compared with milk fed from a bottle. The 'naturalness' of maternal breastfeeding, an idea developed earlier by Rousseau, was emphasised in a campaign to reduce infant mortality. In keeping with that campaign the government cracked down on the ancient business of wet nursing. The Roussel law of 1874 stipulated that every child under two years of age placed with a wet nurse would be subject to surveillance by state authorities. The message was put that 'real' mothers breastfed their children: wet nurses could not be trusted. Finally, the third duty of republican motherhood was education. The mother was responsible for elementary instruction during the first seven years of a child's life. She contributed to the formation of French citizens by ensuring that the principles of secularism and democracy were respected within the family home.[1] Republican motherhood was a politically driven concept. It was strongly promoted by the unprecedented number of left-wing doctors elected to parliament in the three decades before the First World War. Backed by this medical authority the French government introduced new laws for the protection of mothers and children. The laws were welcomed by French feminists of the time who saw in republican motherhood a way to push forward the suffrage agenda.[2]

A different, but no less political, approach to motherhood prevailed among the female aristocracy. Comprised of traditions practised by French noblewomen over many generations, aristocratic motherhood departed in three main ways from the prescriptions of the republican model. First, childbearing among the nobility was understood principally in terms of perpetuating aristocratic bloodlines. To be sure, the future of the 'nation' also mattered to these families, but their primary concern was the survival of the 'race'. Since the quality of being noble was passed down through the male line, nobles laid particular store upon the birth of sons. The eldest son inherited special rights and responsibilities connected with use of the family name. The second major difference between republican and aristocratic motherhood lay in the realm of breastfeeding. French aristocratic families hired wet nurses to suckle babies of legitimate birth. The reasons that nobles opted for wet nursing were multiple and complex, and like the patterns of wet nurse employment in France they changed over time.[3] In the late nineteenth and early twentieth centuries, however, even when doctors and feminists advocated maternal breastfeeding, aristocratic families maintained the longstanding tradition of hiring wet nurses. The third way in which aristocratic motherhood departed from the republican model was noblewomen's deep-rooted support for Catholic education. There were, of course, French nobles who were not Catholic, and the intensity of Catholic faith and practice often varied among members of the same noble family, and historically in France by region.[4] Generally speaking, however, the education of the French nobility was associated with the Catholic Church. Children of both sexes took lessons in the catechism, and noble girls attended convent schools while noble boys were instructed by *précepteurs* and later attended Jesuit colleges. Aristocratic mothers played a crucial role in ensuring this education based on religion was perpetuated. In doing so they undercut the republicans' secularising aims.

The significance of aristocratic motherhood lies in noblewomen's agency to exploit a complex of political issues that highlighted the continuing social power of their families under the Third Republic. The most vocal proponents of an alternative to republican motherhood in France at the turn of the century were the aristocratic leaders of two conservative Catholic women's organisations: the Ligue des Femmes Françaises

(LFF), founded in Lyon in 1901, and the Ligue Patriotiques des Françaises (LPF), founded in Paris in 1902. These two women's organisations shared the same goal to combat republican anticlericalism. By 1914 the LFF and the LPF claimed 200,000 and 545,000 members respectively. Aristocratic women served on the central committees and as regional deputies. Before and after the First World War they used every avenue at their disposal, often enlisting help from male clerics and conservative politicians, to promote their cause. The cornerstone in the campaigns by the LFF and LPF against republican anticlericalism was a concrete vision of Catholic women's role within the family. Leaders of these organisations were staunch opponents of the French feminist movement, which they held responsible for a destructive trend towards 'individualism' tearing at France's social fabric.[5]

The powerful lobbying capacity of Catholic women's organisations, with their membership in the hundreds of thousands, was a public outlet for the political activism of the female aristocracy. Leadership within the LPF and LFF was a very concentrated form of activism that did not appeal to every noblewoman. It provided a platform for some female aristocrats to speak on behalf of all Catholic women, and in so doing find that convictions held by members of their own class, particularly about the centrality of the Church to French society, resonated strongly with women of other classes. Both organisations knew the importance of recruitment. In numerical terms, the memberships of the LPF and the LFF were vastly superior to the 'bourgeois' French feminist movement.[6] Noblewomen were also critically involved in the private dynamics of decision-making about childbearing, nursing, and education within their own families. This investigation of noblewomen's engagement with issues of motherhood places the female aristocracy at the centre of broader historical debates about the relationships between politics, demography, social continuities, and change in nineteenth- and twentieth-century France.[7]

In January 1899 the French feminist newspaper *La Fronde* published an article with the provocative title 'Grèves de mères', or 'Mothers' Strike'. The author, Marie-Louise Néron, blamed the egoism of the urban rich for depopulation in France. 'The most opulent neighbourhoods,' she declared, 'are those that contain the fewest children'. In these districts a woman 'sacrifices the duties of motherhood to luxury and pleasure'.[8] Néron was not the first to make the connection between high social status and low fertility in France. In the mid-eighteenth century well-to-do female writers identified a similar connection and speculated on its principal cause. Madame de Puisieux wrote of the Parisian nobility in 1750: 'Families have never been less numerous than in the past few years. Couples are limiting themselves to one or two children. Is this the effect of conflict between married couples?'[9] These two commentaries published over a century apart present different generalisations about family size and planning among the French elite. Whereas Pusieux saw marital discord as a potential explanation for the perceived decline in births, Néron blamed the selfish attitude of frivolous female socialites. Both accounts raise questions about the rationale for marriage and childbearing at the top of the social ladder.

Statistics presented in Chapter 2 on marital age and fertility among the aristocracy showed a trend developing in the late eighteenth and early nineteenth centuries towards later marriage, particularly among men, and larger families. We saw that over one-quarter (28.5 per cent) of noble couples in high society married between 1900 and 1914 had five or more children, and fertility rates were consistently higher among 'practising' Catholics. Catholic nobles married between 1900 and 1929 had a fertility rate of 4.4 children compared to the noble average of 3.2 children for the same period. What these figures indicate is that the stereotype of a frivolous high society woman, whom feminists accused of leading 'a life of pleasure, exempt from maternity', was false.[10] To be sure, not every nineteenth-century noblewoman achieved the astonishing childbearing record of Alix-Marie-Léontine de Saint-Georges de Vérac. Born in 1818, she bore eighteen children between 1839 and 1868, and according to family speculation endured an additional four miscarriages. This was an extraordinary feat given the mortality rates for mothers and children of the time. Yet the pattern of short intervals between pregnancies was not unfamiliar to many of her contemporaries or their daughters.[11]

There are physiological and cultural explanations for the high birth rate among the nineteenth-century French nobility. Female aristocrats, because they did not breastfeed, were less able to draw on a natural means of inhibiting conception since lactation can produce amenorroea, usually when the mother's diet is lacking in nutrition. When marital sex resumed, after childbirth, there was a good chance of re-impregnation if the couple took no other steps to prevent it. The strong fertility among the French aristocracy, from the late nineteenth into the twentieth century, runs contrary to the Malthusian tendencies evident in the French population as a whole. Research on the greater number of children born to 'practising' Catholics, in comparison with the noble average, suggests that this segment of the nobility followed Church doctrine in rejecting birth control.[12] Later nobles also took pride in the fecundity of their own class. Responses to a questionnaire collated in the 1980s revealed that aristocrats were 'conscious of the advantage that a high birth rate represents and remark for example that it compensates for the natural extinction of families by allowing the number of individuals of noble descent to remain fairly constant even if the number of noble families diminishes'.[13] The survival of the aristocracy was, and still is, directly tied to its ability to reproduce. Not surprisingly, therefore, nobles took a negative view of divorce, singledom, and adoption. Class conditioning meant that anyone who refused the imperative to reproduce was considered destructive, selfish, or even sinful. Women and men of the aristocracy felt duty-bound to ensure the continuation of their bloodline.

Class dictated much about women's physical and emotional experiences of pregnancy and childbirth in the France of the Third Republic. Abortion or abandonment of a newborn baby was often the only option open to a female domestic servant who fell pregnant. Lower-middle-class and working-class women normally continued to work during pregnancy. By contrast, noblewomen never received a salary; they were not personally affected by the French government's employment law of 1892, restricting the daily number of hours that women and children could work in factories, or the Strauss Law of 1913 introducing four weeks' compulsory leave after childbirth with a small allowance paid by the state.

Class also dictated the environment in which women gave birth. Until the 1880s a mother was at greater risk of contracting a fatal disease in a hospital than she was giving birth at home with a midwife; hence, it was only the poorest and often migrant women who were admitted to free public hospitals such as La Maternité.[14] By contrast, homebirth was the norm in aristocratic families, not just for reasons of health protection but also because the family's château might be some distance from a major town. An aristocratic home in which a noblewoman had her own personal apartment, separate from that of her husband, offered a secure, familiar, and more comfortable setting than a hospital. A midwife monitored the health of the expectant mother in the final weeks of pregnancy, and in most cases supervised the delivery. Sometimes a doctor was summoned, and where complications developed during childbirth it was he who made the critical decisions that could result in lives being saved or lost.

A rather too cosy picture has been painted of women and doctors setting out together 'to discipline, to save lives, to make marriages, [and] to restore health' in nineteenth-century France.[15] The general lack of sex education and the cruel initiation to conjugal duties suffered by some noblewomen helps to explain their reticence in discussing very private fears and concerns. Moreover, believers had other persons to whom they could turn for counsel. The diaries of abbé Mugnier, a much-loved priest within Parisian aristocratic circles, reveal that in the 1870s and 1880s some noblewomen confided their marital difficulties to him. This sensitive and tactful priest (who disguised the identities of confessional interlocutors in his private journal) was probably considered a more understanding and discreet listener to someone of profound faith than a medic who kept patient records. The letters of Catholic women to abbé Viollet in the 1920s and 1930s show that female confidence in receiving spiritual and marital guidance from clergy cut across class lines and continued well into the twentieth century, something republicans had long abhorred.[16]

Noblewomen sometimes dissented from doctors' advice, especially where medical authority was perceived to be in conflict with traditional remedies passed down from mother to daughter. For example, in June 1883, the baronne Mathilde de Mackau was taking care of her daughter Anne who was struck by a fever four months after giving birth to a baby girl. From the family estate of Vimer in Normandy, Mathilde kept her husband Armand, who was fulfilling a senator's duties in Paris, informed about Anne's condition. On 2 June she expressed her 'terrible fear' at Anne's symptoms, including incessant thirst, pain, and muscle spasms. Two doctors had examined Anne separately and both prescribed quinine. On 6 June the baronne wrote to her husband that, although she was following their directions for medication, she did not agree with the doctor Lesueur's recommendation to delay bathing Anne. 'I am *very much* in favour of the bath,' she wrote 'and would willingly have given it today. Instead, it was my idea that we rub lotions *that I made myself* over her body. It is beneficial, I think, for fever.'[17]

Anne recovered, but of course there were other mothers and infants who died as a result of a botched delivery or postnatal illness. On 1 August 1882 the princesse Marie-Félix Bonaparte [née Blanc], already suffering from tuberculosis, died of an embolism four weeks after giving birth in the villa de Saint-Cloud. The obstetrician Professor Pinard, who applied forceps in the delivery, had performed emergency mouth-to-mouth resuscitation on the baby. He managed to save the baby, Marie Bonaparte, who had failed to breathe on entering the world. Diaries and memoirs reveal that if a girl lost her mother when she was very young and was raised Catholic, it was often the case that she identified her mother with the Virgin Mary. In Élisabeth de Clermont-Tonnerre's first bedroom was a portrait of her mother, Isabelle de Beauveau, who had died giving birth to her: 'She resembled a Gothic Virgin.'[18]

Of course family members rejoiced and felt relief when a birth went well. News was quickly relayed to relatives by telegram and letter. The duchesse Élaine de Guiche (née Greffulhe) wrote to her father in 1911 assuring him of the good care and attention she was receiving.

> I am touched by the daily tenderness with which aunt Louise surrounds me ... She and uncle Robert joyfully celebrated their fortieth wedding anniversary yesterday. The weather is dreadful here. Thick snow, intense cold. We have not yet been able to baptise Charles ... My father-in-law's concern was sweet. I think his affection for me sets the world record. He pays visits and brings me fruits, flowers, and compliments.[19]

Typically, in addition to the presence of elder relatives, one of the consequences of a homebirth was the presence of other children including siblings of the newborn staying at the château. 'Really I am terrified by this mass of children who surround me,' confessed Élaine to her father. 'Antoine [her eldest son, then aged four] is my consolation. The more he grows up the more he resembles you. I laughed all to myself when, approaching my bed cautiously, he said to me "I am afraid I will be ill like you, if I come closer."'[20]

Feeding and looking after the baby were naturally immediate preoccupations after the birth. The particularity of aristocratic practices in childcare needs to be seen within the context of the Third Republic where childcare was deemed to be a 'feminine' task based on women's biological capacities as well as the longstanding gender order in French society. The republican government saw a mother's responsibility in political terms. Before and after the First World War it promoted the idea that a strong nation was nurtured on mothers' milk. Republicans' attachment to this idea informed their position in parliamentary debates on bills pertaining to female employment. It was also symbolically realised in public art and statuary featuring the buxom Marianne with infants guzzling at both her breasts.[21]

Yet the iconography of maternal breastfeeding scarcely corresponded to social realities before 1914. George Sussman has argued that nineteenth-century France was out of step with other European countries because wet nursing was still evident at all levels of society and the practice declined more slowly than elsewhere. He advances three hypotheses for the wet nursing phenomenon: first, that it was embedded in cultural attitudes toward children and the family; second, that it corresponded to social and economic conditions, especially female employment in urban centres; and third, that it was the safest alternative to maternal breastfeeding before the technological advent of readily available pasteurised milk and rubber-teated bottles. Sussman makes a convincing case that the socio-economic hypothesis best explains the pattern and timing of the end of the wet nursing business in France after the First World War. This was when the level of female employment in urban centres dropped, meaning that fewer working-class mothers needed to delegate the task of feeding their baby to another woman. Sussman is careful not to discard the cultural and technological explanations for wet nursing; he notes that families had different reasons for putting children out to nurse depending on class background.[22]

In the case of the nobility, socio-economic factors applied in a rather different sense to the way they did for urban working mothers. Aristocratic women did not engage in salaried employment, but their social duties at court and in high society constituted a form of 'work' that did not allow for the kind of domestic routine required when nursing an infant. The gradual decline of wet nursing at this level of society was tied to an evolution in social mores. Noblewomen after 1914 were less obligated to spend the afternoon making or receiving calls, and the evening hosting or attending dinners, balls, and theatre engagements. Equally, the financial pressures that began to take their toll on aristocratic entertaining at the turn of the century gradually discouraged these families from maintaining large numbers of staff after the First World War.[23]

The demand for wet nurses among the upper class, however, did help to maintain the industry from the passing of the Roussel law in 1874 to 1914. There were about twelve placement bureau for wet nurses in Paris during this period. The bureau recruited young women, mostly from northern French departments, to work either in their own home in the country or in the home of an employer. The provision of 'live-in nurses for the wealthy ... was the most profitable side of the business'.[24] Of course the ability to pay a wet nurse's wages, something that working-class mothers were not always able to manage, did not mean that nobles were immune to the major problems facing the industry: namely, the insufficient supply and unreliability of nurses. Finding a competent wet nurse was a notoriously hit-and-miss affair, whatever the social status of the employer. A closer look at the culture of childcare among the aristocracy, and nobles' responses to the advent of pasteurised milk, is needed to complement the socio-economic explanation for wet nursing in these elite families.

Since it was difficult to find a reliable wet nurse, nobles were much relieved at a satisfactory hire. In a letter dated 7 March 1883 Mathilde de Mackau wrote to her husband about the wet nurse hired for their granddaughter, Élisabeth:

> Beloved, thanks be to God – the nurse [*la nounou*] has arrived and seems to have settled in well – there are no problems – *everything is fine*. She said she has made sure her own child won't suffer as a result; she brought a woman with her to take him back. So everything is lovely and simple; she won't get bored, she much prefers to be in the country etc. ... etc. ... She has enormous breasts and no longer knew what to do with the milk, although her child had suckled all night. Sister [a nun] finds her magnificent. Baby threw herself upon [the nurse] and suckled mightily. The nurse said: 'Ah! That will do her good and myself as well!' She finds that *she* [*Élisabeth*] *resembles* her own little one and seems to see the positive side to everything. 'Typical wet nurse temperament' said Sister, breaking into laughter.[25]

The scene depicted in the baronne's letter is very different from the representations of motherhood among the French bourgeoisie found in paintings by Mary Cassatt, Berthe Morisot, and other artists of the late nineteenth century.[26] Cassatt, especially, focused on the intimate bond between mother and child, who are usually the only figures who appear in the canvas. By contrast, in Mathilde de Mackau's letter, there is no mention of her daughter Anne's presence while her baby is being fed, and the wet nurse has had her own infant taken away by another woman. In place of these biological mother–child relationships, another set of all-female relationships appear featuring a grandmother, her granddaughter, a wet nurse, and a nun. The scene, as the baronne describes it, is not lacking in intimacy, pleasure, or physicality: this is breastfeeding, after all.[27] But compared to artistic representations of maternity produced in late nineteenth-century France the scene is highly atypical.

The hire of a wet nurse removed the perceived risk that an aristocratic mother would have her milk 'spoiled' by recommencing conjugal sex during the period in which she was breastfeeding. What about the wet nurse and sexual activity? Nobles did take precautions. On 6 April 1875 the princesse Cécile de Béarn wrote to her husband, Gaston, from the capital: 'The husband of Henri's wet nurse is going to be passing through Paris soon. She asked me if she could see him. I gave permission but I told Mary-Anne to remain present *the whole time*. It is most prudent.'[28]

Accounts of the time that aristocratic mothers, with their busy social lives, spent with their children suggest that it was not more than an hour or so each day. The way the time was spent, of course, was determined by the age of the child. A wet nurse fed and minded infants with considerable autonomy until the parents decided they were ready to be weaned. An English or German woman was then hired as a nanny, and one of her tasks was to supervise the children at mealtimes up to the age when they were permitted to sit with adult relatives at the dinner table. The comtesse de Pange remembered that this privilege was granted on her seventh birthday: 'It was a date in my life.'[29] Children greeted their mother in the morning before lessons and play, and on the day of her afternoon reception, known as the *jour*, were sometimes allowed into the *petit salon* to sit very quietly.

In an 1876 letter to her friend, Adolphe Thiers, the duchesse d'Albuféra, who was by then a grandmother, described her daily routine at her family's château. Although she described the life she led as 'entirely consecrated to family', the impression conveyed by the letter is one of brief intervals in the company of children and grandchildren when other duties did not claim her. She was greeted by the young ones in the morning; then strolled with them in the garden after lunch, 'between half-past one and two o'clock', when she took charge of the baby while the wet nurse ate her midday meal; and she saw them again after dinner.[30] A quarter of a century later, around 1900, the marquise d'Harcourt, a mother in her thirties living in Paris, saw even less of her three children. After rising late and making her toilette, the marquise received Paule, Monique, and Hélène who were then taken off to study with a governess, before a trip to explore the gardens along the Boulevard des Invalides or the Champs-Élysées accompanied by an English nurse. Their mother's afternoon was taken up by visits.[31]

In a parenting advice book from 1883 one female author writing under the pseudonym Louise d'Alq presented a realistic assessment of the time an upper-class woman could devote to parenting. 'The young woman of high society cannot always chase after her child. Is it not necessary, during the morning, to find, protected from noise, some sleep to recover from the fatigues of the previous evening's ball? Is it not necessary to pay visits, to go to the *couturière*, etc.? The child would have much to complain about if she had to wait until her mother had time to attend to her!'[32]

Evidence of the social pressures experienced by female aristocrats can be found in the way nobles wrote about, and to, their own mothers. To the extent that a gendered pattern can be detected, girls seem to have been more conscious of maternal attention or lack of it, probably because the mother served as an adult role model for girls in a way that she did not for boys. Distance and respect are the primary elements in noble girls' writings about, and to, their mother. For example, in 1894 Élaine Greffulhe, aged twelve, described her mother:

> The countess of a thousand beauties is a white alabaster statue, with large blazing black eyes, a beautiful and noble figure, and the air of a god transformed into a proud and solitary lily. Her brown hair makes a splendid crown for her virginal figure. The crown suits her well. It is the only face of France worthy to carry the sign of grandeur. No doubt, at her birth, a particle of our ancestors' thoughts entered her brain; this particle has germinated and borne the fruits of intellect.[33]

That Élaine, like any child, jealously craved her mother's time and attention is evident in her letters to Élisabeth Greffulhe.[34] Idolatry, occasional resentment, and a persistent fear of rejection were but a few of the elements that characterised this intense love relationship.

The largely formal style of interaction that aristocratic children experienced with their parents contrasts with the often warm and tactile affection they received from female servants employed to look after them. In their memoirs many nobles recalled small incidents, mannerisms, patterns of speech, and shared activities to try and convey the essence of a treasured relationship with a nurse. Marguerite de Voguë, for example, born in 1920, fondly recalled her 'Neau' (Marie Chopineau), a farmwoman from Barlieu near the family estate in the Cher, who was recommended to her mother by the local *curé*. 'Neau', as Marguerite put it, 'was my real mother until the age of three'.[35] She provides some very interesting background information to explain Marie Chopineau's employment as a dry nurse. Dry nursing (*le nourrisage sec*) has been described as 'a short epilogue at the end of the longer history of wet-nursing'. It originated toward the end of the nineteenth century when 'newborn babies were increasingly placed with rural nurses who, by agreement with the parents, did not breast-feed at all'.[36] This practice was tied to the innovation of bottle-feeding. Parents had to be confident that the dry nurse was properly trained in techniques for sterilising milk.

Marguerite was the youngest of ten children; eight of her elder siblings had wet nurses who were a source of endless complications for the Voguë family. 'Their milk was too rich, or not rich enough, they secretly ate *choucroute* that gave the baby colic; sometimes they "lost their milk" or, struck by sudden depression (perfectly understandable), they returned home (*au pays*).' When the ninth child, Jacques, arrived, the marquise de Vogüé hired a female ass but the first animal fell sick and the milk of the second was spoiled by forty miles' travel to its destination. With the birth of Marguerite the parents resorted to cow's milk fed through a bottle, which it was Neau's responsibility to administer. Marie Chopineau was brought to Paris shortly after Marguerite's birth 'to learn from the midwife how to look after a baby'. Significantly, these lessons, which undoubtedly included training in the sterilisation of milk, took place in the Vogüés' home where the parents could observe Neau and be sure of her competency. The visit to Paris is described as 'a trip to heaven' for the female servant who 'discovered at fifty-five years of age, the joys of maternity'. Marguerite recalled that as an infant she was 'outrageously spoilt' during her transition to solid foods. Neau urged her to eat only the soft white bread, leaving the hard crust for her nurse.[37]

The affectionate way in which Neau is described by her former charge could not be further from the negative portrayals of nurses found in parenting advice books published in turn-of-the-century France. Louise d'Alq warned well-to-do parents that among the rural working class (*le peuple*) 'children are treated slightly worse than animals'.[38] To the 'mercenary hands' of female servants she attributed catastrophes such as:

> brain lesion, mental retardation, spinal deformation, dislocated arms and legs, often death, alas! anaemia, typhoid fever, various horrible illnesses, flaky skin, etc., as well as moral infirmities, questionable characters, perversities dating from childhood, depravity of manners and feeling, etc.[39]

If a child survived these dangers, then their education in speech and manners would be forever jeopardised by exposure to a nurse who spoke with a heavy regional accent or in local dialect.[40] Maguerite de Vogüé does not say whether Neau spoke *patois* to her, but the slight speech impediment (Neau pronounced the letter 'r' as 'l') is mentioned with fondness, as something that signified Neau's uniqueness to her. Whilst we do not know what her parents thought, it seems unlikely, given the more serious problems they encountered with wet nurses, that the Vogüés would have cared much about Neau's confusion of consonants. Moreover, instead of the illnesses enumerated by d'Alq, Marguerite declared that to Neau she owed 'a large part of my health and my joy in living'.[41]

If we consider the information in the Vogüé memoir, within the context of French developments in childcare under the Third Republic, it seems that this family was considerably behind the times. In 1920 the marquis and marquise de Vogüé had decided, as a last resort, to hire a dry nurse for bottle-feeding. This was nearly three decades after municipal authorities in Paris had begun to loan nurses sterilising equipment free of charge (1896), and after doctors had opened the first dispensaries providing medical advice and supplies of sterilised milk, also free of charge (1892).[42] The Vogüés had persisted with wet nurses, despite the problems involved, for their first eight children. 'In the mid-1890s all the elements needed for safe, economical, and convenient bottle-feeding of urban babies were present – the bottle, the milk supply, and the advice on how to use them.'[43] Despite these developments, nobles held fast to the tradition of wet nursing that had been part of aristocratic childrearing since the Middle Ages. That is not to say nobles were ill informed or unconcerned about the high infant mortality associated with wet nursing before 1914. Rather, the ways in which they wrote about the employment of wet nurses in their families suggest that contemporary understandings of hygiene and infant nutrition dominated parental decision-making, and were combined with some pervasive cultural stereotypes.

Nobles born in the decade before the First World War, or in the 1920s, frequently note that their nurse was either Italian or English. Why did nationality matter? Historians of migration have argued that in the case of Italian women it was because they were famous for the quality and abundance of their milk.[44] One male aristocrat, born in 1908, described his nurse Angelina as 'a busty Piemontese brunette, with vast quantities of milk'. He went on to note that 'Italian women have long held a reputation in this realm [of breastfeeding]. Under the *ancien régime*, the children of the royal family drank only Italian milk.'[45] He evidently enjoyed sharing this privilege! In the case of English women it seems that nobles believed they possessed superior standards of bodily cleanliness. A female aristocrat, born in 1918, declared: 'The English were reputed to spend more time and effort on personal hygiene than the French ... It was thought that this hygiene applied to children by nursing professionals would contribute to curbing the mortality rate among children, whatever the social status of the families.'[46]

Of course, these and other accounts by French nobles of wet nursing in the nineteenth and early twentieth centuries are written from an adult's perspective reflecting on childhood experience. It is very difficult to grasp how mothers themselves felt about not breastfeeding. The private journals kept by noble girls in adolescence were usually discontinued upon marriage. Perhaps in a quiet moment of self-reflection, or in speaking with a close friend, a noblewoman might have admitted a sense of grief over lost opportunities for physical intimacy with her baby.[47]

Then again, aristocratic mothers were conditioned to anticipate their return to routine social activity, which some no doubt enjoyed for its own sake and perhaps enjoyed even more for the attention and congratulations they received after giving birth. To make this return, noblewomen had to leave the messy, exhilarating, exhausting, and frustrating business of actually raising children in the hands of wet nurses and nannies. Since they were not breastfeeding, and therefore not subsuming their own physical needs for sleep and nourishment to that of their baby, aristocratic women were more likely to focus on their own body and its needs after giving birth. On one level this was a natural unconscious response, but there was undoubtedly an element of social conditioning as well. It was not uncommon for a noblewoman to feel some pressure, largely self-imposed, to recover her figure for public appearances. Life quickly became very busy, as the letters of the duchesse de Guiche to her mother in the summer of 1907 reveal. From Calvados, two months after the birth of her first child, she wrote:

> There is a mass of gossip. I am making a complete return to social activity [*la grande vie*] around the 15 [August] but I go about everywhere already. I have quite a few friends here and we have an amusing time. The only downside is the appalling immorality of this little group; thank God we do not imitate them!!![48]

The duchesse de Guiche was keen to learn the basics of childcare and noted proudly that she was beginning to know how to wash and powder her baby as well as to administer caster oil as a digestive remedy. But she was still very reliant on hired help, and this reliance only increased two years' later when she fell pregnant for the second time. The duchesse wrote to her mother from her in-laws' estate, Vallière, and it is interesting to note in this letter from 1909 the active fathering that her husband, Armand, was engaged in with the couple's eldest son, Antoine, while she and the servant Maria were otherwise occupied. Following medical examination on 5 September:

> Bronchial tubes and lungs in perfect condition . . . *perhaps* twins!! The obstetrician says the child is awfully lively and healthy . . . There are *a lot* of people here and brilliant polo. The children are sweethearts. Antoine

plays with them constantly. Maria and I pass our time in the nursery talking about baths, wet nurses, nappies, milk etc. etc. I am looking for a good Italian wet nurse for Jeanne ... Armand is crazy about Antoine and spends his time taking him to polo matches and introducing him to all the sports. My father-in-law and Maria leave in a fortnight for Venice leaving us here in charge of the whole nursery!! Every day we bring couturiers and hairdressers in from Paris in order to distract ourselves.[49]

The duchesse gave birth to twin boys three months later. It is an unmistakably privileged world that she describes in her letter with polo matches, house calls from couturiers and hairdressers, and trips abroad. To compensate for the riches they enjoyed, the upper class engaged in charitable activity and many nineteenth-century French noblewomen became patrons of the Société de Charité Maternelle, and other similar organisations.[50] Significantly, the Société's advocacy of maternal breastfeeding by working-class mothers was divorced from the experiences of aristocratic patrons who relied on live-in nurses to feed their babies.

Noblewomen's involvement in the debates on education under the Third Republic began in the early decades of the regime when, as we have seen, noblemen were also active in defending the role of the Catholic Church. The republican initiatives in education were underpinned by two goals: first, to stamp out clerical influence and replace it with the principle of secularism (*laïcité*), and second, to foster patriotism and republican values. Primary school students learnt formal French from Larive and Fleury's textbook that sold twelve million copies between 1872 and 1889; they met with notions of republican unity and the 'greatness' of France in G. Bruno's *Le Tour de la France par deux enfants* that sold eight million copies by 1914; and they saw their respective gendered roles as citizens of the Republic outlined in prescriptive works such as the *Tu seras* series.[51]

This pedagogy bypassed children of the aristocracy who generally did not attend state schools and whose parents were opposed to the government's secularising aims. What kinds of books, therefore, were used to teach aristocratic girls and boys how to read and how to behave? Mostly they were books produced by aristocrats themselves or written explicitly for an aristocratic audience. These included Ferdinand de Gramont's *Les Bébés* (1861) carrying stories such as 'charity' and 'hunting adventure', or, by the same author, *Les Bons Petits Enfants* (1862) with 'the evening ball' and 'first prayer'.[52] Through such stories aristocratic children learnt about the activities of a milieu to which they belonged, and about the kinds of adult roles and behaviour to which they should aspire. Clarisse Juranville dedicated her book *Histoire de la bonne petite Nini ou le modèle de tous les bébés* (1897) to her patron, the comtesse de Bouillé. In the very first chapter, Célinie (referred to as 'Nini' – the use of diminutive nicknames among the aristocracy was deplored by Proust[53]) is described and pictured in a sketch on her knees with her little hands clasped, and eyes raised heavenward, saying her morning prayer. The author, Madame Juranville, declares that she is going to teach her readers the same prayer: 'My Lord, you are very good, I love you very much, oh! With all my heart.'[54]

Not only was this message was all wrong, from a republican secular perspective, but the person who read to and taught an aristocratic child to read was unlikely to be the mother. Noblewomen rarely engaged with their children in daily lessons and recreational time as bourgeoises did with their children.[55] In some households a grandparent took responsibility for a child's upbringing and became a beloved companion. Formal instruction, however, was a task entrusted to governesses, *précepteurs*, and tutors. Mothers and fathers kept in close contact with these educators, and surviving letters show they took an interest in their child's progress. We can see this particularly in the areas of language learning and religious education.

Like the nanny, the governess employed by an aristocratic family was normally an English or German woman. This is explained by nobles' commitment to attaining proficiency in one or more foreign languages; for boys, training in languages was vital preparation for a diplomatic career. *Archives privées* contain examples of children's early attempts at writing. They include letters written in English, usually to the child's mother, and corrected by the governess. For example, in 1896, Alexandre Murat wrote to his mother, the princesse Cécile Murat, on pale blue stationery decorated with a floral pattern. His shaky loopy handwriting, that betrays difficulty in controlling the flow of ink, appeared on pencilled lines ruled one centimetre apart:

> Dear Mamma Cécile
>
> I hope you are quite well. It has been raing ['raining' is written in adult handwriting above] every day since we came to Biarritz and to day [sic] the tide is very high and the waves splash on to the terrace good by [sic] dear Mamma Cécile with love and thousands of kisses from your affectionate little Boy
>
> Alexandre Murat.[56]

The princesse evidently wrote to encourage and praise her son's effort, for on 3 April 1896 he replied:

> My Dear Mamma Cécile
>
> I thank you for your kind letter
> I send you A little picture for Easter
> I have not bought any thing [sic] yet for myself. I play often on the sand
> I make large castles and the sea comes and washes it all away. yesterday I went to Anglet
> good bye [note the correct spelling here, unlike the earlier letter] dear Mamma Cécile I send you thousands of kisses
>
> from your loving little Alexandre.[57]

For some mothers, like the princesse Caroline Murat (née Fraser), English was their native language and the one they used naturally in writing to their child.[58] Others had to make an effort to write in English, their second or third language – perhaps attracting some private mirth from the governess at the result. On 24 July 1875, from Lourdes, the baronne Mathilde de Mackau wrote as a postscript to her daughter Anne, in French: 'Your letters in English *are admirable*. Mme de C. says that you speak *very well. I hope* you will continue.' The baronne's Christmas Eve letter to her daughter was composed in English:

> My dear Anne,
>
> I kiss you a hundred times because grand mamma says you are a good girl. I hope that tomorrow you will say a nice little prayer to the pretty infant Jesus because it is the day that he came in the world [sic]. You know that he loves good little girls; he blesses them and makes them grow; he likes them to be very attentive to their lessons. Papa sends you many kisses, he will give you very pretty things when we come back in Paris [sic]. Goodbye my dearest little Anne. I love you with all my heart. Your Mamma.[59]

Noblewomen's concern for the religious education of their child is evident from the number of books they themselves wrote on the subject, and the books that were dedicated to them by priests. The upbringing and social position of female aristocrats, as well as the close relationships they formed with clergy and religious, gave them a measure of lay authority in spiritual matters.[60] The Catholic Church supported noblewomen's interest in and contributions to the field of religious education. This support took various forms, including expressions of homage for Christian parenting. For example, on the occasion of her son Joseph's First Communion, the princesse Marie de Caraman-Chimay (née de Montesquiou-Fezensac) received a letter from the Carmelite nun Sister Marie Joséphine. Congratulating Joseph and his parents on the happy occasion, the Sister observed that the nuns' enclosure prevented them from paying their respects in person. The princesse's visit to the community, however, had enlivened their prayers for the young communicant and his family.[61]

The religious education of nobles began at a very young age. Christian infants were baptised, a ceremony that served symbolically to unite maternal and paternal families through the vow taken by the child's godparents. Children accompanied their parents or nanny to religious services, and heard grace at the adults' table. It was the nanny who answered a child's 'simple' questions about religion and supervised their prayers. The duchesse Élisabeth de Clermont-Tonnerre recalled she did not like God when she was a child, in the 1880s, because every time she did something naughty someone would stand her in front of his portrait, which hung in her bedroom, and say, 'It is the good Lord who punishes you!'[62] Élaine Greffulhe, born in 1882, created her own visual images of God and the Holy Family. In pencil drawings painted over in watercolours she depicted 'Jesus at five years', the Virgin Mary in a blue shawl radiating light, Joseph and Mary escaping Bethlehem with baby Jesus, and six women holding up infants with the caption, 'Let the children come to me.'[63]

Marguerite de Vogüé's memoir details the personal interest taken by both her parents, but especially her mother, Louise, in the religious education of Marguerite and her siblings. Louise de Vogüé was strongly influenced in her pedagogical ideas by the works of a well-known theologian and orator of the time, père Laberthonnière. She owned a copy, personally signed by him, of his book *Théorie de l'éducation* that was into its eighth reprinting by 1923. Marguerite recalls that this book sat among her mother's favourites on the bookshelf in her *petit salon* at the family's château, La Verrerie. Her father, meanwhile, was a follower of the social Catholic movement. He had been encouraged in this by his father and grandfather, as well as a group of friends inspired by the Catholic reformers Lacordaire, Ozanam, de Montalembert, and de Mun. Another cleric, abbé Boyreau, became a close friend of the Vogüés and spent his vacation with them at La Verrerie.[64]

Personal connections such as these provided some incentive for public campaigning by noblewomen to protect the Church's role in education. Perhaps the greater impetus, however, was indignation at the boldness of republican attacks. Faced with the closure of Catholic schools, the disbanding of religious orders, and the Separation of Church and State in 1905, Catholic noblewomen repeatedly urged parents to defend and oversee the religious education of their children. The vicomtesse de Vélard, a spokeswoman and later president of the LPF, defined a mother's educative role in her 1906 speech to the Congrès de la Société d'Économie Sociale:

> It is through a mother that religion must penetrate the soul of children. She must teach them, by words and deeds, the respect for God and his laws. By the seriousness and generosity of her life, she will prove the utility of religion, the place it must have in the family, the strength it provides in difficult times.[65]

The aristocratic leaders of the LPF and LFF believed that tough action was necessary to halt the demise of Catholic education in France. In the climate of mounting anticlericalism at the turn of the century they made concerted use of their networks to refute secularisation. Between September 1901 and May 1902 the LFF received more than seven hundred letters from all departments of France. It is estimated that around one-half were written by nobles. Local committees sprang up, typically at the instigation of '*la noble dame du château*'. The LFF's bulletins and leaflets were distributed to church congregations and at public meetings. A propaganda campaign was conducted through the national and regional press. Songs were composed and items such as medals, crucifixes, and engravings were disseminated.[66]

The LPF, meanwhile, exhorted its members to support Catholic schools in three ways. First, by making financial donations and sending their children to the schools; second, by modelling Christian values; and third, by ensuring that if their child was sent to a state school any 'bad' atheist influences were protested against and removed. The LPF's reports and pamphlets reminded readers of the negative consequences of secular education. Republican schools 'distorted history to the benefit of the "glorious post-1789" era, forgetting the civilizing action of the Church and kings'. They were hotbeds of seditious activity owing to teachers' affiliation with France's major trade union, the Confédération générale du travail (and the Confédération générale du travail unitaire after the war). Fundamentally, they were 'against God and do not hide the fact'.[67]

The LPF continued its campaign against secular schooling into the 1930s and enjoyed one notable success. In 1923, working with other organisations, it launched petitions and an open letter of protest against a decision by the Minister of Education, Paul Lapie, to erase any mention of 'duty toward God' from the programme of public schools. The ruling was overturned following Lapie's dismissal.

Although this battle was won, the LPF and LFF were gradually losing the war as the conflict between anticlericals and committed Catholics shifted to the sideline of the political scene. Before the First World War the French state struggled to meet the demand for teaching that had been provided by religious orders. By the end of the Third Republic, however, a comprehensive system of secular schooling was firmly established. Aristocratic parents, whose sole prayer to God for their children was that they should possess faith, now needed to rely more heavily on cross-generational influence and example to combat the trend toward secularism they observed in wider society.[68]

Class as well as gender shaped the cultural practices and experiences of motherhood among women at the top level of French society. In decision-making on the bearing, nursing, and education of children noblewomen were influenced by the example of previous generations, the dictates of religion, and contemporary concerns such as hygiene. Most importantly, female aristocrats prioritised the interests of their family, their class, and the Catholic Church. This put them at odds with feminists of the Third Republic who, although by no means homogeneous in their views on motherhood, considered issues affecting mothers from the perspective of women's rights.[69] The French feminist strategy, to advance the cause of female emancipation by stressing women's national duty to bear children, ran parallel with the message put out by the medical profession. In the context of fears about 'depopulation', this strategy enabled republican feminists to criticise women of the aristocracy whose eighteenth-century forebears were known to have practised birth control. Charges against noblewomen, of rejecting motherhood to pursue a carefree life of luxury and leisure, were founded upon preconceptions rather than reality, however. Maternity was highly valued among the nobility. It was just that aristocratic family practices – including the hiring of wet nurses, nannies, and governesses, and usually Catholic baptism – did not conform to the model of republican motherhood advocated by bourgeois feminists and doctors.

Noblewomen were not passive observers to the political climate in which republican motherhood was promoted. Rather, they used an acutely gendered strategy available to them as mothers to launch a sustained counter-attack. Motherhood conferred upon women of the aristocracy an important degree of authority within domestic and social spheres. In exercising that authority they drew on personal connections with priests and religious to aid and inspire them in various forms of activism from speechmaking to writing books on religious education. These women's engagement with issues of motherhood provides further illustration of the way in which 'politics' in the Third Republic was based on interplay between the 'private' domestic setting and the 'public' realm. Noblewomen were not mere pawns in a chess game of dynastic interests. They were in a real sense 'queens' with at least as much ability as the 'kings' to manipulate and to use to their advantage the complex dynamics of gendered power within their own families and in wider society.

Notes

1 On the concept of 'republican motherhood' see Elinor Accampo, *Blessed Motherhood, Bitter Fruit: Nelly Roussel and the Politics of Female Pain in Third Republic France* (Baltimore, 2006), pp. 3–7; Suzanne Desan, *The Family on Trial in Revolutionary France* (Berkeley, 2004), pp. 10–11, 72–3, 76–8, 210–13, 217–18. France exhibited a low birth rate from the mid-eighteenth century: for statistical comparison with other modernising nations see Accampo, *Blessed Motherhood*, p. 7. On the duties of republican mothers see Anne Cova, *Maternité et droits des femme en France (XIX et XXe siècles)* (Paris, 1997), pp. 29–49, 102–4; Valérie Lastinger, 'Re-defining motherhood: breast-feeding and the French Enlightenment', *Women's Studies* 25 (1996), 603–17.

2 Jack D. Ellis, *The Physician-Legislators of France: Medicine and Politics in the Early Third Republic, 1870–1914* (Cambridge, 1990); Jean Elisabeth Pedersen, 'Regulating abortion and birth control: gender, medicine, and republican politics in France, 1870–1920', *French Historical Studies* 19 (1996), 673–98; Karen Offen, 'Depopulation, nationalism, and feminism in fin-de-siècle France', *American Historical Review* 89 (1984), 648–76; Marie-Monique Huss, 'Pronatalism in the inter-war period in France', *Journal of Contemporary History* 25 (1990), 39–68.

3 George D. Sussman, *Selling Mothers' Milk: The Wet-Nursing Business in France 1715–1914* (Urbana, 1982).

4 Ralph Gibson, *A Social History of French Catholicism, 1789–1914* (London, 1989).

5 Odile Sarti, 'The Ligue Patriotique des Françaises (1902–1933): a feminine response to the secularization of French society' (PhD Indiana University, 1984), p. 80; Bruno Dumons, *Les Dames de la Ligue des Femmes Françaises*

(1901–1914) (Paris, 2006), pp. 82–9, 269–76; Elizabeth C. Macknight 'Why weren't they feminists? Parisian noble women and the campaigns for women's rights in France, 1880–1914', *European Journal of Women's Studies* 14 (2007), 127–41.

6 Steven Hause and Anne Kenney estimate that the French feminist movement at the turn of the century comprised at most '20,000–25,000 women whose recruitment to activity could be expected'. Steven C. Hause with Anne R. Kenney, *Women's Suffrage and Social Politics in the French Third Republic* (Princeton, 1984), pp. 42–3; Sarti, 'The Ligue', pp. 73–132, 274–8; Dumons, *Les Dames*, pp. 191–263.

7 See, for example, Robert A. Nye, *Crime, Madness and Politics in Modern France: The Medical Concept of National Decline* (Princeton, 1984); Elinor A. Accampo, Rachel G. Fuchs, and Mary Lynn Stewart (eds), *Gender and the Politics of Social Reform in France, 1870–1914* (Baltimore, 1995); Cheryl A. Koos, 'Gender, anti-individualism, and nationalism: the Alliance Nationale and the pronatalist backlash against the femme moderne, 1933–1940', *French Historical Studies* 19 (1996), 699–723; Joshua Cole, *The Power of Large Numbers: Population, Politics, and Gender in Nineteenth-Century France* (Ithaca, 2000).

8 Cova, *Maternité*, p. 101.

9 Christine Théré, 'Women and birth control in eighteenth-century France', *Eighteeth-Century Studies* 32 (1999), 553.

10 Margaret H. Darrow, 'French noblewomen and the new domesticity, 1750–1850', *Feminist Studies* 5 (1979), 41–65; Cyril Grange, *Les Gens du Bottin mondain: y être, c'est en être* (Paris, 1996), pp. 154–5, 160–1, 507; Cova, *Maternité*, p. 101.

11 René de La Croix de Castries, *Papiers de famille* (Paris, 1977), p. 279; Patrick de Gmeline, *La Duchesse d'Uzès (1847–1933)* (Paris, 1986), p. 31. On maternal mortality see Accampo, *Blessed Motherhood*, p. 29. On child mortality see Sussman, *Selling Mothers' Milk*, pp. 66, 181.

12 Lastinger, 'Re-defining motherhood', p. 611; Grange, *Les gens*, pp. 154, 162.

13 Éric Mension-Rigau, *Aristocrates et grands bourgeois: éducation, traditions, valeurs* (Paris, 1994), pp. 24–5.

14 Rachel G. Fuchs and Leslie Page Moch, 'Pregnant, single, and far from home: migrant women in nineteenth-century Paris', *American Historical Review* 95 (1990), 1007–31; Leslie Page Moch, and Rachel G. Fuchs, 'Getting along: poor women's networks in nineteenth-century Paris', *French Historical Studies* 18 (1993), 34–49.

15 Jean-Pierre Peters cited in Michelle Perrot (ed.), *A History of Private Life* vol. 4 *From the Fires of Revolution to the Great War*, trans. Arthur Goldhammer (Cambridge, 1990), p. 651. See also Angus McLaren, 'Doctor in the house: medicine and private morality in France, 1800–1850', *Feminist Studies* 2 (1975), 39–54; Jill Harsin, 'Syphilis, wives and physicians: medical ethics and

the family in late nineteenth-century France', *French Historical Studies*, 16 (1989), 72–95.
16 AP 258/1 and 258/2 Fonds Chanoine Mugnier; Martine Sevegrand, *L'Amour en toutes lettres: questions à l'abbé Viollet sur la sexualité*, 1924–1943 (Paris, 1996). Jules Michelet decried the confessional intimacy of wives and priests in *Du prêtre, de la femme, de la famille* (1845).
17 Letters 2 June and 6 June 1883 in AP 156 (I)/298 Fonds Mackau.
18 Celia Bertin, *Marie Bonaparte: A Life* (London, 1982), pp. 48–50; Élisabeth de Clermont-Tonnerre, *Au temps des équipages* (Paris, 1928), pp. 16, 42–3. On Marian devotion see Gibson, *A Social History of French Catholicism*, pp. 254–6.
19 Undated letter in AP 101 (I)/24 Fonds Gramont.
20 Undated letter in AP 101 (I)/24 Fonds Gramont.
21 For a striking example see Honoré Daumier's *La République* in Accampo, Fuchs, and Stewart, *Gender*, frontispiece.
22 Sussman, *Selling Mothers' Milk*, pp. 8, 162–3, 182–3.
23 Elizabeth C. Macknight, 'Cake and conversation: the women's *jour* in Parisian high society, 1880–1914', *French History* 19 (2005), 342–63.
24 Sussman, *Selling Mothers' Milk*, p. 176. See also George D. Sussman, 'The wet-nursing business in nineteenth-century France', *French Historical Studies* 9 (1975), 304–28; Serge Zeyons, *La Femme en 1900: les années 1900 par la carte postale* (Paris, 1994), pp. 44–8; Yvonne Knibiehler, 'Bodies and hearts' in Michelle Perrot and Geneviève Fraisse (eds), *A History of Women* vol. 4 *Emerging Feminism from Revolution to World War* (Cambridge, 1995), pp. 347–9, 352–3.
25 AP 156 (I)/298 Fonds Mackau.
26 Stewart Buettner, 'Images of modern motherhood in the art of Morisot, Cassatt, Modersohn-Becker, Kollwitz', *Woman's Art Journal* 7 (1987), 14–21. For eighteenth-century precursors see Carol Duncan, 'Happy mothers and other new ideas in French art', *The Art Bulletin* 55 (1973), 570–83. Feminist art historians have suggested that Berthe Morisot's painting of her own daughter and wet nurse reflect the mother's ambivalence about wet nursing in practice. See Linda Nochlin, *Women, Art and Power and Other Essays* (New York, 1988), pp. 37–56; Anne Higonnet, *Berthe Morisot's Images of Women* (Cambridge, 1992), ch. 9; Anne Higonnet, *Berthe Morisot* (Los Angeles, 1995), pp. 101–3, 154–60.
27 Lastinger, 'Re-defining motherhood', p. 611; Cindy A. Stearns, 'Breastfeeding and the good maternal body', *Gender and Society* 13 (1999), 308–25.
28 6 April 1875 in AD Charente J 1078 Fonds Galard, Brassac, Béarn, Chalais.
29 Comtesse de Pange, *Comment j'ai vu 1900* (Paris, 1962), p. 24.
30 Undated letter (c. Oct. 1876) in AP 77/1 Fonds Thiers-Albuféra.
31 Michel Chabot, *Histoire de Jean et Yvonne domestiques en 1900 racontée par Paul, leur fils, à Michel, son petit-fils* (Paris, 1988), pp. 54–5. See also Pange,

Comment j'ai vu, pp. 44–9; Clermont-Tonnerre, Au temps des équipages, pp. 104–5; Anne de Noailles, Le Livre de ma vie (Paris, 1976), pp. 21–2.
32 Louise d'Alq [Alquié de Rieupeyroux], Notes d'une mère: cours d'éducation maternelle (Paris, 1883), p. 58.
33 AP 101 (II)/35 Fonds Gramont.
34 AP 101 (II)/36 Fonds Gramont.
35 Marguerite de Vogüé, La Fontaine du cerf. Histoire de Louis et Louise, marquis et marquise de Vogüé 1868–1958 (Poitiers, 1983), p. 19.
36 Sussman, Selling Mothers' Milk, pp. 2–3.
37 'Mangez l'blanc, ma Bébelle, moué, j'mang'lai l'poûrri', ou encore: "Plenez don' la bonne mie blanche, pis donnez-moi la cloûte, qu'est ben tlop dûrre poul vous...', Vogüé, La Fontaine du cerf, pp. 19–20.
38 D'Alq, Notes d'une mère, p. 60.
39 D'Alq, Notes d'une mère, p. 53.
40 D'Alq, Notes d'une mère, pp. 177–8. On language and speech see Marguerite Stevenson Barratt, 'Communication in infancy' in Mary Anne Fitzpatrick and Anita L. Vangelisti (eds), Explaining Family Interactions (London, 1995), pp. 5–33.
41 Vogüé, La Fontaine, p. 19.
42 Sussman, Selling Mothers' Milk, pp. 165–6. Working-class mothers and their babies especially benefited from free clinics and milk dispensaries, see Moch and Fuchs, 'Poor women's networks', p. 47.
43 Sussman, Selling Mothers' Milk, p. 166.
44 Renée Lopez and Émile Temime, Migrance. Histoire des migrations à Marseille vol. 2 L'Expansion marseillaise et 'l'invasion italienne' 1830–1918 (Aix-en-Provence, 1990) quoted in Mension-Rigau, Aristocrates, p. 305.
45 Mension-Rigau, Aristocrates, p. 305.
46 Mension-Rigau, Aristocrates, p. 303. Even by 1954 only around half of French homes had running water. A poll conducted in 1951 showed that 39 per cent of the readers of Elle magazine bathed only once a month. Susan K. Foley, Women in France since 1789 (New York, 2004), p. 244.
47 Elizabeth C. Macknight, 'In memory of myriad selves: the baronne Mathilde de Mackau (1837–1886)', Magistra 14 (2006), 46–72, esp. 69–70.
48 8 August 1907 in AP 101 (II)/37 Fonds Gramont.
49 5 September 1909 in AP 101 (II)/37 Fonds Gramont.
50 See, for example, Christine Adams, 'Maternal societies in France: private charity before the welfare state', Journal of Women's History 17 (2005), 87–111; Susan K. Grogan, 'Women, philanthropy, and the state: the Société de Charité Maternelle in Avignon, 1802–1917', French History 14 (2000), 295–321.
51 Peter McPhee, A Social History of France 1789–1914 2 ed. (New York, 2004), p. 253.
52 Ferdinand de Gramont, Les Bébés. Vignettes par Oscar Pletsch (Paris, 1861), pp. 15–17, 61–3; Ferdinand de Gramont, Les Bons Petits Enfants Vignettes par Ludwig Richter (Paris, 1862), pp. 49–50, 67–8.

53 'These stupid abbreviations are a sign of the utter inability of the aristocracy to appreciate its own poetry.' Marcel Proust, *In Search of Lost Time*, trans. C.K. Scott Moncrieff and Terence Kilmartin revised by D. J. Enright, vol. 3 *The Guermantes Way* (London, 1993), pp. 437–8.

54 Clarisse Juranville, *Histoire de la bonne petite Nini ou le modèle de tous les bébés* (Limoges, 1897), pp. 5–6.

55 Marie-Françoise Lévy, *De mères en filles: l'éducation des françaises 1850–1880* (Paris, 1984), pp. 17–52.

56 AP 31/71 Fonds Murat.

57 AP 31/71 Fonds Murat.

58 Letters of 1853 to the prince Joachim Murat IV in AP 31/66 Fonds Murat.

59 AP 156 (I)/301 Fonds Mackau.

60 Prolific female authors include the comtesse Drohojowska (pen name of A. J. Symon de Latreillle) and Clarisse Juranville. See Marie-Claire Grassi, 'Le Savoir-faire au féminin 1820–1920' in *Du goût, de la conversation et des femmes* ed. Alain Montandon (Clermont-Ferrand, 1994), pp. 213–32. Books by priests include Félix Dupanloup, *Femmes savantes et femmes studieuses* (Paris, 1867). On the personal connections between women, clerics, and religious see Elizabeth C. Macknight, 'Faiths, fortunes, and feminine duty: charity in Parisian high society, 1880–1914', *Journal of Ecclesiastical History* 58 (2007), 482–506; Jean Delumeau (ed.), *La Religion de ma mère: le rôle des femmes dans la transmission de la foi* (Paris, 1992), pp. 301–25, 327–42.

61 Undated letter in AP 101 (II)/39 Fonds Gramont.

62 The portrait of 'God' is most likely to have been a representation of Jesus. Clermont-Tonnerre, *Au temps*, p. 16.

63 AP 101 (II)/35 Fonds Gramont.

64 Vogüé, *La Fontaine*, pp. 24, 82–4; Louis Laberthonnière, *Théorie de l'éducation* 8 ed. (Paris, 1923).

65 Sarti, 'The Ligue', p. 201.

66 Dumons, *Les Dames*, pp. 193–263, 284–304, 334–40.

67 Sarti, 'The Ligue', pp. 203–4.

68 Sarti, 'The Ligue', p. 206; Judith F. Stone, 'Anticlericals and *bonnes soeurs*: the rhetoric of the 1901 Law of Associations', *French Historical Studies* 23 (2000), 103–28, esp. 111–17, 127; Vogüé, *La Fontaine*, p. 78.

69 Offen, 'Depopulation', 648–76; Karen Offen, 'Challenging male hegemony: feminist criticism and the context for women's movements in the age of European revolutions and counterrevolutions, 1789–1860' in Sylvia Paletschek and Bianka Pietrow-Ennker (eds), *Women's Emancipation Movements in the Nineteenth Century: A European Perspective* (Stanford, 2004), pp. 11–30; Accampo, *Blessed Motherhood*, pp. 37–9.

7

Children's worlds

The prince Roland Bonaparte was a small boy with a fondness for toys. He especially liked model sailing ships and was rather good at sketching real ones. Anything connected with seafaring interested Roland for he wanted to be a naval commander when he grew up. In addition to his seagoing ambitions the young prince also manifested from an early age a 'very marked disposition for safeguarding his own interests'.[1] In the 1860s his companion for afternoon walks in Paris was Goffinet, the Belgian *valet de chambre* of Roland's father, the prince Pierre Bonaparte. During their outings together Roland would often ask Goffinet to buy him toys and snacks. Goffinet duly kept a record of expenses for these items, which he submitted monthly to the boy's father. One day, having remarked on the frequency of Roland's toy purchases, the prince Pierre Bonaparte decided to introduce a new system. Pierre explained to Roland that he would henceforward receive pocket money. The sum of 100 francs paid on a monthly basis seemed quite reasonable to Pierre for satisfying his son's taste in toys. At the end of the following month, however, Pierre was astonished to see that Goffinet's expenses book continued to include the same frequent records for toy purchases on Roland's behalf. He asked his son to shed some light on the subject. The boy explained his dilemma. Every day, when he and Goffinet set out on their walks in the capital, Roland very carefully carried the 100 francs with him. And every day he came close to making, but always put off, a terrible sacrifice. How could he exchange even one of his precious banknotes for a much desired toy?

The story of Roland's introduction to capitalism, in which Goffinet served as unwitting middleman, offers some insight into the world of an

5 Boy sketching, by Paul-César Helleu (c.1900)

aristocratic child. It was a privileged world. Pocket money and a servant companion were advantages that very few children in nineteenth-century France enjoyed. The majority of the nation's population still lived in rural areas so excursions through the streets of Paris were not a regular leisure activity for most youth.[2] How then did boys and girls of the nobility learn about their privileged status in society? What kinds of daily routines and interactions did they experience? Answers to these questions lie in study of the roles played by parents, grandparents, servants, siblings, and other relatives in nobles' upbringing. Governesses and *précepteurs* were responsible for scholastic instruction but the formal lessons they gave were only one dimension of a much broader education designed to enrich the cultural capital of aristocratic children. In preparing those children for adulthood the influence of family and milieu was of the greatest importance.[3]

Girls and boys of the nobility began their scholastic instruction with a governess in the family home. The governess was typically a single woman in her early twenties from a bourgeois background. She could make a respectable living by taking on this kind of private teaching post, and it was a comparatively secure form of employment for an unmarried woman whose family did not have the financial means to support her. Usually the governess resided in the home of her employer and her role of providing instruction and company for the children gave her a unique position in the household. Aristocratic parents invested trust and responsibility in the governess, and her constant proximity to the children meant that nobles tended to consider her one of the family. She was served meals in the same room, and at the same time, as her employers, where she sat with the children either at a small table or, when the children were old enough, at the adults' dining table. The fact that the governess did not take her meals with the servants in the kitchen quarters was an indication of her separate, and superior, status. In some households she became a target for servants' resentment and envy.[4]

Around the age of four, aristocratic children were taught by the governess to read and write. We have seen that boys and girls often practised writing in English as well as in French in letters to their parents. The importance to nobles of acquiring fluency in several languages helps to explain why many families employed a governess of German or British nationality who spoke in her native language, rather than in French, to children. The presence of a *Fräulein* in the home may seem unusual in the post-1870–71 context when many French people harboured attitudes of bitterness and desire for revenge toward Germany. Yet interest in German culture was prevalent among the French elite and was expressed, for example, in the enthusiasm of the upper class for Wagnerian opera. The comte de Maillé advised his daughter Blanche in 1897: 'It is well worth ensuring [your sons] speak German well.'[5] At the turn of the century many nobles also admired British culture, personified as they saw it in the prince of Wales who frequented certain salons of Parisian high society. The English spoken by French nobles tended to be characterised by an Oxford accent.[6] In addition to modern languages, one of the advantages for aristocratic girls of being educated in the home was that they could receive lessons in Latin. This was not the case for girls taught in state schools where, until 1924, Latin was taught only to boys and was a prerequisite for university study. Following Anne d'Uzès's request to learn Latin private lessons were arranged for her at the family's château.

In the Paris of the 1890s Élaine Greffulhe followed a very structured study routine. On weekdays she rose by 8 a.m. and her first lesson of the day was taken with her governess, Madame Cordier, from 8.30 to 10.15 a.m. Then came a walk in the park until 11 a.m., usually followed by a piano lesson before lunch. Afternoons commenced with a German lesson, followed by a French lesson, and a short recreation break. On Mondays and Wednesdays Élaine then took a Latin or English lesson, while on Tuesdays, Thursdays, and Fridays she completed German homework. From 6.45 p.m. until dinner at 7.30 p.m. Élaine was in the company of her grandmother. Élaine's mother, the comtesse Élisabeth Greffulhe, was not involved in delivering this primary education, but she certainly took an interest in her daughter's progress.[7]

Similarly, on the Béarn family's estate near Pau in the 1880s, the children of the prince and princesse de Béarn received private instruction from a governess. When Mademoiselle Doker informed her employers that she would be resigning from her post to get married, the princesse Cécile expressed regret to her eldest son Henri: 'She brought up your sister [Blanche] so well and was always excellent with all of you, particularly Hélie.'[8] The Béarns kept in touch with Mademoiselle Doker after her marriage to Monsieur Dumas. They rejoiced with her at the birth of her first child, Germaine, and she sent lace from her husband's shop so that Blanche could make dresses for her doll, Blenette. Her immediate replacement, Mademoiselle Suiter, stayed only six weeks before the princesse decided she was unsuitable and another single woman was hired to fill the post.

It was very important for boys as well as for girls to receive training in a variety of social accomplishments (*les arts d'agrément*).[9] Perhaps the most essential of these were the ability to play an instrument and to dance. For girls, the piano was considered the most suitable instrument. They often became accompanists to their brothers and to other male relatives who sang or played instruments such as the violin or cello. Dancing was both a form of exercise and an essential 'courtly' skill. Lessons were given by a *professeur de danse* and, if there were no boys in the household, girls learned to lead as well as to partner by practising with sisters and female cousins. While it was common in Paris and regional cities and towns to hire specialist tutors for *les arts d'agrément*, the majority of children also heard their mother and other relatives and acquaintances play music, and saw them paint, draw, dance, and sew.[10]

In this way professional tuition and informal learning opportunities were complementary parts of an aristocratic education. Physical environment also played a role. The homes of the nobility, furnished with valuable works of art, including paintings and sculpture, were fertile ground for the growth of cultural knowledge and appreciation, albeit only in certain directions. At the turn of the century when Pauline de Broglie asked for her mother's opinion of the paintings in the Salon des Indépendants, she received the reply: 'All these young painters are frightfully common. They only paint vulgar things.'[11]

Bills and receipts in the Berthier family archive provide a picture of the various private lessons that the prince Alexandre and his two sisters, Élisabeth and Marguerite, received in Paris. Dance lessons were taken weekly with Émile Fischer in 1891 (20 francs per lesson) and with G. Stilb in 1893 (40 francs per lesson). Horse-riding lessons were taken weekly at the École d'Équitation Gabriel Paillard Neveu in May 1892 (12 francs per lesson). Gymnastics classes were taken monthly at Lopez's Grand Gymnase Hygiènique et Médical des Champs-Élysées in 1891 and 1892 (25 francs per lesson). The girls' sheet music for learning the piano was purchased at A. Durand et fils, where orders were placed for Widor's *Valses*, Tropelli's *École élémentaire*, Grieg's *Peer Gynt*, and Marmontel's 30 *Petites études*. Drawing pencils were purchased at F. Dupré, Papeterie. Subscriptions to children's magazines included *Le Journal de la jeunesse* for Élisabeth (20 francs per annum) and *Mon journal* for Marguerite (8 francs per annum), both published by Hachette.[12]

These expenses formed part of the financial investment by the prince and princesse de Wagram in their children's education. The cost of lessons came on top of other expenses, of course, such as those for clothing and toys. Handkerchiefs, stockings, blouses, gloves, and hats were bought at the fashionable department stores, Le Bon Marché and the Galeries Lafayette. Alexandre's trousers were made by a specialist children's tailor, Lacroix et Voisin, on the boulevard Haussmann. His boots in calfskin and in patent leather came from Norén's Chaussures de Luxe in the rue Marbeuf. It was probably for Alexandre that a butterfly case was bought from Guyon, in the rue de Bourdonnais, together with pins and a cask of liquid poison to bring instant death to the hapless specimens.[13]

One of the ways in which a noble boy's education differed from that of noble girls was that he progressed from lessons with a governess to lessons with a *précepteur*. This transition from a female to a male teacher occurred before a noble boy reached puberty. The presence of a *pré-*

cepteur in the household was much more common in aristocratic families before the First World War than after it, although examples can be found in the interwar period. The princesse de La Tour d'Auvergne Lauraguais had her two sons, Godefroy and Charles-Louis, educated by the *précepteur* Hénaff in the 1920s. Like the governess, the *précepteur* was typically single. Young males in training for the priesthood often filled this position, although some *précepteurs* were older clerics.[14] On 8 October 1895 Maillé wrote from La Jumellière reporting proudly of his grandson, Armand, 'he seems to work well with the priest' and 'plays well at billiards and dominoes'.[15] In the 1890s Alexandre Berthier's *précepteur*, Monsieur Ruin, was a bachelor, and when the Wagrams departed for summer holidays to Normandy he went south to Lourdes where he stayed at Béthanie Maison Lécuyer, a lodging house for ecclesiastics and single men. Most of the year, however, Ruin spent either in Paris or at the château de Grosbois as the personal tutor and companion to Alexandre. In the same way that Goffinet paid for the prince Roland Bonaparte's toys and snacks, Ruin paid for such items in advance and then claimed reimbursement from the princesse de Wagram. The *précepteur* had to keep a careful record of expenses. Cab fares, snacks, bicycle hire, stamps, books, notebooks, an atlas, return tickets from Paris to Grosbois, and a carriage fare to the dentist were all claimed by Ruin in November and December 1895, in total some 56 francs.[16]

Relations between a *précepteur* and an aristocratic family were typically cordial, with elements of a patron–client bond. In some cases nobles provided financial support during the *précepteur's* seminary studies that was supplementary to wages. Letters written by *précepteurs* to the parents of their aristocratic pupils provide some insight into the cares and preoccupations of these men. On 6 July 1873 the abbé Rosenberg wrote to the princesse Murat from Tours where he was convalescing after a period of illness. She had previously sent a letter enquiring about his condition. He replied:

> This is my first day of perfect health ... Although I have no intention of succumbing to the terrible affliction of boredom, it is surprising to discover a certain feeling of emptiness. I really believe I miss my student ... In what frame of mind will he return? ... I am optimistic about his judgement, but his lack of energy alarms me. Moral fortitude is about the only thing that I wish intensely for him ... If, according to my best hope, he passes his exams successfully then it will truly be due to his good nature. With any other student, I assure you, I would have obtained meagre results.[17]

Although the abbé himself was humble about his pedagogic capabilities, the princesse Murat seems to have been more than satisfied that he was a good teacher to her son. This was encouraging for the abbé: 'I take this opportunity to express my real gratitude for the confidence you have shown in me which has touched me deeply.'[18]

In rural France this type of relationship between a cleric teacher and an aristocratic family was often embedded within a wider network of personal ties that connected château and parish. Nobles' support for the work of the church benefited communities in all kinds of material ways. This did not guarantee harmony, for there were occasions of political tension and of *châtelains* making unreasonable demands on the time and energy of clergy. Monsieur Dury, the *précepteur* who gave lessons to Boni de Castellane at the château de Rochecotte in the Loire valley, was also employed by the Castellane family to give lessons to young girls in the communes of Saint-Patrice (Indre-et-Loire), Saint-Michel (Charente), and Langeais (Indre-et-Loire). Mère Philomène, who was the head of one of the schools in which Dury taught, made regular visits to Rochecotte to pay her respects to the *châtelaine*, Boni's grandmother, to tell her about the schoolchildren's progress and to collect alms for the poor. Although Dury cuts a rather sorry figure in Boni's *Mémoires* it is quite possible that he and his wife, who together took charge of the annual distribution of prizes to the schoolchildren, were well respected within the local community. To the small boy at Rochecotte he was a figure of fun. Clean-shaven, in an era when a moustache was a sign of independent manhood, and with a pointed nose, Dury came to the château dressed in a worn-out redingote suit and an excessively flared satin top hat of a style normally worn to the opera. He gave the six-year-old Boni his first lessons in mathematics, which must have been frustrating for both of them. 'You will never know how to count, Monsieur Boni', Dury is reported to have said. Even the immodest aristocrat agreed.[19]

Each year the Castellane family took up residence at Rochecotte for the autumn hunting season and the descriptions of these times constitute the most lyrical passages of Boni's memoirs. He and his younger brother Jean revelled in the hunt: 'We adored the horse, the dogs, the movement. The memory of obstacles that we had jumped over obsessed us during the week.' In the evenings before dinner, in a smoking room on the second floor, the boys' mother received the officers from the military academies at Tours and Saumur who had been her hunting companions during the morning. Social gatherings in this room were of a less formal nature than ones held in the ground-floor salon and held a special charm for the two boys who were usually admitted. Boni recalled listening to 'the thoughts being expressed around me while inhaling the scent of molten resin and gazing fixedly at the pretty flames leaping forward in the shape of blue fidgeting hands'.[20] After Christmas the marquis and marquise de Castellane returned to the capital for the Paris Season while their two sons stayed on until the spring in the care of their grandmother.

Grandparents occupied a very considerable place in the lives of aristocratic boys and girls. Typically they had more time to spend with a grandchild than the child's parents.[21] We have already seen, for example, that Élaine Greffulhe had daily contact with her grandmother at the end of the day's lessons. This was during the hours that her mother, the comtesse Greffulhe, received guests at home, a tradition known as the five o'clock tea or *le cinq à sept*. In what ways, then, did grandmothers and grandfathers contribute to shaping a child's values, behaviour, and beliefs?

The marquise de Breteuil reflected on the principal role her paternal grandmother played in her upbringing in a journal entry for 1886. Constance, who was aged three when her mother died, was raised at the château de Caumont by her grandmother, the marquise de Castelbajac (née La Rochefoucauld). She describes very clearly how the time she spent in the latter's company fell somewhere between recreation and formal instruction. According to her granddaughter, the marquise de Castelbajac excelled at 'these intimate lessons from which one learns a great deal more than from the dry content of textbooks'.

> She allowed me to think freely, approved of my good little ideas, helped me to clear away those that were not right, teaching me how to do and to say certain things and patiently correcting the bad expressions that I, like all children, had picked up from nurses and servants. If she saw that I was a bit annoyed or embarrassed by my own ignorance (since I have always had a good opinion of myself) she briskly changed the subject and told me a pretty story or cleverly picked out a small rhyme so that I would go to bed in a positive frame of mind. I think that nothing in the world can replace the experience of one's earliest education and it is easy to understand why. The ideas taught to a child do not remain as they were at the time that they were sown. They grow and develop with the child, but always in the direction in which they were planted. I only realised that later on in life. Many things that my grandmother repeated to me constantly, that lodged in my mind and that I only partly understood at the time, gradually came to make sense to me. Now I see very clearly that my dear

grandmamma made a very large contribution to the good memories that have stayed with me from those years of study and upbringing.[22]

We saw in the previous chapter Louise d'Alq's warning to parents that a child's education in speech and manners would be forever jeopardised by exposure to a nurse who spoke with a heavy regional accent or in local dialect. In the marquise de Breteuil's account it was her grandmother who 'saved' her from this danger. She depicts her grandmother as the personification of good fortune in her life, rather than the nurses and servants whose presence in the household she seems to have forgotten was another sign of her privileged upbringing.[23]

Of course, ways of speaking and interacting undergo gradual change in every society as each generation absorbs, and modifies to some degree, the customary speech patterns and styles of communication of the previous generation.[24] The marquise de Breteuil meditated on the effect produced by her mother's death which created a gap in this cross-generational transmission process. Without the influence of her mother, she had adopted all her grandmother's ways; the marquise de Castelbajac in turn had learnt those ways from her mother, the duchesse de La Rochefoucauld.

> Considering that my great-grandmother, the duchesse de La Rochefoucauld, was married before the [1789] Revolution, and that my grandmother was born in 1799, it is not surprising to find that, although I have very modern ideas about certain things, I also have some dusty and antiquated manners. Hence, I say: 'Monsieur, votre père' and 'Madame, votre mère', which is extremely out of fashion. I bow deeply before elderly ladies and make small bows to young women, while many of my peers only nod their head in greeting. I always conclude my letters to elderly ladies with an expression of respect, which pleases them, and I never call men by their surname alone, as is the habit these days.[25]

In this passage with its few select examples (the respectful terms of address, the deep bows before elderly women) the marquise de Breteuil evokes a whole 'style' of interpersonal behaviour, which she admitted was 'a bit behind the times'. It is clear from the marquise's account, and other evidence in *archives privées*, that females were the principal guardians and transmitters of the gestures, attitudes, and linguistic habits that signalled aristocratic 'distinction'.[26] Mothers and grandmothers, but also aunts, mothers-in-law, and great-aunts, were responsible for ensuring that young nobles maintained formality and sophistication in the way they moved and spoke. Noblemen also had to set an example, of course, and keep a close eye on the standards of behaviour of their offspring. The prince Gaston de Béarn repeatedly stressed to his son Henri the importance of correct manners in letter writing. Daily correspondence contained a 'multitude of small nuances by which one distinguishes well-bred people'.[27] Any lapse into casualness damaged the air of cultivation that was so prized among the nobility.

The princesse Marthe Bibesco received the polish she needed to move in royal society from her mother-in-law, the dowager princesse Valentine Bibesco. There was no better person to teach the newly wed sixteen-year-old Marthe. Valentine knew the crucial ingredients for moving in the most prestigious social circles. She was highly educated, a brilliant conversationalist, and kept impeccable standards of speech and deportment. At the Bibesco country residence, Posada, in the Carpathian foothills, where Marthe was forced to stay whilst her husband attended military camp, Valentine took her daughter-in-law in charge and over four and a half years imparted all that was necessary for Marthe to really 'shine'. There were elocution lessons in several languages, a literary diet of classical and modern authors, and coaching in how to enter and move about a room with style. Marthe, who found in this gruelling regime a distraction from the melancholy that her husband's infidelities and total lack of concern for her inspired, applied herself with diligence. Her escape from the strict and constant monitoring of her physical movement and intellectual application, as well as the monotony of the dowager princesse's company, was to take long walks in the Romanian countryside, '[her] very own land of the willows'.[28]

'And what of grandfathers?' asked the comtesse Isabelle de Paris in her memoirs. 'One rarely talks about them. Yet mine was wonderful. I only knew one of my two grandfathers, Bon-papa d'Orléans, the comte d'Eu. He was very tall. Since he was largely deaf and enjoyed hearing his grandchildren play, we were very noisy. But, in love, he taught me silence and tenderness.'[29] When the comte d'Eu and 'Bébelle', as he called her, went on walks together in the decade before the First World War the comte left behind his silver ear trumpet so they did not feel obliged to speak. After visiting the broods of peacocks in the grounds of the château they made their way to a row of trees where in springtime violets poked up through the new grass. Instructed by her grandfather, the little girl would carefully pick a small bouquet for her mother before the pair returned to the château d'Eu, hand in hand. The comtesse de Paris reflected that to be able to know one's grandparents is a source of great happiness and gives a child 'the sense of the family's continuity'. In the grounds of the château d'Eu, that continuity was symbolised by a line of oak trees. Accompanied by her grandfather, Isabelle planted her own oak near to those of the former king, Louis-Philippe, and other members of the royal family. 'To plant a tree is to think of the future.'[30]

Another striking picture of the influence of a grandfather is contained in the *Souvenirs* of the comtesse Sibylle de Mirabeau-Martel, who was born in 1849 and known to contemporaries by her pen name 'Gyp'. The comtesse's ancestors included the revolutionary orator Mirabeau and the impassioned counter-revolutionary, Mirabeau-Tonneau. She was an only child and following her father's death, when she was aged eleven, her maternal grandfather, Gonneville, took charge of her early education. This included playing with toy soldiers that he gave her and leafing through a picture book of famous generals. Gyp adored her grandfather 'savagely and tenderly', as she put it, and stories of his experiences as a soldier in Napoleon I's army, then subsequently in the personal guard of Charles X, made a deep and lasting impression on her. Gonneville was described by one of his commanding officers as 'one of our finest cavalry officers . . . an officer of the utmost distinction'.[31] The military reputation of this man mattered intensely to his beloved granddaughter who wanted to be buried with his portrait. It was largely though Gonneville's influence that Gyp became 'fiercely patriotic' and a model of devotion to the French army in which she longed to serve as her male ancestors had done.[32]

There are other examples of aristocratic girls playing 'soldiers' and idealising cavalry officers. At the age of eight in 1890 Élaine Greffulhe became president of the Société des Amis des Jeux. Aline Berthier, a descendant of the maréchal Berthier, Napoleon I's Minister of War, had founded the Société in 1882. It had one hundred members ranked from chief to soldier who each paid a monthly subscription of ten centimes that entitled them to a snack and military outfit. Under Élaine's presidency, the Société met every Sunday at l'hospice Greffulhe, 71 avenue de Villiers. Games varied but were normally competitive with the winners receiving prizes: a doll for a girl and a book in English or German for a boy. Only in the types of prizes given is there any indication in the Société's 'rules' that this highly organised children's play was gendered along conventional lines.[33]

By the time nobles reached puberty there was less scope to experiment with gender roles because of adults' concern that the 'normal' paths for each sex be followed. Girls were expected to work conscientiously at developing 'feminine' character traits of modesty, prudence, and familial devotion.[34] This was preparation for attracting a spouse and it went hand-in-hand with encouragement to appreciate 'masculine' attributes in men of the same class. When the prince Joachim Murat V became engaged to Cécile Ney d'Elchingen, the princesse's guardian Madame Furtado-Heine wrote to her future son-in-law, the sub-lieutenant: '[Cécile] adores your profession.'[35] Boys, meanwhile, were expected to pursue training at a military academy followed by a period of armed service. Although some did show talent for military command, many were simply following family tradition and, like their ancestors, would later use their experience in the army to move into politics or diplomacy. Henri de Breteuil, for instance, was destined for training as a cavalry officer well before he entered St Cyr in 1867; a book and gun belonging to Abd el-Kader that his father had carried off in 1843 while serving as aide-de-camp to the duc d'Aumale in Algeria were kept at the château de Breteuil.[36]

Beyond the circle of influence represented by family, another important source of learning about adult gendered roles for most nobles was the Catholic Church.[37] We have previously examined the efforts of aristocratic fathers and mothers to defend Catholic education. By shifting perspective on to the world of children we may see the effects of this parental concern for religious formation.

Many aristocratic children had their first memorable encounter with religion when death touched the household. It was not uncommon for a child to lose a parent, sibling, grandparent or favourite servant to illness, disease, or complications in giving birth. Recalling the family's state of confusion upon her father's sudden death, when she and her sister were very young, the comtesse Anna de Noailles reflected:

> Children are in the way at a time of grief; adults, convinced of the indifference of childhood and agitated by all the painful tasks that encumber them, brush aside the little ones and push them out of the way, not knowing where to put them or how, for the moment, to be rid of them.[38]

The comtesse recalled the oppressive atmosphere of the family home especially during the first six months of mourning, when repeated funerary devotions and the relentless wearing of stifling black crepe seemed to hold recovery from grief at bay. A child could find it awkward and alienating to have her playmates, in their bright garments, ask why she wore black all the time.[39]

On reaching adolescence, generally at the age of twelve, Catholic girls and boys were given a structured initiation to religion as they prepared for their First Communion. The comtesse de Pange writes that up until the age of twelve '[her] ignorance in religious matters was total'.[40] This was rather unusual, she suggests, for a child of her milieu, but she explains it in reference to the mild anticlericalism of her maternal grandparents and the mix of Protestants and Catholics in her paternal family line. Her father was irritated by debate on religious issues, and her mother had other interests she preferred to discuss with friends.[41] Pauline received catechism lessons at the Église de Saint-Philippe-du-Roule under the direction of the parish priest and her First Communion took place on 17 May 1900, the tenth anniversary of her younger brother's death, which nobody mentioned although she was aware of it. Her description of the occasion, written from an adult perspective, has none of the gravity and deep devotional sentiment that characterises the journal entries of girls on the cusp of adolescence. Generally the prayers and poems composed at the time of First Communion are consistent in the theme of a young person's soul set aflame by Christ's passion.[42]

Some noble girls, after initial instruction from a governess, were enrolled in convent schools. Personal accounts written in later life indicate that pupils at these schools 'gained an appreciation for the companionship and security of an enclosed, feminine community'.[43] In mature women's memoirs, 'the convent of childhood, compared to the disappointments of adult life, seems an earthly paradise'.[44] The *archives privées* of aristocratic families do not provide a clear picture of whether noble girls were happy attending convent schools; there are relatively few letters since these girls were more likely to attend as day pupils rather than board. Yet there is evidence of diligence in study. In 1870 Marie-Thérèse de Foresta was a day pupil in the convent school run by the nuns of Sacré-Coeur de Jésus in Marseille. Dressed in her uniform of black tunic, black straw hat, veil, and gloves she resembled all the other girls. Marie-Thérèse was singled out on prize day in April, however, receiving an honourable mention for good conduct and the Prize for Application in Religious Instruction.[45]

For Zenaïde des Cars learning about Christ's passion inspired such an intensity of faith that, at the age of twenty-one, she became a nun. In October 1881 this young noblewoman, in the presence of ecclesiastics, friends and relatives, joined the community of Carmelites at the Parisian convent in rue d'Enfer. Her journal of 1875–76 offers some insight into the mind of Zenaïde in the years before she committed her life to Christ. We will never know, however, what she wrote in the passages that were cut with scissors from its pages. On Sunday 2 July 1875, she noted that after Vespers there had been a gathering at which, 'the curé spoke about sacrifice in general and about the small daily sacrifices that one should practise in order to prepare for the more serious challenges that are encountered in any life'. Over the following weeks Zenaïde tried to make *petits sacrifices* but was ultimately critical of her own efforts: 'I know my own weakness and the ease with which I succumb.' Zenaïde des Cars prayed to God for 'some time of peace to strengthen [her] for new battles'.[46]

The struggle that Zenaïde des Cars, like other young women of the aristocracy, identified was an internal one.[47] By contrast, young noblemen were conditioned to aspire to public demonstration of martial virtues on a real battlefield. In a collection of essays Father Didierjean commemorated the lives of Jesuit-educated men. According to Didierjean, the vicomte Charles de la Noue 'felt irresistibly drawn towards the military profession [*le métier des armes*]' by the traditions of his Breton family. His ancestors included Gilles de la Noue, a fourteenth-century equerry who had served under Bertrand du Guesclin in the Hundred Years War, and François de la Noue, a Calvinist lieutenant under Henri IV, who was mortally wounded in the siege of Lamballe in 1591.[48] Similarly, the three brothers Goué 'from a noble and patriarchal family of the Vendée' went to fight in the Franco-Prussian War and 'by their bravery added to the honourable heritage that they had received from their ancestors'.[49]

Didierjean's essays were published in 1882 just two years after the republican government's executive decree that dissolved the Society of Jesus in France forcing Jesuits to abandon control of the colleges they had established. By paying tribute to former students, Didierjean was promoting a defiant message that Jesuit education produced courageous and pious soldiers who had willingly sacrificed their lives for France. John Padberg has shown there was a strong military tone at Jesuit colleges where on celebratory occasions high-ranking officers were invited to review the students' march and drill before dinner. In 1874 at a college in Lille, for example, the général de Martray and the baron Le Guay attended a feast day where the général proposed a toast at dessert 'to the honor of the Society, recalling the close relations of St Ignatius [patron saint of Catholic soldiers] and the Society with military life'.[50] After initial crackdown on their communities caused by the 1880 decree Jesuits gradually managed to resume positions in colleges where the military tone remained in evidence. In the 1890s the Jesuit colleges in France supplied about 18 per cent of the intake into St Cyr, 13 per cent into the École Polytechnique and 22 per cent into the École Navale.[51]

In the summer of 1893 Auguste de Caumont La Force had received good grades in his third year at the Jesuit college in the rue de Madrid for which his grandfather, the comte de Maillé, wrote to congratulate him. A letter from Maillé to his daughter Blanche from 1897 indicates that the younger boys, Jacques and Armand, were also progressing well in their studies. 'I send you my compliments on your two sons, even Jacques who often lacks drive and diligence. Armand has a fine collection [of results] ... I find it very satisfying for them ... and a grandfather.'[52] Armand followed his elder brother into the Jesuit college in the rue de Madrid. After a visit in November 1899, his doting grandfather reported:

> I was delighted to see him in good condition. It is certainly very good for the health to work hard, to get up early in the morning and to eat nutritious things when one is hungry ... He seemed to me to be satisfied with his class but still not entirely sure of his academic standing in relation to his fellow students. I think I detected in him a thrilled sense of pride for being at the head of his class. The visit went well although I forgot to bring him a box of sweets but it did not bother him since his father had brought him a box of mints on Saturday evening.[53]

Entry into college brought substantial changes to a young noble's daily routine, living environment, and sociability.[54] In 1873 the prince Roland Bonaparte entered the Royal Naval School at New Cross, Kent, as a boarder. This institution prepared boys of elite families 'for the Universities, for the Military, Naval, and East Indian Services, for the Civil Service and other Competitive Examinations, and for Mercantile Pursuits'. The School was incorporated by an act of parliament in 1840 and its patrons included Her Most Gracious Majesty, the Queen, and other members of the British royal family. Roland's medical and scholastic examination took place in September 1873 when he was aged fifteen. His General Knowledge was reported to be 'fair'; he was capable of 'simple equations' in Mathematics; and in Classics he was 'quite a beginner'. Fortunately for Roland the Royal Naval School did not forbid the keeping of toys, although these had to fit into a play box of about one square foot in dimension. Although the regulations do not mention a school uniform, there were clear specifications on the types of clothing and numbers of garments required.

The correspondence that survives from Roland's time at New Cross shows that his father Pierre took an active interest in his son's studies, advising Roland to work hard at mastering the English language which he stressed it was important for a marine to possess. He also encouraged Roland to learn about strategy in modern land warfare, sending him a handmade mnemonic card representing the twelfth Germany army corps in the war of 1870–71. Roland spent only one term at the Royal Naval School during which his conduct was reported to be 'very good'. It required several attempts by Eames, the School secretary, to extract payment of outstanding fees from the Bonapartes – eventually he referred to an instruction from the School's president and council. On returning to France Roland was enrolled at the Institution Hortus, 94 rue du Bac. Once again he was a boarder. Pupils at the Institution Hortus followed the courses of the Lycée Saint-Louis. They received religious instruction from a resident chaplain and they took a range of lessons in sports and *les arts d'agrément*. Roland had music lessons three times per week and fencing, dancing and gymnastic lessons twice each per week. He also had lessons in swimming and horse riding.[55]

During the 1880s Henri de Béarn attended the École de l'Immaculée-Conception in Toulouse, returning to his family's property near Pau for holidays at Easter and Christmas. Reports of the boy's academic laziness inspired brusque criticism from father Gaston and cajoling from mother Cécile: 'I would be so happy if you were first in your class … I am convinced you will become a great Latin scholar.'[56] Although intellectual precocity was not in evidence, Henri showed every sign of shooting up physically. Gaston was obliged to send a suit from Paris to accommodate 'the giant Goliath'. Cécile commiserated over an outbreak of acne: 'these are merely pimples of youth; they will soon pass, and youth as well unfortunately.'[57]

For noble boys who boarded it could be upsetting to lose the companionship of siblings as well as to be separated from parents. The Foresta children, Maxence, Henriette, Sibylle, and Albéric, spent some time in the late 1890s at their grandmother's home, the château des Tours near Marseille, where they received instruction from a *Fräulein*. On 21 May 1899, Maxence and Henriette told their mother, Thérèse de Foresta, that the château 'seemed empty' following their parents' departure, but promised to be very well behaved. Maxence found it terrible to be taken from this environment the following year and enrolled as a boarder at the Collège Saint-Joseph in Avignon. There he complained to his mother that he suffered from headaches, which the male nurse made light of, and protested that one teacher was especially strict: 'with him we always have to finish our homework otherwise it is a zero'. Maxence begged his mother to write to him often. 'I am not happy at college, I am even unhappy …

Come and visit me soon because I am longing to see you again. How is everyone at home?'[58]

Prior to Henri Greffulhe's entry to college, his two sisters, Jeanne and Louise, their cousin Pauline d'Armaillé and nurse Zizi had been his principal playmates. In the early 1860s Jeanne and Louise each wrote to their brother in Paris to keep him up to date with life at the château de La Rivière. In an undated note Louise reported that a bout of influenza meant she had been unable to ride the black pony, their cousin Pauline had come down with measles, and there were rats under her cubbyhouse. Jeanne reassured Henri that his goat, donkey, and horses were all in good condition, adding that the pigs, sheep, pigeons, rabbits, and hens were also doing well. One of her undated notes ended teasingly, with the use of a nickname playfully written in large letters: 'I hope that you are still working very hard, Plombard. Adieu, my dear Henri, everyone here joins me in sending love, your sister, Jeanne.'[59]

Sibling bonds were important among the aristocracy because they laid the basis for the next generation's experience of an extended network of cousins. Following the death of the prince Gaston de Béarn in 1893, his younger brother Jean became the legal guardian of Gaston's children. Henri visited and sent letters and presents to his Béarn cousins in Corsica where they hoped he might be able to complete his military service. Sabine de Béarn was particularly keen to have her 'kindest, friendliest, most charming and suave' cousin stationed near Bastia. Henri's gifts of tiepins, stamps, and rings delighted Hector, Centule, Joseph and Jeanne who sent photographs in return.

> Last Thursday we had a picnic on the boulders but Hector disturbed the party by starting a grass fire. The *maquis* was burning for an hour then the party resumed. In the photo you see our faces looking very calm despite some blackened legs and cindered trouser bottoms.[60]

Henri Greffulhe was close to his two sisters, Jeanne and Louise, who married respectively the prince Auguste d'Arenberg and the marquis Robert de L'Aigle. He was a devoted and indulgent uncle to his assorted nieces and nephews to whom he loved giving presents. Ernest d'Arenberg received a box of 'excellent cigarettes'. 'Each time I smoke one I will experience a double pleasure, first the one that a smoker feels on inhaling fine tobacco, then the one of saying to myself it is a gift from you.' Emma d'Arenberg, who adored flowers, was the happy recipient of 'magnificent roses', 'splendid carnations' and 'a bouquet of violets that gave [her] the greatest pleasure'. Marie de L'Aigle was given a 'beautiful apple' to help her recover from a leg injury. She wrote to thank him, reporting that she could again 'run and skip with my cord'.[61] Henri's daughter, Élaine, also appreciated the company of her aunts and uncles. Whilst on holiday in the Netherlands, in August 1903, she wrote to her father, 'Papouta' (her nickname for Henri):

> Here we have found the sea and an admirable breeze. The weather is extremely fresh and fine; the beach is superb; we are staying in an exquisite villa and having great fun and games all day with uncle Pierre, aunt Marthe, and aunt Gui Gui [Ghislaine] who is always made fun of by all. One forgets to put tea in her teapot, etc. etc. . . . At The Hague we saw the very handsome paintings by Rembrandt. We have had great laughs here fishing on a Sunday. We are all merry and getting along wonderfully. . . . Kisses from Élaine. [p.s.] Here we are eating the amazing cheeses of Holland![62]

This was not the first or only letter from Élaine to convey delight in the simple pleasures of family gatherings and food. Another of her notes, undated, captures the activities and pace of life at the château de La Rivière through a series of small sketches: 'Our lunch together', 'Billiards', 'The Riding Lesson', 'Maman's 2 p.m. reception' and 'Bedtime' (the latter depicts a person in bed with a servant bringing a lighted candle and a little arrow pointing in the direction of the 'W.C.'). Élaine also pressingly requested certain items from her father, which she drew to show him. These included a large rosary of blue beads, several brooches, a lace shawl, dried preserved fruits, a large plum, a bunch of cherries, and a pot of jam.

In the France of the Third Republic, like in other societies, food was fundamental to human identity for the types of food people ate, especially during childhood, as well as the environment they grew accustomed to eating in, contributed strongly to the sense of who they were. People developed appreciation for certain foods as they grew older but, as Proust reminds us, the tastes and smells of dishes they loved as children retained their evocative power and place in personal memory.[63] The comtesse de Pange was admitted to the adult table at the age of seven and her earliest memories of food were largely bound up with members of the Broglie family, especially her grandmother, who ruled with an iron fist over every aspect of mealtime from menus to conversation. Pauline recollects how her father (who loved pickles) often questioned her grandmother about how she had spelt certain dishes on the menu: 'Does one write "Niocchi" or "Guiniocchi"? Potatoes *en robe de chambre* or *en robe de champs?*' The family ate few vegetables because her grandmother did not like them and was in the habit of calling the purées often served with roasts 'poultices' and macaroni 'gruel for cats' – enough to put anyone off eating those dishes.

Striking to us today is the amount and variety of meats served in the Broglie household, which was typical among the upper class at the turn of the century in France and other Western countries. 'One served on silver platters enormous pieces of meat all rare and bathed in strong sauces . . . whole hams garnished with paper ruffs, game pâtés, casseroles, cold meats, [and] terrines,' writes the comtesse de Pange. In Paris most meats as well as fruit and vegetables were purchased from the central market, Les Halles, but aristocratic families also ate the game shot on country estates. The comtesse de Pange's grandmother 'only liked the game that the game-keepers of Normandy and Anjou sent each week in winter'. Such pride in, and preference for, the local produce of country areas perhaps meant that to some degree the regionalism of French cooking was reproduced in Parisian aristocratic households; it is difficult to tell from the few menus that have survived.[64] Certainly some non-French nobles made an effort to eat the food familiar to them. In Russian households 'one serves [before the soup] hors-d'oeuvres of fish, oysters, [and] caviar,' reported an etiquette writer, the baronne d'Orval. Russian dukes were staunch patrons of Prunier's, the Parisian restaurant famed for its oysters.[65]

The comtesse de Pange gives a general depiction of the Broglies' daily menu: 'The menu, morning or evening, was composed always of seven or eight dishes [arranged in services]. An entrée (generally with eggs), a meat dish with potatoes, a roast fowl, a vegetable dish, a side dish . . . In addition one served desserts spread out on the table "à la russe", as my grandmother said.' For Pauline the highlight of the meal was the confectionery. She was sometimes given permission to go and watch the sugar being cooked in great tubs in the kitchen. The ball of pink, chocolate, or coffee tinted sugar that emerged resembled 'a skein of wool that twisted and stretched'; the great art was to form it into curved wreaths that appeared on the table at gala occasions.[66] The comtesse de Pange looked back nostalgically on the dietary pattern of her childhood when she could eat everything without surveillance: 'I drank large glasses of red wine and took second helpings of every dish.'[67] To the comtesse Anna de Noailles the impulse of children to eat rapaciously and with gusto was an expression of wonder at the universe and a precursor to adult desires:

All that attracts the child in life, through every sense, he wants to carry to his lips and absorb it. Which child has not wished to drink rain, to savour snow, to bite the buds where the future rose lies sharp, piled together, and crinkled up, to crush the inedible chestnut ... This desire to snap up, this joy of tasting, the sly satisfaction of concealing in oneself what one covets and making oneself the owner of it is surely the formula of all desire.[68]

Given the customs we have seen of sharing meals together as a family, and of giving small edible gifts, especially fruits, it is not surprising to find food used as a metaphor in nobles' writings to convey very personal messages about love and desire. Between intimates such messages were warmly anticipated. But expressions of love could also come as a surprising revelation to the recipient. Sometimes this enabled the development or deepening of intimacy where loving feelings were reciprocal. The particularity of each bond was part of what made the intimacy so precious.

The général marquis de Galliffet was not a man known for having a warm heart. As military commander during the Week of Blood in 1871 he was dubbed 'the executioner of the Commune' and in 1899 he was appointed Minister of War by Waldeck-Rousseau. Even a friend of the général, the duchesse Anne d'Uzès, found his manner 'ruthless': 'I knew him well, we were like family; but, apart from his bravery, I hardly liked him.'[69] Yet the Montesquiou-Fezensac family archive reveals a very different side to the général. In the late 1890s, and up until his death in 1909, Galliffet wrote notes and letters to Mathilde de Montesquiou-Fezensac, the daughter of his friends, whom he dubbed 'Mademoiselle Pierrot'. There is nothing untoward about these notes. The général was deeply fond of Mathilde, whom he had known since she was a baby. He sent her Easter eggs. He sent her 'the best dates from the far south of Algeria' urging her to 'eat lots of them so [your] father won't eat too many'. He sent her a 'symphony of roses': 'They are like you, Mademoiselle, fresh and without affectation.' Galliffet had a soft side. In 1897 he told 'Pierrot' about the death of his dog 'poor Freestone, my best and most faithful friend' who on the day following a hunt suffered an attack of paralysis and died, 'suffering atrociously'. 'Boulacq, your devoted servant', as the général usually signed these letters, asked Mathilde to send him 'one of the photographs that you took of this poor animal'. A similarly melancholic letter the following year informed Mathilde of the death of his cat and wished her *bon voyage*: 'Your uncle told me you are departing to Germany on a concert tour ... rest assured

6 The général marquis de Galliffet (1893)

that on your return you will find me in the condition of an ancient Mummy.'[70]

Galliffet was then in his sixty-eighth year and becoming increasingly aware of his own mortality. The company of his young friend, 'the young swan' or 'little wild animal', brought a joy that was bittersweet and he mused frequently on the difference in their ages. He was, it seems, not a little in love with her:

> I hope, Mademoiselle, that Your Grace is in good health. I will deprive myself of the pleasure of catching up with you since a young Reinette apple like yourself would not, without damage, meet the old bruised pear that I am! ... It would be much better to be taken by your aunt *chez* Colombin,

the *pâtissier* on the rue Cambon, to eat excellent small pastries and to drink a wonderful hot chocolate. Please remember me to your dear parents and believe me your very respectful, Boulacq (hermit).[71]

Mathilde de Montesquiou-Fezensac was by then a young adult woman who had made her debut in high society. Unlike the petals of edelweiss that the Minister of War sent her, carefully packed in cotton wool, her childhood ways could not be so readily preserved.

When Paul Bourget wrote that for a high-society woman 'constant mastery of herself is the professional virtue' he likened it to 'courage in men of the military'.[72] The novelist captured the very essence of aristocratic upbringing that was designed to instil a high level of discipline and self-control in nobles' behaviour as well as a sophisticated understanding of social and sexual mores. The motive behind this training was social differentiation, for it was primarily through comportment and language that the nobility signalled their superiority over the bourgeoisie. To demonstrate aristocratic status through the body nobles were required to dress and carry themselves elegantly and to speak, eat, and interact in a refined manner. Nobles' upbringing contained checks and balances so that they developed an understanding of social hierarchy through daily contact with men and women from the middle and working classes whilst continually learning from relatives the nuances of behaviour that signalled 'distinction'. This transmission of cultural capital from generation to generation made nobles confident of sustaining their position 'at the polished summit of good society'.[73]

Defence of the Catholic Church's role in education was important to the majority of nobles not only for reasons of faith but also because clerics and members of religious orders reinforced messages about honour, duty, and sacrifice. Girls and boys were raised on such messages through relatives' storytelling about ancestral accomplishments, and the Church assisted parents by steering youngsters towards what were considered to be appropriate gendered roles. Private education was not intended to function as a closed system but rather to act as a springboard for nobles into positions of public authority, influence, and esteem. This was a model of education that for centuries had prepared noble girls and boys to occupy high-profile roles and to embody the concept of service for France.[74] Among the Foresta family, a great Provençal house of nobility, the men were renowned for their service at senior levels of the Church hierarchy, in politics, the army, and diplomacy. Maxence de Foresta had been an unhappy child at the Collège Saint-Joseph in Avignon but forty years later, in 1939, he would write to his mother: 'Everything is going well. I am increasingly interested in my role as unit commander in the countryside in spite of the cares and responsibilities it entails. In what capacity shall I serve after the war?'[75]

Notes

1 Undated note in AP 103/39 Fonds Lucien Bonaparte.
2 Colin Heywood, *Childhood in Nineteenth-Century France: Work, Health and Education among the 'classes populaires'* (Cambridge, 1988), chs 1–3; Laura Lee Downs, *Childhood in the Promised Land: Working-class Movements and the Colonies de Vacances in France, 1880–1960* (Durham, 2002). Colin Heywood pays careful attention to class and to urban and rural experiences in *Growing Up in France: From the Ancien Régime to the Third Republic* (Cambridge, 2007).
3 Pierre Bourdieu, *Distinction: A Social Critique of the Judgement of Taste*, trans. Richard Nice (London, 2000), pp. 13–14, 24–6, 63, 65, 120, 122.
4 Éric Mension-Rigau, *Aristocrates et grands bourgeois: éducation, traditions, valeurs* (Paris, 1994), pp. 37–8.
5 3 August 1897 in AP 353/30 Fonds Caumont La Force. On French elites and Wagner see André Michael Spies, *Opera, State and Society in the Third Republic, 1875–1914* (New York, 1998), pp. 82–90; Frederic Spotts, *Bayreuth: A History of the Wagner Festival* (New Haven, 1994).
6 Elizabeth C. Macknight, 'Cake and conversation: the women's *jour* in Parisian high society, 1880–1914', *French History* 19 (2005), 342–63; Mension-Rigau, *Aristocrates*, pp. 306–18.
7 AP 101 (II)/36 Fonds Gramont.
8 24 December 1888 in AD Charente J 1093 Fonds Galard, Brassac, Béarn, Chalais.
9 These social and courtly skills were of longstanding importance for nobles across Europe. See Jonathan Dewald, *Aristocratic Experience and the Origins of Modern Culture: France, 1570–1715* (Berkeley, 1993), pp. 79–96; Jerzy Lukowski, *The European Nobility in the Eighteenth Century* (New York, 2003), p. 60; Dominique Picco, 'Peut-on parler de modèle nobiliaire à propos des familles des demoiselles de Saint-Cyr entre 1686 et 1793?' in Josette Pontet, Michel Figeac, and Marie Boisson (eds), *La Noblesse de la fin du XVIe au début du XXe siècle: un modèle social?* vol. 1 (Anglet, 2002), pp. 173–98.
10 'Note sur les activités musicales de la comtesse Greffulhe' in AP 101 (II)/128 Fonds Gramont; Anna de Noailles, *Le Livre de ma vie* (Paris, 1976), pp. 19, 73, 180–3; Comtesse Jean de Pange, *Comment j'ai vu 1900* (Paris, 1999), pp. 59, 61, 86, 209. On dancing lessons, Claude Francis and Fernande Gontier, *Mathilde de Morny: la scandaleuse marquise et son temps* (Paris, 2000), p. 95.
11 Pange, *Comment j'ai vu*, p. 30.

12　AP 173 bis/426 Fonds Maréchal Berthier.
13　AP 173 bis/426 Fonds Maréchal Berthier.
14　Marcel Launay, *Le Bon Prêtre: le clergé rural au XIXe siècle* (Paris, 1986), p. 71.
15　8 October 1895 in AP 353/30 Fonds Caumont La Force.
16　AP 173 bis/426 Fonds Maréchal Berthier.
17　6 July 1873 in AP 31/67 Fonds Murat.
18　6 July 1873 in AP 31/67 Fonds Murat.
19　Boni de Castellane, *Mémoires* (Paris, 1986), pp. 33–4; Launay, *Le Bon Prêtre*, pp. 245–51.
20　Castellane, *Mémoires*, pp. 23–9.
21　Pange, *Comment j'ai vu*, pp. 53–64; Élisabeth de Clermont-Tonnerre, *Au temps des équipages* (Paris, 1928), p. 15; Celia Bertin, *Marie Bonaparte: A Life* (London, 1982), pp. 34–5, 40, 44.
22　Éric Mension-Rigau (ed.), *Journal de Constance de Castelbajac, marquise de Breteuil* 1885–1886 (Paris, 2003), pp. 181–2.
23　The remark about all children picking up bad expressions from household staff illustrates the notion of 'misrecognition', when a person fails to appreciate that they are the product of particular conditioning. See Pierre Bourdieu, *Masculine Domination*, trans. Richard Nice (Cambridge, 2001), pp. vii–viii, 84–8.
24　Pierre Bourdieu, *Langage et pouvoir symbolique* (Paris, 1982).
25　Mension-Rigau, *Journal de Constance de Castelbajac*, pp. 132–3.
26　Macknight, 'Cake and conversation', 342–63.
27　11 October 1890 in AD Charente J 1092 Fonds Galard, Brassac, Béarn, Chalais.
28　Christine Sutherland, *Enchantress: Marthe Bibesco and Her World* (New York, 1996), pp. 27–32.
29　Isabelle de Paris, *Mon bonheur de grand-mère* (Paris, 1995), pp. 14–15.
30　Paris, *Mon bonheur*, p. 19.
31　Gyp, *Souvenirs d'une petite fille* 2 vols (Paris, 1927); Willa Z. Silverman, *The Notorious Life of Gyp: Right-Wing Anarchist in Fin-de-Siècle France* (Oxford, 1995), p. 15.
32　Silverman, *The Notorious Life*, pp. 9–16; Willa Z. Silverman, 'Gyp et l'Affaire Dreyfus', *Modern and Contemporary France* 43 (1990), 5–16.
33　AP 101 (II)/35 Fonds Gramont.
34　Comtesse de Gencé, *Code mondain de la jeune fille* (Paris, 1909).
35　Letter 9 March 1884 in AP 31/68 Fonds Murat.
36　Mension-Rigau, *Journal de Constance de Castelbajac*, p. 8.
37　Jean Delumeau (ed.), *La Religion de ma mère: le rôle des femmes dans la transmission de la foi* (Paris, 1992), pp. 310–25, 327–42; Claude Langlois, *Le Catholicisme au féminin: les congrégations françaises à supérieure générale au XIXe siècle* (Paris, 1984); Paul Seely, 'O Sainte Mère: Liberalism and socialization of Catholic men in nineteenth-century France', *Journal of Modern European History* 70 (1998), 880–91.

38 Noailles, *Le Livre*, pp. 122–3. See also Clermont-Tonnerre, *Au temps*, p. 16; Pange, *Comment j'ai vu*, pp. 16, 204–6; Bertin, *Marie Bonaparte*, pp. 25–6, 44.
39 Noailles, *Le Livre*, p. 144.
40 Pange, *Comment j'ai vu*, p. 177.
41 Pauline's paternal great-uncle, the abbé Paul, was brought up by a Protestant aunt before converting to Catholicism. His murder in 1895, committed by a woman, was exploited by the press, causing considerable pain for the family and contributing to the suppression of religious talk in the home. See Pange, *Comment j'ai vu*, pp. 150–6.
42 AP 101 (II)/1 Fonds Gramont; Élisabeth Higgonet-Dugua, *Anna de Noailles, coeur innombrable: biographie-correspondance* (Paris, 1989), pp. 24–5; Clermont-Tonnerre, *Au temps*, pp. 103–8; Bertin, *Marie Bonaparte*, p. 49.
43 Whitney Walton, *Eve's Proud Descendants: Four Women Writers and Republican Politics in Nineteenth-Century France* (Stanford, 2000), pp. 35–7.
44 Colette Cosnier, *Le Silence des filles: de l'aiguille à la plume* (Paris, 2001), pp. 145–50.
45 AD Bouches-du-Rhône 140J/113 Fonds Foresta.
46 18 July 1875 in AP 399/215 Chartrier de Malesherbes.
47 Elizabeth C. Macknight, 'In memory of myriad selves: the baronne Mathilde de Mackau (1837–1886)', *Magistra* 12 (2006), 46–72.
48 François suffered an arm amputation in 1569 and was henceforth known as La Nouë Bras-de-Fer. His *Discours politiques et militaires* (1587) is a historical account of the Wars of Religion.
49 Le Père Didierjean, *Élèves des jésuites: souvenirs des collèges de la Compagnie de Jésus en France*, 1850–1880 2 vols (Geneva, 1882), pp. 129–50, 209–22.
50 John W. Padberg, *Colleges in Controversy: the Jesuit Schools in France from Revival to Suppression, 1815–1880* (Cambridge, 1969), p. 232.
51 Maurice Larkin, *Religion, Politics and Preferment in France since 1890: La Belle Époque and Its Legacy* (Cambridge, 1995); p. 37; P. J. Harrigan, 'The social appeals of Catholic secondary education in France in the 1870s', *Journal of Social History* 8 (1975), 122–41, esp. note 62.
52 3 August 1897 in AP 353/30 Fonds Caumont La Force.
53 28 November 1899 in AP 353/30 Fonds Caumont La Force.
54 Guy de Rothschild, *Contre bonne fortune* (Paris, 1983), pp. 55–9; Theodore Zeldin, *France 1848–1945* vol. 2 *Intellect, Taste, and Anxiety* (Oxford, 1977), pp. 244–58, 291–99; Paul Gerbod, *La Vie quotidienne dans les lycées et les collèges au XIXe siècle* (Paris, 1968).
55 AP 103/39 Fonds Lucien Bonaparte.
56 29 October 1885 in AD Charente J 1093 Fonds Galard, Brassac, Béarn, Chalais.
57 18 March 1889 in AD Charente J 1093 Fonds Galard, Brassac, Béarn, Chalais.
58 21 May 1899, 27 February 1902, and 4 October 1902 in AD Bouches-du-Rhône 140J/121 Fonds Foresta.
59 Undated notes from Louise Greffulhe in AP 101 (I)/28 Fonds Gramont. Undated notes from Jeanne Greffulhe in AP 101 (I)/29 Fonds Gramont.

60 Undated letter in AD Charente J 1094 Fonds Galard, Brassac, Béarn, Chalais.
61 Undated notes and cards from Ernest and Emma d'Arenberg and note from Marie de l'Aigle 30 October 1911 in AP 101 (I)/29 Fonds Gramont.
62 AP 101/(I)/24 Fonds Gramont.
63 Bourdieu, *Distinction*, pp. 177–99.
64 Pange, *Comment j'ai vu*, pp. 26–7. For menus see AP 31/95 Fonds Murat; Gabriel-Louis Pringué, *Trente ans de dîners en ville* (Paris, 1950), pp. 254, 266.
65 Baronne d'Orval, *Usages mondains. Guide du savoir-vivre moderne dans toutes les circonstances de la vie* 3 ed. (Paris, 1901), p. 171.
66 Pange, *Comment j'ai vu*, p. 28.
67 Pange, *Comment j'ai vu*, p. 28.
68 Noailles, *Le Livre*, pp. 137–8.
69 Patrick de Gmeline, *La Duchesse d'Uzès (1847–1933)* (Paris, 1986), pp. 78–9.
70 Notes and letters in AP 349/35 Fonds Montesquiou-Fezensac.
71 16 May 1898 in AP 349/35 Fonds Montesquiou-Fezensac.
72 Paul Bourget, *Un coeur de femme* (Paris, 1890), pp. 90–1.
73 David Higgs, *Nobles in Nineteenth-Century France: The Practice of Inegalitarianism* (Baltimore, 1989), p. 217.
74 Dewald, *Aristocratic Experience*, pp. 86–93.
75 8 October 1939 in AD Bouches-du-Rhône 140J/121 Fonds Foresta.

8

Space and memory, loss and nostalgia

There are moments that appear to us to be perfect. For the baronne Mathilde de Mackau such a moment came on 22 May 1883 at the Vimer estate in Normandy. She wanted to share it with her husband, Armand, to whom she had been married for twenty-five years:

> My beloved, I am writing to you in the pathed woods ... on your path under the beautiful beech trees. Anne [the couple's daughter] is seated there on her *chaise longue*. Everything sings; everything is bathed in sunlight. The woods are full of *life*, of *youth*, of joyous sounds. I hear all that *so well*! ... But nothing finds echo in me, except our old memories. How much pleasure I have taken in our life together where everything was so perfumed, so sweet, so radiant! Our visits here ... and all that we did when we were 'little ones'.[1]

Mathilde, then in her mid-forties, had just become a grandmother. Filled with joy by the arrival of her first grandchild, Élisabeth, the daughter of Anne and the comte Humbert de Quinsonas, she delighted in gently teasing 'grandfather Mackau' about his own deep emotions evidenced at this time. 'You are moved like a woman,' she wrote, 'when you say goodbye, when something finishes, when, when ... in short, always. It is a great torment to be like that, but all the same I think that it is better to feel too much than not enough.'[2]

Neither Mathilde nor Armand knew in that spring of 1883 that they had less than three years left together. Mathilde's death came suddenly. In December 1885 she contracted typhoid fever and the baron de Mackau, under pressure to remain in Paris for work at the Senate, was desperate to join her at Vimer. He wrote:

I wanted to leave this evening. I have been asked, as a personal service to many colleagues, to chair an important meeting tomorrow that was called two days ago. It is a professional obligation ... I am making the sacrifice to stay and I will leave tomorrow night, Sunday ... I hope to be at Vimer by six o'clock in the morning.[3]

It is impossible to say whether Mathilde, in the grip of the fever, could have read the letter or whether it was read to her before she died. The letter was found by her daughter, Anne, among other correspondence in the baronne's bedroom on 22 January 1886, a few days after Mathilde's death. Armand, overwhelmed by grief, wrote to his deceased wife's cherished friend, Constance Bautte de Faveau, on 19 January: 'It is finished. Constance, my dear, you who loved her completely. You know what I lose. Thus it is to you alone that I send out this cry of despair! ... After tomorrow I will see her no more.'[4]

Death is a pervasive theme in the archives of aristocratic families. This is not surprising, given the legal and financial ramifications of property transmission, but archival materials also point toward some of the emotional ramifications. The practice of sending condolence letters, one of the many rituals associated with mourning, made death a subject about which to read and write. Moreover, the advent of photography in the late nineteenth century meant that pictures of funeral ceremonies and portraits of the deceased could be published and disseminated with unprecedented ease.[5] Nobles kept newspaper clippings of obituary notices for their relatives, in the same way that they did for wedding notices, and these are preserved in the archives. All of these factors mean that death at the upper levels of society has been readily documented in personal correspondence, photographs, press clippings, and wills. What do these documents reveal about nobles' attitudes towards death? In a milieu that cultivated an image of perpetuity how did aristocratic men and women deal with death's finality?

Sources about death in aristocratic families contribute to a wider investigation into the subjects of space and memory, loss and nostalgia. Grieving is a process most commonly associated with the death of a loved one, but grieving can also be triggered by the recognition of some other form of ending. It involves coming to terms with, and perhaps cherishing, memories. We have seen examples elsewhere in this book of endings that brought sadness to individuals who felt a sense of loss at the time. The comte de Maillé, for instance, consoled his daughter Blanche when she felt upset about leaving behind her old life with her parents to live as a married woman. Nostalgia is usually generated by a retrospective sense of loss, after the end has come. Examining the ways in which nobles expressed nostalgia provides an opportunity to consider the degree to which perceptions of social change were mirrored in reality.

Jonathan Dewald has underlined the need for historians to think critically about nostalgic portrayals of aristocratic societies 'in decline' because sometimes they can be 'fundamentally misleading'. 'Around the nobility, it appears, there has clung a permanent rhetoric of nostalgia; what was once solid and assured, so observer after observer tells us, has reached the verge of collapse.'[6] In the mid-nineteenth century the French nobleman Alexis de Tocqueville portrayed the decline of nobilities from the eleventh century as a central motif of European history. Yet, as Dewald points out, Tocqueville's thesis is deeply problematic for it does not account for long periods of growth and consolidation in aristocratic wealth, status, and power over eight hundred years. Since the Middle Ages nobles in many European countries have complained about poverty and the ruin of their estates in order to seek tax breaks or some other form of government assistance.[7] Whilst French nobles experienced material losses as a result of the 1789 Revolution, we need to remember that behind subsequent litanies of complaint these men and women still experienced on a daily basis what it meant 'to have'.[8] Since the command of different types of capital remained core to nobles' sense of identity in the Third Republic, the functions of memory in aristocratic families and the multiple forms and meanings of loss for nobles deserve further exploration.

Space and memory are closely intertwined themes in nobles' memoirs. For the comtesse d'Armaillé, writing in the mid-1840s, the salon of the château de La Rivière, with a Louis XVI clock on the black marble chimneypiece, was more than just a room. It was the focal point of her family home where, in her mind's eye, relatives occupied customary positions:

> to the right of the chimneypiece a Louis XVI sofa, on which my mother and my elder sister were having a lively conversation. Opposite my father, ensconsed in a deep armchair, sounding off against the weakness of the government; my brother next to him, expressing an exact opposite point of view. Then my brother-in-law Monsieur de Bonneval, always a dyed-in-the-wool Legitimist; the rest of us at our work around the table; my nephews at the far end of the salon, playing billiards or at the games-table.[9]

Eight decades later, in the 1920s, a visitor to the château de Bonnelles, home of the duchesse d'Uzès, recalled a similar scene in the salon with its 'enormous vases of flowers, clavichord, old billiard table and tables covered in photographs':

> There, next to madame d'Uzès, are six of us, hurriedly lining up the cards for a game of patience. Our venerable partner intones 'ten of hearts ... knave of clubs ... king of diamonds.' 'Oh, not so quickly,' softly begs her granddaughter, mademoiselle Yolande de Luynes. Next to her are her son, the duc d'Uzès, and her eldest daughter, the duchesse de Luynes, and then her granddaughter Anne, the comtesse de La Rochefoucauld, and myself.[10]

Comparing the descriptions of these two scenes, in different residences and in different centuries, one is struck by their apparent similarity. Conversation between relatives, billiards, and other games continue, so that in the eight decades that separate the two scenes time seems to have 'stopped'. The presence of familiar furnishings gave rooms a timeless quality for those who knew them well. One way for the aristocracy to preserve the values of the past was to live surrounded by tangible reminders of the privileged social position it had long enjoyed. To occupy the same property, and make use of the same objects as their ancestors, helped nobles to create a sense of family unity. Boni de Castellane wrote of his ancestral home, the château de Rochecotte: 'Each generation served there as a link in the chain of the line. In the styles of furniture one saw what united them all, one to another.'[11]

Furnishings also carried potent reminders of intimacy for lovers. This was the case for the marquis Jacques d'Anguilhon arriving at the home of the duchesse Christiane de Blanzac in a novel by Pierre de Coulevain set at the turn of the century. A footman shows Jacques into Christiane's red drawing room:

> On finding himself once more in this room, which he knew so well, he was moved as he never had been before. Now that he was in love, his senses entered into direct communion with all the things which belonged to Christiane and which seemed to contain something of her. The faint perfume in the air was delicious to him. He looked at the little sofa, on which she always sat. The cushions had kept the imprint of her shoulders and arms. There was the little desk at which she sat when attending to her social affairs, the old harpsichord on which she accompanied herself when she sang her exquisite little songs. He had *seen* all these things hundreds of times, but now he *felt* them, and they seemed sacred to him and wonderful [italics in original].[12]

After two years of extraordinary happiness Jacques's extramarital love affair with Christiane ended in tragedy. In real life too, there were sad

7 The *grand salon* at the château d'Ermenonville (1884)

endings to passionate intimacy. The prince Napoléon, in 1890–91, sent over one hundred letters, telegrams, and hand-delivered notes to his lover, the marquise de Saint-Paul. On 8 April 1890, after a sojourn together in Rome, he described his anguish at her departure:

> The blow is severe; hope is my aid ... Hébert took me back to his place. He spoke to me about you. He understood that to see once again the rooms in which you had been just a few hours ago, the piano that resonated under your delicate hands, those chairs in which you had been seated, was my one desire, my comfort. I closed my eyes and wished never to open them again in order to block out the reality. ... The desire so pro-

found and true to know you are happy dominates everything! Is it possible? The future is upon us. Everything comes down to the hope of seeing you again, of having a place in your life, as small as events will allow for. Nature needs the sun; a shooting star will not suffice ... I kiss your hands. Napoléon.[13]

Space and memory also feature prominently in letters exchanged between siblings. As nobles grew older, and particularly once their parents had passed away, the bonds of siblinghood often grew in importance. There were of course cases of breakdown in sibling relations. We have seen that these could be triggered by disputes over inheritance that escalated into legal contests. But for those who were fortunate enough to escape such disputes, or at least sensible enough not to let them become a reason for permanent estrangement, sibling bonds could be a source of great comfort in adulthood.

In 1888 the comte Charles Greffulhe, father to Henri, Jeanne and Louise, passed away and a few years later, in June 1891, Louise was staying at one of the properties in which they had spent time as a family. Her brother wrote to her:

> This work in the library to which you are devoting yourself will bring back to life moments that are melancholy but sweet even so, for the gentle cultivation of a profound sadness is often mellowing; it awakens old memories that absence rejuvenates. I hope that this period of calm and repose will be interrupted only by the twittering of birds in the sky and by the subtle noises of jubilant nature.[14]

Familiarity with the same living spaces was part of the sibling connection. There was also a strong sense of shared values on Henri's part, which he conveyed in another letter to Louise written in 1927:

> If punctuality is the hallmark of a gentleman, it is also, for sensitive hearts, the sign of fidelity. How may I return with enough grace your punctual visits that have brought charm to my solitude? Do you know the joy that your dear presence caused me in awakening a past that remains, between the two of us, like an enchanted suite of imperishable memories? In these turbulent times, where the traditional virtues are rattled about, where the ironies of progress seem to hound in order to destroy all that we have learnt to respect and to love, it is so sweet to find ourselves near to one another in order to recall the happiness of past times! No, the joyful days of our childhood have not prepared us for today's lifestyle, and it is really for that reason that we are so content to relive our beautiful youth together.[15]

Jeanne, Henri's other sister, expressed the same nostalgic longing for 'our beautiful youth' in her 'Histoire vraie d'une petite fille heureuse, 1860 Bois-Boudran'. This is a charming, if heavily romanticised, account of a child 'who lived happily under the good Lord's sun, loved by all, and who grew up in freedom without restrictions and without conflicts'.[16] Jeanne's 'Histoire' is based on her memories of growing up on the Greffulhe estate; it is a 'true story' but with a certain fictional quality. What emerges very clearly from the 'Histoire' is that nostalgia is as much a process of forgetting as it is of remembering. To grow up as Jeanne did in the company of a brother and a sister, 'without restrictions and without conflicts', would be quite a feat!

One of the key times in life at which siblings looked to each other for support was at the death of a parent. In the previous chapter we saw how the comtesse Anna de Noailles recalled the impact of a parent's death on herself as a young child. The Gramont family archive contains a very rare and immediate account of the impact of a parent's death on a young adult, written by the comtesse Élisabeth Greffulhe. In December 1884 the princesse Marie de Caraman-Chimay (née de Montesquiou-Fezensac) contracted a gastro-intestinal infection that, combined with bronchitis, led to her death on Christmas Day in Brussels. She was fifty years of age. Élisabeth, then aged twenty-four, kept an account of her mother's decline in the form of a daily journal which is prefaced by a note 'to re-read with my sisters'. The account extends over just nine days but to the young woman in a state of extreme emotion it must have seemed an eternity.

16 Dec. 1884
I left Paris, arrived in Brussels at 1.58.
   A bit nervous and irritable at 2 p.m. Around 5 o'clock she [Marie de Caraman-Chimay] had an attack ... that lasted a quarter of an hour. ... She ate, apart from her milk (3.5 litres), half a biscuit at dinner. She did not dine [with us] at the table.

17 Dec.
Restless first half of the night ... she stayed in bed this morning. She rose at midday, felt tired in getting up, she drank some *jus de viande* as well as her milk. She had a quiet day. She came into the *petit salon* and enjoyed listening to Pierre [one of Élisabeth's brothers] and I playing. An attack at quarter to 6, she lay down on her bed ... She got up again at 7 p.m., a little rested, and returned to the armchair. She spent a quiet evening, perhaps better.

18 Dec.
She rose at midday quite exhausted after a bad night. She is very anxious ... In getting up she feels very, very weak. O Lord, have pity on us. It is too

awful to see her like this ... I found her much worse although yesterday she asked for her *jus de viande* and drank all her milk. We called for Martiny [the doctor] to come during the day. He found her very irritable.

19 Dec.
She stayed in bed ... was cheerful, we chatted for an hour and a half ... [Her] pulse is good. She passes her time between the armchair and her bed, a relatively better day ... My aunt arrived with the children.

20 Dec.
She is irritable. Martiny came. ... We chatted, her, Gui Gui [Ghislaine, one of Élisabeth's sisters] and I about Henri [Élisabeth's husband]. Memories of her first ball made her laugh ... At 6 o'clock Monsieur Lefèvre came with Martiny. Consultation. Afterwards Gui Gui and I took Martiny aside ... She asked to see Father D. to take communion.

21 Dec.
Restless day, pulse stronger. Quiet evening. Martiny gave her a morphine injection at half past nine. She is sleeping calmly.

22 Dec.
Vague eyes peering out from the armchair ... We chatted for a long time; she looked well.

23 Dec.
Martiny found her noticeably better; pulse stronger, nerves calmer. We chat as if she had only a simple migraine.

24 Dec.
She was restless in the early morning waiting for Father D ... I brushed her hair with the little lead brush. We chatted for three quarters of an hour ... Henri arrived this morning but we haven't told her yet. She doesn't expect him until tomorrow ... We set up a place for him to wash in the dining room. We woke young Alexandre who was sleeping. His brothers and Robert arrived.

25 Dec. Christmas Day, Brussels
In the morning I found her weaker. There was barely a pulse. Martiny was concerned ... Gui Gui and I realised that she was waiting for Henri, indeed the idea preoccupied her all day. I found her much worse, oh much worse. Eyes a bit vague. Many times she said to me 'My dear little Bébeth'. For the first time I felt complete despair. At 5 o'clock Papa called for Henri; she was asking for him insistently. Henri was moved. She told him she was very ill. I saw that Henri found her very poorly. O Lord. Her voice was so faint; she said 'adieu' so sadly. Gui Gui and I took the title deed to Geneviève who is ill. We made her drink some tea when we got back ... At 8 o'clock she took her extract of *jus de viande* again ... Papa had dined earlier and

stayed with her during dinner. She was extremely impatient waiting for Martiny. Papa was obliged to talk to her about her affairs. She could not wait until 9 o'clock. Papa was at the top of the stairs; he did not want to go back in without Martiny. We gave her her injection ... she calmed down immediately after such incredible agitation. She called for Jo, Ghislaine, and me; she wanted us to hold her in our arms. Three times she said 'You always see me when I am so ill, come and see me when I am well.' Her voice was hoarse ... She said to us 'My dear little Bébeth, my dear Jo, my little Gui Gui.' ... We left and closed the door to let the morphine take effect. Gui Gui and I waited in the salon next door. Papa went downstairs to see all the brothers. After half an hour together Gui Gui and I were very upset. I talked to her about my uncle. I went back into her room while Gui Gui hugged little Alexandre. [Mother] called out to the nun ... Then I saw her ... *ah, mon Dieu*.[17]

This stark account speaks powerfully of the sense of abandonment that a parent's death can trigger in a grown adult. Élisabeth, in denial for the first eight days as she searched for signs of recovery, can no longer ignore the brute fact on the 25th: 'For the first time I felt complete despair.' For this twenty-four-year-old, only recently married and with a baby daughter not yet two years of age, the death of Marie de Caraman-Chimay placed a new and frightening weight of responsibility on her shoulders. As the eldest child, she now had to fulfil a maternal role for her younger siblings. Her father, the prince de Caraman-Chimay, occupied a demanding professional post in the Ministry of Foreign Affairs in Brussels. The family's finances were not in good shape. It was Élisabeth who, in 1887 and 1889, took charge of vetting potential marriage candidates for her sister Ghislaine and her brother Pierre, a task that her mother, had she been alive, would most certainly have done.[18] There was a lot to organise in the days immediately after the princesse's death. A funeral ceremony took place at the Église de Saint-Gudule in Brussels, then the coffin was taken back to Paris on the train where another ceremony was held at the Église de Saint-Germain-des-Près, then relatives journeyed south for the princesse's burial in the family tomb of the Montesquiou-Fezensac in the Sarthe.

In the wake of a relative's death Catholic custom dictated a retreat from normal socialising and usually only a restricted circle of kin attended the burial ceremony. Nobles issued *lettres de faire part* informing friends and acquaintainces of a death in the family. Recipients wrote letters of condolence in reply. Grief was essentially a private experience and the manner in which grief was expressed varied from person to person. On

31 March 1884 Rose Ney d'Elchingen wrote to console her future brother-in-law, the prince Joachim Murat V:

> Thank you for the kind greetings you sent us via Cécile [Joachim's fiancée and Rose's sister]. I was deeply touched to learn that you have cried on the inside with me, and I even thought one ought to invent tissues for tears on the inside that are sometimes more plentiful than tears on the outside; it goes to show that the habit does not make the monk.[19]

Exchanging letters was one way in which nobles reached out to one another in bereavement. Faith was often a source of consolation. But, even for the very devout, grieving for the loss of a loved one was not a straightforward or predictable process.

Whilst the death of a family member produced sorrow on the part of relatives, it also sharpened the perpetual aristocratic preoccupation with succession and bloodline. The death of a son was a particularly severe loss for nobles for it reduced the likelihood for transmission of the family name to the next generation. Pauline de Pange and Anne d'Uzès each had a brother who died during childhood and the deep impression made by those deaths is apparent in their memoirs.[20] Since aristocratic children did not attend school they relied on siblings and cousins as playmates. In Anne's case the death of her brother Paul from cerebral congestion, just three years after the death of her elder sister Pauline, meant she was brought up as an only child. Furthermore, with no male heir in her generation, Anne became the sole inheritor of an immense fortune deriving from her ancestor, the 'veuve Clicquot'. The consequences of her brother's death resonated throughout her adult life and engendered complex emotions in part because of the extensive responsibilities and privileges she attained as a result of it. To compound matters, in 1893 at the age of forty-six, the duchesse d'Uzès lost her own first-born son, Jacques, who died of a fever in the Congo. Her deceased husband's rights over the d'Uzès title and estate passed to Jacques's younger brother, Louis Emmanuel.[21] The life of Anne d'Uzès contained classic examples of the ways in which a noblewoman and her family had to adapt, in practical and emotional terms, to changed circumstances resulting from the death of a son.

Responses to death in aristocratic families are instructive on the penetration of theology and the practice of piety within this upper-class milieu under a secular state regime. During the Third Republic the evolving nature of Catholic theology combined with political concerns to shape people's interpretations of the meanings of death. Two particular strands of French Catholic thought about death can be identified.

The first of these strands centred on the notion of sacrifice. In post-revolutionary France ideas of sacrifice 'powerfully informed French royalism, republicanism, and Catholicism' and the nobleman Joseph de Maistre, who fled France in 1792, is credited with being 'the first French intellectual to offer a theoretical critique of sacrificial violence in the service of political foundation'.[22] Maistre's writings contain many of the roots of right-wing reactionary thinking about the utility of sacrifice for conservative regeneration. Through the nineteenth century sacrifice remained a key concept for many who shared Maistre's class background and, like him, 'passionately defended monarchism and Catholicism, the political and religious pillars of hierarchy, order, and faith'.[23] The notion of sacrifice featured strongly within clerical and conservative interpretations of death in the France of the early Third Republic. Both during and after 'l'année terrible' of 1870–71, sacrifice was commonly linked with the notion of regeneration at a national level.[24] The second strand in French Catholic thought prioritised the notion of mercy. Around the middle of the nineteenth century some theologians began to adjust perceptions of a God of fear to those of a God of love. This theological shift was accompanied by the 'feminisation' of the Church in France that saw a rise in the number of female orders and the spread of Marian devotion. The notion of mercy was incorporated into the sermons of high-profile clerics who advanced the idea of a benevolent rather than punitive God. Although this message became increasingly widespread, 'moral rigorism, hell-fire preaching, and other attributes of the old religion were certainly not dead by the twentieth century'.[25]

These two theological strands co-existed to varying degrees across different parts of France. In Périgord, for example, there was a tension in Christian preaching between 'the vision of a God of justice and even vengeance, and that of a God of mercy'.[26] In the diocese of Angers in the early nineteenth century parish clergy as well as visiting missionary preachers were 'inclined to preach about an angry rather than a loving God'.[27] Meanwhile in Paris from the 1830s and 1840s, lectures by Henri Lacordaire and Gustave de Ravignan attracted large audiences who heard little about the last judgement, heaven and hell. Instead, these clerics developed the themes of human obligations toward God and fellow humans, and the role of Christianity in the moral history of humankind. Re-establishing the Church's intellectual legitimacy was part of the purpose of these lectures, but so too was conversion. In contrast to the tactics employed in rural parishes, 'hellfire and brimstone were apparently not considered an effective means of winning back the urban elite'.[28]

Some of the explanations for the Church's changing message across the nineteenth century include the influence of Alphonse de Liguori's moral philosophy; general improvement to the living standards of French people brought about by technological and economic developments; and a rise in 'family sensibilities' that emphasised the connectedness of individuals.[29] Signs of God's mercy seemed apparent to the living, and these in turn informed attitudes toward and preparations for death.

From the literature directed at clergy it is possible to reconstruct the manner in which the Church defined a priest's duties at the bedside of the dying. The following description captures the extent of symbolism involved:

> This sacrament began with an exhortation in which the dying person was called on to have hope and confidence in God's mercy as he looked forward to eternal life. There then followed several prayers in Latin, including the Confiteor, the granting of plenary indulgence, and then the actual anointing, during which the priest made the sign of the cross with the holy oil on the eyes, ears, nostrils, hands and feet. Then came the Kyrie Eleison, the familiar prayer for mercy said at every mass, and a final brief exhortation in French.[30]

The references to mercy in the initial exhortation and Kyrie Eleison indicate the priest's intention to comfort the dying by fostering hope for salvation and belief in eternal life. In practice, the conduct of the ceremony was not always as calm as the above prescription would have it. Religious disaffection and rumours of spiritual blackmail by priests led to some tense deathbed scenes and arguments within families about the Church's control over this rite of human passage.

Catholic nobles' writings about death provide information about the extent to which the two contrasting Church messages, about sacrifice and mercy, permeated the minds of the faithful. These messages were not necessarily exclusive of one another. Very often, and particularly in the context of war, the concepts of sacrifice and mercy are mingled in interesting ways within nobles' writings. Just a few days before her mother's death the comtesse Greffulhe wrote: 'O Lord, have pity on us', suggesting she looked upon God as a benign and merciful figure. A similar view was frequently expressed in the letters of the baronne Mathilde de Mackau. As a girl Mathilde received guidance from a confessor, choosing the abbé Langénieux when the priest selected by her mother, according to her preferences as a Spanish noblewoman, proved to have little empathy for a young and enquiring mind. At eighteen years Mathilde read the lectures of Henri Lacordaire and was enraptured by their revelation of a benevolent and consoling God who bore little resemblance to the severe and imposing God worshipped by her mother. The relation between Mathilde and her God seemed an extension of her father's tenderness toward her. References to sacrifice were more common in cases where death was associated with heroism, or more potently martyrdom, in the public imagination. Examples are contained in press statements about the death of over one hundred, mostly upper-class, women in the Charity Bazaar fire of 1897, and in Catholic responses to the Battle of Loigny of 1870.[31]

In the event of a death the close ties that Catholic aristocratic families maintained with clerics, nuns, and monks informed the performance of last rites, masses for the repose of the soul, and burial ceremony. A priest's ability to convey the message about God's mercy at the final hour depended largely on the nature of his relations with parishioners. For most people in nineteenth-century France, 'the presence of the priest in their home would be regarded as an exceptional event'.[32] This was not the case among the Catholic nobility. Many aristocratic families received clergy in the home on a regular basis. When a member of the family died their local priest usually administered the last rites and nuns were present at the bedside to offer prayers for the deceased and support for relatives. The appearance of a cross in literary and visual portraits of the body, prayers in Latin on death notices, and condolence letters from nuns and clerics are signs that faith and spiritual community continued to matter, often very intensely, to the nobility. In the wills of nobles bequests to religious communities were frequently made in return for masses for the repose of the soul.[33]

Sources that touch upon death open up questions for historians about the ways in which the lives of individuals are remembered and whether or not those lives enter the historical record. What happened to the personal documents of a noble after their death? Were letters normally included in the terms of a will or was it simply assumed that someone would take responsibility for preserving them within the family? How did such materials end up catalogued in archives for researchers to read? To answer these questions, and to provide some insight into the archiving process, let us return to where this book began with the subject of nobles' family papers.

On 5 October 1924 Mademoiselle Fernande Lafitte wrote to the prince Henri de Béarn about some papers relating to his mother's family, the Talleyrand-Périgord:

Since the death of the prince de Chalais [Élie de Talleyrand-Périgord] in 1883, there has remained here, at the château de Chalais, quite a large store of old documents that the prince d'Arenberg, executor of the will, entrusted to my father, Monsieur Hilaire Lafitte. Sadly for me my father died and four months later, in January of this year, the prince d'Arenberg also passed away. The archivist of the Charente has written to me to ask what will become of these papers and whether they might be left to the state. There are very old documents of interest to the region dating back to the thirteenth century, and a great number of court records and titles concerning the families of the region, as well as some documents of a private nature: correspondence of the Périgord family, personal deeds, marriage contracts, legal records etc. My late father made an initial sorting of the documents when the château was taken over by his commission for elderly care, so as to have restored those articles and plans necessary to ensure the integrity of the bequest. What has remained, therefore, belongs exclusively to the heirs of the prince de Chalais and still awaits partition between them ... I am writing to inform you of this, supposing that you must have inheritance rights by your mother, and will address this same letter to the princesse Pierre d'Arenberg so as to keep you both informed of the situation. I would be grateful to know your position on the matter.[34]

At the time she wrote this letter Fernande Lafitte was still in mourning for her father, hence it was composed on black-bordered stationery. What sort of man was Hilaire Lafitte and why had the archives been entrusted to his care by the prince d'Arenberg back in 1883?

In his will, Élie de Talleyrand-Périgord, who had no surviving children from his marriage, left the château to the hospital at Chalais and some separate funds to his nephews, the princes d'Arenberg.[35] The purpose of the bequest to the hospital was to establish an old people's home in the château for which Hilaire Lafitte would take charge; this home was opened in 1889. Clues to the nature of Lafitte's relationship with the family can be found in a letter he wrote to the prince and princesse de Béarn on 17 September 1888. Lafitte began the letter apologetically for he regretted having missed an opportunity to meet with the prince and princesse during a visit the couple made to the estate.

> I was informed much too late of your visit to Chalais on Saturday and for this reason was not able to come and greet you at the château and to offer my respects to Madame la princesse. It would have been my sincere pleasure to do so. Equally, I only learned yesterday of the pause in your journey at Coutras station where you had to wait for twenty minutes; otherwise I would have met you there and presented Madame Lafitte and my four boys.

This I regret all the more since opportunities to see you both, and especially the princesse with whom I have had the honour of being acquainted for such a long time, are already very rare and this occasion would have been one of the most agreeable and easy. My memories of the Périgord family have remained, Monsieur le prince, of the best and most respectful nature. I will treasure them always … In looking back on the past, as far as my memory permits, I never fail to encounter a thousand and one reasons why I should think of and love the Périgords. It is with profound emotion, Madame la princesse, that I recall the noble figure of Monsieur le duc, your grandfather [Augustin-Hélie de Talleyrand-Périgord], and his great generosity toward all my family, and especially toward me during my student days. I recall those happy days of my childhood when he would come to the château, the boundless joy my brother and I felt in his presence, and his affectionate gestures. I also recall, Madame la princesse, the grace and friendliness that you showed to each of us on your visits as a young girl. Nor can I forget the kindness with which I was received at the *hôtel* in the rue St Dominique when, during my six years of medical study, Monsieur le duc did me the honour of inviting me to dine at his home almost every month. Believe me, Madame la princesse, when I say that such memories can never be erased from my mind. With your gracious permission, I shall always maintain a very lively interest in whatever the future holds for you.[36]

Lafitte's letter depicts his own experiences of space and memory associated with an aristocratic family of which he was not a member either by blood or by marriage. There is an inescapable air of nostalgia to the letter and one rather wonders what Lafitte had unconsciously forgotten, or chosen to omit, in composing such a radiant account. He conveys a strong loyalty to the Talleyrand-Périgords in which the emotional qualities of the relationship, especially with Augustin-Hélie de Talleyrand-Périgord, 'Monsieur le duc', provide a kind of layering over the financial dimension. The latter is only gently and tactfully alluded to in the phrase 'great generosity toward all my family, and especially toward me during my student days'. Augustin-Hélie de Talleyrand-Périgord took a particular interest in education and supported at least twelve children through their schooling as well as providing funds for the establishment of a library in the parish of Maffliers. What is powerfully evident from the letter is the way in which the lives of the two families, the Talleyrand-Périgords and the Lafittes, were entwined through their mutual connection with the Chalais estate. Space and memory lay at the core of a bond that extended over more than one generation. Hilaire Lafitte's daughter was sensitive to this fact, referring to the sentiments of her father in a second letter she wrote to the prince de Béarn on 2 November 1924: 'His affection for all the Périgord family was sincere, an expression of his veneration of the past, and to see the old château of Chalais fall into indifferent hands was something he often deplored.'[37]

At the prince de Béarn's behest in 1924, Fernande Lafitte went to the trouble of obtaining a detailed breakdown of costs for transporting the Talleyrand-Périgord papers over the five-hundred-odd kilometres from Chalais to Paris by train. It was not an inexpensive exercise; the total cost, she estimated, would be around 2,000 francs. Three months later, however, the papers were still at the château. The delay in transporting them was not due primarily to lack of money, although that may have been a contributing factor. Rather, the prince de Béarn and the princesse d'Arenberg could not reach an agreement about who should take possession of the papers. They both wanted them (the princesse claimed the collection should rightfully go to her son who had attained his majority) and neither was prepared to give way to the other. On receiving different sets of instructions from the prince de Béarn and the princesse d'Arenberg there was little that Fernande Lafitte could do. She was caught in the centre of the relatives' disagreement and unable to act for fear of displeasing one of them. Awaiting some form of resolution between the two, Fernande took the least troublesome path and returned the boxes to the room designated for storing the papers in the château.[38] At the same time, however, she took the precautionary step of informing the department of Charente's chief archivist, Burias, of what had taken place in her dealings with the family. He in turn asked the mayor of Chalais to keep an eye on things and let him know of any new developments regarding the papers at the château.

It was Burias who took up the business again, two decades later, after the Second World War. On 18 October 1945 the archivist for the Charente wrote to the director of the Archives nationales de France. The object of his letter was to obtain a solution for the safe preservation of the papers at the château de Chalais. Burias recounted to his senior colleague in Paris that the papers had been left in the care of Lafitte who together with his daughter had been authorised under the terms of the prince d'Arenberg's will to continue living at the château for the remainder of their lives. He also told the director of how Fernande had been perplexed by the difficulty of attaining some form of agreement between the two relatives. Fernande was an elderly woman by 1945 and it was she who was once again trying to get the issue of the family papers resolved, probably fearing that in the event of her death they might just be forgotten or irreparably damaged through neglect. The mayor of Chalais had informed

Burias of Fernande's concerns. Burias himself had his own opinion of what should happen:

> It seems to me that there is good reason to keep these archives in the Charente and in the department's archival store. They do not directly concern the heirs ... I do not have precise information on the volume of the archives. Apparently they take up about one half of one cubic metre. If the archives are to be transported out of the Charente please provide me with guidance on the appropriate course of action. Perhaps if you were to send letters to the heirs, a happy solution might be found? Given the advanced age of Mademoiselle Lafitte, these documents will sooner or later be left abandoned and at risk of being lost or damaged. The current conditions of conservation are far from ideal in the château, which is in quite a bad state of disrepair after this long war.[39]

The archives of the Talleyrand-Périgord entered the collection of the Archives départementales de la Charente in 1972, as a donation from the abbé Ducouret. Seven years later in 1979, via donation from Monsieur Esclafer, the papers of Hilaire and Fernande Lafitte were added to these same *fonds*. What documents remain therefore of the lives of the Talleyrand-Périgord and Lafitte families in respect to the château de Chalais are inventoried and preserved together.

No doubt this book would have been written differently if the personal papers of servants employed in aristocratic households were stored at the Archives nationales or in departmental archives. What the possibilities might be for writing a history based on such documents must remain a matter of speculation. There is some evidence available, in the form of letters and oral accounts, to suggest a history of aristocratic families told from the servants' perspective might complement or challenge the history told in this book.[40]

In the archives of the La Rochefoucauld family is a set of letters that reveals slippage in the way that nobles and their working-class employees perceived their relationship. Whilst there are gaps in this documentation, letters that have not survived and were either lost or intentionally omitted from the archive, the letters that have been kept by the La Rochefoucaulds convey a deep sadness about a form of loss that was unexpected, and shocking, for them. Importantly, these historical documents are not about a way of life that 'ended' with the 1789 Revolution, or with the agricultural crisis of the late nineteenth century, or with the First World War – powerfully destabilising and traumatic as each of those episodes was for nobles and for many other people. Rather, it is a way of life,

8 Alcove in the prince's bedroom at the château de Chalais (1977)

conducted within 'a closed world' of 'customs and illusions', that aristocratic families were still striving 'to preserve to the extreme' on the eve of the Second World War.

In October 1939 Jules Faisandier took leave from the employ of the comte and comtesse Xavier de La Rochefoucauld to join the 331st regiment of the second batallion of state infantry. The world war then breaking was anticipated to be prolonged and bloody, so it was not clear either to Jules or to the La Rochefoucaulds when or if he would come back. Marie Gillard, who had been employed since April of that year as the cook in the La Rochefoucauld household, also decided to depart at around the same time as Jules. She took up a new post in the home of Madame Lambert Champy who lived near the town of Romorantin (Loir-et-Cher), not far from the La Rochefoucaulds' estate at Pellevoisin. Both Jules and Marie had possessions, not a great amount between them, but some of what they owned in the way of clothing and other personal belongings was at Pellevoisin and some at their employers'

Parisian residence in the rue Daru. Jules, who did not have time to return to Paris before joining his regiment, asked Marie to take responsibility for his possessions, for he knew that she was planning to resign from her post as cook and would need to go to the rue Daru to collect her own things. Jules did not, however, inform the comte and comtesse de La Rochefoucauld of the arrangements he had made with Marie for her to take charge of what he owned.

Xavier de La Rochefoucauld wrote to Jules on 17 October concerning what he knew of Marie Gillard's intentions:

> She insisted on going to Paris to move her possessions, collect some important personal papers, and bring back the winter clothing she needs. She requested the key to your room at rue Daru where, she told us, there are items she must also collect for you. The comtesse and I are not aware of the nature of those items. It seems to be a matter of understanding between you both.[41]

The comte felt uncertain and rather concerned about this state of affairs. Jules Faisandier had been in his employment for many years. Marie, by contrast, had been the family's cook only for a few months. He could not be sure that what she told him of Jules's wishes was correct and true. Moreover he and the comtesse were surprised: 'You [Jules] have not mentioned anything to us on this subject. [Marie] told us that she would write to you for your written confirmation of what she has said.'[42] Wanting some direct word from Jules, and recognising that postal delays were likely, Xavier enclosed with his letter the means for him to send a forty-word telegram. He asked that this contain a short message to confirm that the arrangements of which Marie had spoken were *bona fide*: 'I authorise Marie Gillard to remove all my belongings that I have left either in my room at rue Daru or in my room at Pellevoisin. Jules Faisandier.'[43] In concluding his letter the comte gave Jules some news regarding the La Rochefoucauld family, the accommodation of Alsacian refugees at Pellevoisin, and the requisitioning of a nearby property as a hospital. He expressed hope that Jules was doing well.

On Monday 30 October, within a few hours of Marie's scheduled departure, the comte de La Rochefoucauld received a letter from Jules written on the 24th in the place of the requested telegram. Jules explained that he did not wish the comte to go to any personal trouble regarding his belongings: 'I gave Marie complete permission to mind my affairs and I showed her various things that I may have need of here and of which she alone has understanding.'[44] By the time Jacques's letter arrived, however, Xavier's anxiety at not receiving word from Jules had already led him, on Friday 27th, to ask Marie whether she had received anything. He explained to Jules on 3 November:

> She replied that she had received a letter dated 18 October and spontaneously offered to show it to us; hence we know of its existence. This letter notably contained this phrase: 'Bring the money as well as everything else you can, my letters above all. I don't believe that after the war I will have the courage to return to their service.' Confronted with your wishes, so clearly expressed, we could only assent and, with Marie Gillard's agreement, we obtained a certified testament from the notary at Pellevoisin ... It is hardly worth saying that Madame la comtesse and I were extremely hurt and surprised by the terms of your letter to Marie Gillard. We were quite oblivious to the idea that your presence in our household had been so particularly disagreeable for you that it would require real 'courage' to return. Whatever the facts of the matter, and whatever your feelings towards us may be, we retain nothing less than excellent memories of the many years you have spent in our service, in the course of which we believe to have shown you, in all circumstances, not only great kindness but also affection.[45]

The comte de La Rochefoucauld was clearly stung. He had an almost paternal regard for Jules Faisandier, and was completely taken aback by the revelation of the servant's true feelings. Xavier wrote to Jules's father at Latour in the Loire valley with whom he had previously exchanged correspondence on the subject of a nose operation Jules had needed. A draft of this letter is in the archive and the multiple crossings out suggest the comte struggled to find words to express his dismay. Under the impression that the young man had left Pellevoisin on the best of terms with them, he and the comtesse were, he wrote, 'very upset by the decision Jules has taken'.[46] Faisandier senior, for his part, replied that his son had 'acted very badly if, after so many years of service, his intentions have caused hurt to you and Madame la comtesse, and this is painful for us'.[47]

It was two months before Jules Faisandier himself replied to Xavier de La Rochefoucauld's letter of 3 November and when he did it was to send greetings and best wishes for the New Year. This letter, unfortunately, is not in the archive but there is a copy of Xavier's reply written on 4 January 1940:

> My dear Jules
>
> Thank you for your kind letter received on the morning of the 1 January; it brought great pleasure to myself and to Madame la comtesse. Rest

assured, all is forgotten. A moment of thoughtlessness is understandable and readily excused. Let us speak no more of it. For us it is as if nothing had happened, and you remain, as always, our dear, loyal Jules . . . We are in the midst of an exceptionally cold winter. It must be the same in your region; we hope that you are not suffering too much because of it. Have you been granted leave yet? You know that your room at the Hermitage awaits you.[48]

We do not know whether the infantry soldier ever did have the courage to go back to the La Rochefoucauld household. The comte and comtesse may have erased from their minds the true sentiments of the person they wanted to believe was 'our dear, loyal Jules'. For the former servant it was more difficult to forget.

Notes

1 22 May 1883 in AP 156 (I)/298 Fonds Mackau.
2 23 May 1883 in AP 156 (I)/298 Fonds Mackau.
3 19 December 1885 in AP 156 (I)/304 Fonds Mackau.
4 19 January 1886 in AP 156 (I)/302 Fonds Mackau.
5 Thomas Kselman, *Death and the Afterlife in Modern France* (Princeton, 1993); Philippe Ariès, *L'Homme devant la mort* (Paris, 1977); Julia Hirsch, *Family Photographs: Content, Meaning and Effect* (Oxford, 1981).
6 Jonathan Dewald, *The European Nobility* 1400–1800 (Cambridge, 1996), pp. 9, 13.
7 Dewald, *The European Nobility* 1400–1800, pp. 7–14; Alexis de Tocqueville, *Democracy in America*, ed. J. P. Mayer (New York, 1969).
8 Robert Forster, *The House of Saulx-Tavanes: Versailles and Burgundy, 1700–1830* (Baltimore, 1971), ch. 5 and conclusion.
9 Mark Girouard, *Life in the French Country House* (London, 2000), p. 325.
10 Girouard, *Life*, p. 325.
11 Boni de Castellane, *Mémoires* (Paris, 1986), p. 23.
12 Alys Hallard, *American Nobility: From the French of Pierre de Coulevain* (New York, 1913), p. 320.
13 8 April 1890 in AP 353/85 Fonds Caumont La Force.
14 6 June 1891 in AP 101 (I)/28 Fonds Gramont.
15 20 June 1927 in AP 101 (I)/28 Fonds Gramont.
16 'Histoire vraie d'une petite fille heureuse 1860 Bois-Boudran' in AP 101 (I)/55 Fonds Gramont.
17 'Disparation de ma mère, à relire avec mes soeurs' in AP 101 (II)/39 Fonds Gramont.
18 AP 101 (II)/38 Fonds Gramont.

19 31 March 1884 in AP 31/69 Fonds Murat.
20 Comtesse de Pange, *Comment j'ai vu 1900* (Paris, 1962), p. 16; Anne d'Uzès, *Souvenirs de la duchesse d'Uzès née Mortemart*, préface de son petit-fils le comte de Cossé-Brissac (Paris, 1939), pp. 1–2.
21 Patrick de Gmeline, *La Duchesse d'Uzès (1847–1933)* (Paris, 1986), pp. 31–3, 81.
22 Jesse Goldhammer, *The Headless Republic: Sacrificial Violence in Modern French Thought* (Ithaca, 2005), pp. 5, 71.
23 Goldhammer, *The Headless Republic*, p. 71.
24 Raymond Jonas, *France and the Cult of the Sacred Heart: An Epic Tale for Modern Times* (Ewing, 2000), pp. 158–68; Elizabeth C. Macknight, 'Honor and the military formation of French noblemen 1870–1920', *Historical Reflections/Réflexions Historiques* 35 (2009), 95–114.
25 Claude Langlois, *Le Catholicisme au féminin: les congrégations françaises à supérieure générale au XIXe siècle* (Paris, 1984); Ralph Gibson, *A Social History of French Catholicism*, 1789–1914 (London, 1989), pp. 251–4, 267.
26 Ralph Gibson, 'De la prédication de la peur à la vision d'un dieu d'amour – La prédication en Périgord aux XVIIe–XIXe siècles' in *Le Jugement, le ciel, et l'enfer dans l'histoire du christianisme* Actes de la douzième rencontre d'histoire religieuse tenue à Fontevraud les 14 et 15 octobre 1988 (Angers, 1989), pp. 153–67.
27 Kselman, *Death and the Afterlife*, pp. 70–2.
28 Kselman, *Death and the Afterlife*, pp. 82–3.
29 Kselman, *Death and the Afterlife*, pp. 84–8.
30 Kselman, *Death and the Afterlife*, p. 91.
31 Elizabeth C. Macknight, 'Faiths, fortunes, and feminine duty: charity in Parisian high society, 1880–1914', *Journal of Ecclesiastical History* 58 (2007), 482–506; Macknight, 'Honor', pp. 95–114.
32 Kselman, *Death and the Afterlife*, p. 90.
33 Adeline Daumard, 'Une enquête sur la noblesse à Paris au XIXe siècle', *Cahiers du centre de recherches historiques* 3 (1989), 27–38; Claire Biquard, 'Piété et foi dans le Faubourg Saint-Germain au XIXe siècle', *Histoire, économie et société* 2 (1993), 299–318; Macknight, 'Faiths', pp. 482–506.
34 5 October 1924 in AP 69/2 Fonds Béarn de Chalais.
35 Georges Martin, *Histoire et généalogie de la maison de Talleyrand-Périgord* (La Ricamarie, 2009), pp. 102–3.
36 17 September 1888 in AP 69/2 Fonds Béarn de Chalais. Martin, *Histoire et généalogie de la maison de Talleyrand-Périgord*, pp. 99–101.
37 2 November 1924 in AP 69/2 Fonds Béarn de Chalais.
38 2 November 1924 and 8 February 1925 in AP 69/2 Fonds Béarn de Chalais.
39 18 October 1945 in AP 69/2 Fonds Béarn de Chalais.
40 Michel Chabot, *Histoire de Jean et Yvonne domestiques en 1900, racontée par Paul, leur fils, à Michel, son petit-fils* (Paris, 1988); Geneviève Fraisse (in collaboration with Martine Guillin), *Femmes toutes mains: essai sur le service domestique, recherches, discussions, documentation et interviews* (Paris, 1979).

Pierre Guiral and Guy Thuillier, *La Vie quotidienne des domestiques en France au XIXe siècle* (Paris, 1978).

41 17 October 1939 in AP 142/13 Fonds Xavier de La Rochefoucauld.
42 17 October 1939 in AP 142/13 Fonds Xavier de La Rochefoucauld.
43 17 October 1939 in AP 142/13 Fonds Xavier de La Rochefoucauld.
44 24 October 1939 with handwritten note: 'reçue le 30 à 11hr; Marie partait à 2hr' in AP 142/13 Fonds Xavier de La Rochefoucauld.
45 3 November 1939 in AP 142/13 Fonds Xavier de La Rochefoucauld.
46 3 November 1939 to Faisandier senior in AP 142/13 Fonds Xavier de La Rochefoucauld.
47 8 November 1939 in AP 142/13 Fonds Xavier de La Rochefoucauld.
48 4 January 1940 in AP 142/13 Fonds Xavier de La Rochefoucauld.

Conclusion

'It's a boy! It's a boy!'[1] For the duchesse de Sabran-Pontevès, these simple words meant a very great deal. Her deepest desire during first pregnancy was to deliver a son who would possess the name, and later inherit the title, of her husband Foulques, comte (later duc) de Sabran-Pontevès. Motivated by this desire she read history during the pregnancy. She reflected in particular upon the history of the aristocratic family into which she had married. 'In drawing upon the examples there I hoped to serve better the memory of those whose tradition and name I had been called to continue.'[2] The duchesse gave birth to the couple's first son on the morning of 30 April 1937 in the Villecresnes clinic. The boy was baptised Elzéar, which was his paternal grandfather's name, and also the name of a more distant ancestor, Elzéar de Sabran, who in 1266 had taken part in the Naples expedition initiated by Charles I of Anjou. The duchesse de Sabran-Pontevès gave birth to a second son, Jean, on 15 January 1939 and to a third son, Géraud, on 18 March 1940. With their three children and a nurse the couple joined the exodus from Villecresnes in the summer of 1940 as the German troops advanced into France. There was a fourth addition to the family, a baby girl baptised Gersende, who was delivered without a doctor present in a house where telephone wires had been cut on 26 August 1943. Foulques's parents died during the exodus, his brother Jean was killed in battle, and Foulques himself was maimed so badly in the fighting that he became a permanent invalid.

Four decades after Elzéar's birth, on 2 August 1977, an *arrêté* authorising the inscription of the successor to the title of comte de Sabran-Pontevès on the Registre du Sceau was issued by the Ministère de la

Justice. Whilst the name and title of this aristocratic family had survived into the Fifth Republic, many others did not. In 1900 it is estimated that there were 5,033 aristocratic families in France; by 1975 the number had shrunk to 4,057. This rate of extinction – 19 per cent over seventy-five years – reflects the lack of sons to perpetuate some noble bloodlines. The presence of just one male in 257 aristocratic families put those bloodlines at strong risk of extinction in the 1970s.[3]

This demographic attrition among the twentieth-century nobility must be seen within the context of two world wars that sharply reduced the numbers of men in the French population as a whole, skewed the ratio of women to men, and had far-reaching consequences for gender relations that rippled out over subsequent decades. The 1921 census in France recorded 6.2 million women and 5.1 million men in the age bracket of 20–39 years; large numbers of women did not marry as a result of the shortage of men. Nationally the birth rate remained low, with 2.05 being the average number of offspring for French couples in 1935.

For noblemen, stories of ancestors' military heroism and achievements had long created particular pressure to serve with distinction in the army. Fathers and grandfathers played a key role in the transmission of military values, as did the Jesuits in their colleges. After France's defeat by the Prussians in the war of 1870–71, wider societal forces increased the weight of expectation too. During the early Third Republic, when the Catholic Church was under siege and the conservative right was losing ground to the republicans, the aristocracy cultivated an ideal of military manhood that its men were expected to fulfil. Defending a distinctive notion of honour 'in the blood' was important to nobles in those politically turbulent decades when bourgeois elites were promoting a secular republican brand of hero capable of restoring national glory.[4]

Yet this determination to retain the aristocracy's cultural authority in the profession of arms was fraught with complication and risk. The virulent anti-Semitism with which the conservative right in general, and the French officer class in particular, lashed out against Dreyfus in the 1890s was inflected for those who were noble with fears and insecurities about their own 'race' and heterosexual virility. The public's obsession with depopulation, degeneracy, and national honour fed anxieties about masculinity widely in French society during this period.[5] For noblemen the tensions over honour 'in the blood' were insuperable. Some of them were marrying rich Jewish women, which in 1898 it was said, 'prevents their claiming to be part of *la noblesse française*: that of Agincourt and of Denain'. In 1914 another pamphleteer quipped 'It is no longer the [Almanach du] Gotha – it is the *Goldgotha!!*'[6] Moreover, the concern to uphold aristocratic military reputations and remind the public of nobles' heritage of ancestral accomplishment heightened the threat of bloodlines becoming extinct. On 15 August 1914 Joachim Murat wrote to his wife Cécile about a decision she had made in light of the national call-up: 'Dearest, how I admire your courage – you speak of sending Louis [the couple's second youngest son] as well? You are right. [Our sons] are worthy of the blood that runs in the veins'.[7] For the nobility, raised on messages from relatives and the Church about duty and sacrifice, heroic death on the battlefield represented a pinnacle of male aspiration. It was precisely this form of sacrifice that could spell a family's eclipse. On hearing that the marquis de Saint-Loup was killed in action, Proust's Narrator grieves for a man who 'throughout his life ... had seemed to be restraining an impulse to charge' and who 'died more himself than ever before, or rather more a member of his race, into which slowly he dissolved until he became nothing more than a Guermantes'.[8]

War was not the only reason for demographic attrition among the twentieth-century nobility. The Third Republic saw the introduction of new legislation that contributed to the fall in the number of aristocratic families. Although birth rates were high for noble couples – with 3.2 offspring being the average and 4.4 for practising Catholics in the first three decades of the twentieth century – the decree issued on 14 December 1906, that the French government would no longer create new titles or authorise foreign titles meant there was no replacement to noble stock when a bloodline became extinct. The fall in numbers was already apparent during the nineteenth century when there were not enough new titles being created quickly enough to offset the extinction of older ones.[9] High fertility was thus crucial to nobles since it increased the likelihood of at least one son being born and was the only way to sustain the number of individuals of noble descent, in the face of a gradual reduction in the number of families.

Political circumstances that closed off recruitment to noble status, which was the effect of the 1906 decree, were not without historical precedent in Europe. In the Dutch Republic, for example, the noble population diminished through the seventeenth and eighteenth centuries when new titles were not being created. The rate of decline varied from province to province but the pattern was essentially the same. Holland had twenty-one aristocratic families in 1650 dropping to six by 1730; Friesland had fifty-eight aristocratic families in 1600 but only thirty-four in 1700; Groningen had forty-five in 1600 but only ten by 1800, and so on. Only when the Dutch Republic ended was this trend reversed. The Orange Monarchy recommenced ennoblement among leading landowners and established regent families in the early nineteenth century.[10]

In the France of the Third Republic, the potential for monarchy to be restored became ever fainter with the electoral defeats for conservatives in the late 1870s, the death of the comte de Chambord in 1883, and the law on exile in 1886. Of course members of the aristocracy blamed one another, as well as blaming republicans, for this situation: the rivalry between Orléanists and Legitimists had not helped the cause for restoration. Within this context, however, nobles such as Maillé and Gouvello continued to educate sons and daughters about monarchism and about masculine and feminine duties within a patriarchal Christian order. Monarchism was a tradition and set of convictions to which many noblemen and noblewomen remained passionately committed.[11] They perpetuated the 'silent but persistent struggle' against republicanism through the educative strategies of their families. In aristocratic households those strategies were designed to equip sons with the ambition to hold political office and the self-belief to stand for election. For monarchists as well as for Bonapartists conserving political traditions within the home was key to promoting the 'permanence of dynasties' in local and national politics.

When the republican government sought to increase state control in childrearing and education, for example through the 1874 Roussel law on wet nursing and the Ferry laws of 1880–82, the aristocracy responded by using explicit messages about gendered parental roles as the basis for political counter-attack. Noblemen argued that republican legislation usurped the *chef de famille*'s authority to 'govern' his family; they were defending the concept of patriarchal rule that was historically core to aristocratic social theory and to nobles' vision of Christian doctrine. Noblewomen argued that mothers had a duty to teach children Christian values and that wives needed to respect the authority of their husbands in accordance with God's will interpreted within papal encyclicals. At the same time, aristocratic families continued to perform their private functions in the teeth of a regime that was intent on demeaning and outlawing the resources and values that they so highly prized. The drive to assist the embattled Catholic Church, morally and financially, was congruent with aristocratic aims to protect the command of capital in the next generation. Nobles already had mutually supportive relationships with clerics, monks, and nuns who were involved in children's instruction and helped cultivate ideals of masculinity and femininity in adolescents.

Regular contact between aristocratic families and clergy helped to underpin the formation of pressure groups promoting Catholic motherhood and the rights of *pères de famille* as the government pushed forward with its policies for secularisation. Through high-level Church contacts, public speaking, publications, local networking, and their own domestic practices nobles deployed social and cultural capital to oppose republican goals in gendered and politicised ways.

They did so at a time when for a range of reasons their command of economic capital was slipping and under renewed political threat. The value of land fell by one-third between 1880 and 1912 and, although the proposals from the left for a tax on titles were never implemented, new taxes on inheritance (1901) and income (1914) added to the financial pressure caused by inflation during and after the First World War. Moreover, the early Third Republic brought new obstacles to the transmission of titles and the end of the *majorat* system. Such measures continued a series of legislative interventions on nobiliary matters that had punctuated the nineteenth century. By abolishing the Conseil du Sceau in 1872, then discontinuing recruitment to the position of *référendaire au sceau* by decree in 1891, the republican government made specialist knowledge of titles and nobiliary law more rare among those with administrative responsibility in the area. Nobles seeking verification of a title continued to pay the fee for *droits de sceau*, which was updated in the Fourth and Fifth Republics through new laws on finance passed on 8 August 1947 (article 65) and on 27 December 1968 (article 82).[12] The 1905 law on finances that approved the state buyback of *majorats* meant that the remaining holders of this form of entail became eligible to receive compensation. In the 1940s the Massa *majorat*, the last of these entails to survive in France, was still the subject of legal and bureaucratic complications with no procedure in place for indemnity payment.

Concerns over property, of course, have historically always been alive among nobles in Europe. In Spain the perpetual and hereditary entail known as the *mayorazgo* – far more ancient than the Napoleonic *majorat* for it was legally codified in the 1505 Laws of Toro – was abolished in 1836. The following year saw the abolition of the lay lordships (*señorío*), which also dated back to the Middle Ages. The Spanish aristocracy thus lost the stability of income provided by the *mayorazgo* but cash compensation for ancient *señorial* rights restored liquid funds at a time when these nobles were competing with other investors for free property (*bienes libres*).[13] French nobles in 1905 did not reap financial recompense in this way.

For French aristocratic families generally, and for practising Catholics especially, the desire for many offspring sat uneasily against the knowledge of the awkward implications for their estates due to the 1791 law on partible inheritance. By trying to produce sons to perpetuate the aristocratic bloodline, the potential for 'war between brothers and sisters' over inheritance was exacerbated. A similar problem can be observed in early modern Denmark where the Danish law on inheritance stipulated that daughters should inherit property but only half as much as sons. Danish nobles tried to get around the problem of estate fragmentation by accumulating more land so that the property holdings passed on to each child were bigger.[14] In France, however, it made more sense for nobles to shift investment away from land during the late nineteenth century. High fertility indicates that protection of the name (social capital) was the most important priority for nobles. This factor set aristocratic family strategies apart from others. A contrast exists, for example, with the strategies of rural workers who owned small landholdings. For them it was imperative to protect economic capital by keeping farms intact so this motivated couples to limit the number of children they had in the nineteenth century.[15]

Nobles' concern to protect names and bloodlines, whilst at the same time trying to offset financial difficulties, also informed the continuities in aristocratic marital strategies in the Third Republic. The nobility retained a strong rate of endogamy – calculated at 0.86 for marriages contracted in the period 1850–1918 dropping to 0.75 in the period 1919–45 – with 'exceptions' made for men, principally younger male siblings, to form lucrative marriages with wealthy commoners. Noblewomen in the nineteenth century had equal rights to inherit property but, as in earlier times, the 'rules' set by kin imposed tighter limits for them over the selection of a spouse in order to safeguard social capital. When it was difficult to dower a daughter, or to find a suitable husband for her, nobles made 'choices' that conformed to the logic of their conditioning and the historical practice of tying court service and monasticism into family strategy.[16] Instead of marrying the Protestant Hottinguer, Ghislaine de Caraman-Chimay remained single and became a *dame d'honneur* at the Belgian court; others entered convents in which they often held senior roles like Blanche de Béarn, Soeur Vincent Supérieure de la Miséricorde in Rouen. The female aristocracy had to be knowledgeable about lineage and dynastic strategy because they cared about the survival of their 'race'. Noblewomen often took the lead in negotiating marital alliances, although the decision-making process involved senior relatives of both sexes.

Invested in noblewomen too was the primary responsibility for transmitting the cultural capital of 'distinction' to younger members of their families. Grandparents helped parents to instil values, discipline, and an understanding of the family's heritage. Educative strategies supported this transmission process so that, in addition to scholastic instruction from governesses and *précepteurs*, children spent time with senior relatives learning more than 'the dry content of textbooks'. Distinction was capital exercised through the body with different codes for each sex. Through the elegance of their language, gesture, poise, and demeanour, nobles were considered to express the inner 'natural' quality of aristocratic breeding. Deployment of this capital relied on public performance in all the many rituals of aristocratic sociability. It was supported by the conspicuous consumption of maintaining a large household. In their interactions with servants, nobles practised on a daily basis the 'theatre of rule'.

We can see then that all the multiple dimensions of an aristocratic family – 'simultaneously a lineage, a historical legacy tied to specific fiefs, a nuclear family, a kin group interwoven with other equally ambitious dynasties, and a financial enterprise' – are relevant for understanding nobles' tactics for preserving command of capital in the France of the Third Republic.[17] To reproduce itself an aristocratic family employed a series of interconnected strategies that resemble the strategies Bourdieu observed among the Kabylians and Béarnais. Matrimonial and inheritance strategies were designed to protect and transmit patrimony; fertility strategies were designed 'to produce as many men as possible as quickly as possible'; and educative strategies were designed to inculcate 'an exalted adherence to the lineage and to the values of honour'.[18] Of course, family strategies do not work optimally all of the time at any level of society. Bourdieu's metaphor of the difference between a hand of cards and the way it is played captures the blend of shrewd decision-making and luck involved in familial reproduction.[19] To understand the evolution of aristocratic family strategies it is necessary to look across the broad political, social, and economic landscape, without losing sight of 'the varying impact different family members had on familial decisions'.[20] Both sexes had to navigate the currents of circumstance that could push an aristocratic family either towards dynastic prosperity and longevity or towards material failure and ultimate extinction.[21]

In nearly every part of Europe – with the exception of Poland-Lithuania – the nobility survived into the twentieth century despite considerable threats and pressures. The situation in France was distinctive because of the intense blows that the nobility and the Catholic Church had experienced in 1789–91. It is all the more telling, therefore, that aristocratic families retained a significant presence in French society and made substantial contributions to political, cultural, and intellectual developments throughout what has been dubbed the 'bourgeois century'.[22]

The convention among historians has been to ignore or underestimate French nobles' capacity to tackle the formidable challenges to their way of life, convictions, and identities in the France of the Third Republic. Within this vein of interpretation the 1789 Revolution had set in motion a process whereby the aristocracy was transformed into a 'shrivelling caste', a 'dwindling band of martyrs' who accepted their own demise because there was 'no resisting' the advance of republican ideals and democracy.[23] This book has argued to the contrary that nobles in the Third Republic actively responded to attempts to undermine or remove their command of capital in all its forms. The many and varied acts of resistance to republican goals documented in *archives privées* contradict the notion of nobles stoically accepting decline. There is extensive evidence over the period from 1870 to 1940 not only that noblemen and noblewomen defended their own family's interests and projects but also that some of them led much wider social movements to campaign against republican initiatives and secularising policies.

Historians' investment in the notion of a triumphant republican bourgeois culture has led to condescending remarks about the nobility and served to limit investigation of this social group.[24] This reluctance to engage seriously with the subject of nobility is paradoxical since there were half a million bourgeois false nobles in the Third Republic and the aspirations of the bourgeoisie were firmly centred upon aristocratic distinction and mimicking nobles' lifestyle. Part of the reason nobles continued to exert authority and influence in the France of the nineteenth and twentieth centuries was that there were people from all classes who respected and cultivated social hierarchies through their attitudes and behaviours. Certainly the very ancient dynamics of deference no longer functioned in the way that they had done before 1789.[25] Yet for every sign that the French nation was attempting to fashion itself along democratic lines, there was a countersign of the longstanding fascination with the nature, value, and uses of aristocratic capital. The names and titles of nobility evoked a world that was not the world the republican government sought to create. They evoked a culture that was not the culture of a secular France. They evoked principles that were not the principles of egalitarian democracy.

The resilience of conservative ideologies that became powerfully evident during the interwar decades and the Vichy regime should make historians more, not less, attentive to nobles' participation in public debates and to the roles that these men and women played in the political, social, and intellectual life of modern France. Conservative attitudes about gender roles dominated legislators' policy-making, political propaganda, and large elements of cultural production after the First World War. The harsh new laws against abortion passed in 1920 and 1923 were one sign of the aim of preventing women from aspiring to anything beyond domesticity and motherhood. In rare instances an aristocratic woman did become interested in the aims of female emancipation, as the duchesse d'Uzès did through her contact with the English-born feminist Jeanne Schmahl. But even d'Uzès's support for female suffrage in 1911 was couched in terms of a woman's roles within the home. Other noblewomen of her generation, as the leaders of Catholic women's organisations, publicly distanced themselves from feminism and poured scorn on women with career aspirations that might distract from motherhood that was perceived to be the most sacred feminine duty.[26] This was not a tiny elitist movement in which they were involved. In 1932 the Ligue Patriotique des Françaises and the Ligue des Femmes Françaises agreed to merge. Together they formed the Ligue Féminine d'Action Catholique Française that had two million members by 1939.[27]

The longstanding emphasis on 'race' in European aristocratic thought assumed ever-increasing force in the political sphere. According to Proust, by the end of the First World War, 'there no longer were Dreyfusards in politics' so that 'Brichot himself, that great nationalist, when he alluded to the Dreyfus case now talked of "those pre-historic days"'.[28] Yet the sentiments of the conservative right in the 1890s were far from forgotten, and connections have been drawn between nationalism and anti-Semitism at the time of the Dreyfus Affair, interwar fascism, and the Vichy government's collaboration with Nazi Germany.[29] Pétain's authoritarian parliamentary regime, which promoted a traditional family model with the father as head, paralleled the longstanding belief among Catholic monarchists that the foundation for monarchic government lay in households structured on patriarchal lines. The formation of right-wing political groups from the turn of the century helps to explain the origin of some of the support for such a leader. There were nobles who became involved in, or favoured the aims of, organisations such as Charles Maurras's L'Action française and Colonel de la Roque's Les Croix-de-feu. When the Vatican condemned L'Action française in 1926 the condemnation caused divisions within aristocratic families with members having to choose whether they owed fidelity to the pope or to Maurras. For other nobles the shame of France's defeat in 1940 motivated them to oppose Pétain and become resisters.[30]

Race remained a sensitive issue among the nobility, especially at times of escalating international tension. In 1914 the author of *Droit de la Race supérieure* claimed that children 'noble by one buttock, Jewish by the other' would be the legacy of intermarriage 'because Israel is prolific!'[31] An article published in *Au Pilori* on 8 July 1943 listed the names of nobles who had married Jewish women and asked: 'As a result of this crossbreeding, has the French aristocracy remained Aryan or has it become Jewish?'[32] That such an article should be kept in the archives of an aristocratic diplomat is indicative of the emotional impact such writings could have for nobles in the corrosive social environment of Vichy France where 'choices' very often had lethal consequences.

In 2011 a wealth of scholarship exists on the subject of nobility from the Middle Ages through to the late twentieth century and exciting comparative research is being done. Too often, however, historians pay minimal attention to the interdependency of gender roles and may refer to noblewomen only to illustrate a point about marriage. Such an approach is problematic for advancing historical knowledge about nobility. It avoids key issues relating to the exercise of power. It overlooks the fact that in their daily lives and long-term ambitions aristocratic women and men relied upon, struggled against, competed with, and showed affection and desire for one another. In the domestic environment as well as in their public roles nobles had to negotiate the jealousies, thrills, and competitiveness of a social world suffused with sexuality. Expressions of enmity and revenge are a fertile field for historical investigation.[33] So too are expressions of friendship, eroticism, and love of kin.[34]

A core aim of this book has been to demonstrate the value of *archives privées* for writing modern French history and there is every reason to believe that further investigation of similar archives in other countries is a productive way forward for researchers working on gender roles within the European nobility. For a historian to suggest that research in family archives is too laborious, too time-consuming, and therefore 'quite impossible' is disconcerting from a professional point of view; so too is the argument that such research 'virtually precludes any appreciation of the broader ebb and flow of historical process'.[35] With so much still to learn about the intricacies of interest and emotion, as well as about gender and the dynamics of power within families, archival research is more essential than ever. 'Otherwise, we may find ourselves at the very outset, when it makes all the difference, denying contemporaries the opportunity to speak as clearly, freely, and fully of their times as they might.'[36]

Over one hundred and fifty years have passed since the French archivist Henri Bordier wrote that 'the most precious documents' in family archives are 'the letters and writings of all kinds' that complement titles, deeds, and accounts dating back to the Middle Ages.[37] In drawing upon a wide array of those documents this book has shown that aristocratic families, whilst they wished 'to ignore the passing of time' in the France of the Third Republic, were in fact adapting and responding constantly to changes imposed by the world around them. This pattern of gradual adaptation, always with an eye to ensuring the persistence of noble traditions, continued the pattern of their ancestors.[38] The challenges that French nobles faced between 1870 and 1940 were undoubtedly difficult and discomforting for them. There are abundant expressions of distaste for and regret about some of the transformations they witnessed in France during those decades. Yet one also finds in the archives nobles' expressions of hope and anticipation about possibilities and projects that, for them, lay in the future. To a degree that most people could only dream of, aristocratic men, women, and children understood what it meant 'to have'.

Notes

1 Duchesse de Sabran-Pontevès, *Bon sang ne peut mentir* (Paris, 1987), p. 287.
2 Sabran-Pontevès, *Bon sang*, p. 191.
3 Alain Texier, *Qu'est-ce que la noblesse?* (Paris, 1988), pp. 137, 409.
4 Elizabeth C. Macknight, 'Honor and the military formation of French noblemen, 1870–1920', *Historical Reflections/Réflexions/Historiques* 35 (2009), 95–114; Paul Gerbod, 'L'Ethique héroique en France (1870–1914)', *Revue historique* 268 (1983), 409–12.
5 Christopher E. Forth, *The Dreyfus Affair and the Crisis of French Manhood* (Baltimore, 2004); Robert A. Nye, 'Honor, impotence, and male sexuality in nineteenth-century French medicine', *French Historical Studies* 16 (1989), 48–71.
6 David Higgs, *Nobles in Nineteenth-Century France: The Practice of Inegalitarianism* (Baltimore, 1989), p. 28; Urbain Gohier, *Droit de la Race supérieure* (1914) cited in Georges Maurevert, *Fisc et blason ou l'impôt sur la vanité* (Paris, 1923), pp. 61–2.
7 15 August 1914 in AP 31/71 Fonds Murat. Louis Murat was killed in action in 1916. On the importance attached to 'courage' for both sexes in this period

see Robert A. Nye, *Masculinity and Male Codes of Honor in Modern France* (Oxford, 1993), pp. 216–28.
8 Marcel Proust, *In Search of Lost Time* vol. 6 *Time Regained* trans. Andreas Mayor and Terence Kilmartin, revised by D. J. Enright (London, 1996), p. 197.
9 Higgs, *Nobles*, p. 219.
10 J. L. Price, 'The Dutch nobility in the seventeenth and eighteenth centuries' in H. M. Scott (ed.), *The European Nobilities in the Seventeenth and Eighteenth Centuries* vol. 1 (London, 1995), pp. 85, 87–8; H. F. K. Van Nierop, *The Nobility of Holland: From Knights to Regents*, 1500–1650, trans. Maarten Ultee (Cambridge, 1993). On demographic attrition in Italy see James C. Davis, *The Decline of the Venetian Nobility as a Ruling Class* (Baltimore, 1962).
11 Éric Mension-Rigau, *Aristocrates et grands bourgeois: éducation, traditions, valeurs* (Paris, 1994), pp. 466–74.
12 Texier, *Qu'est-ce que la noblesse?*, p. 195.
13 I. A. A. Thompson, 'The nobility in Spain, 1600–1800' in Scott, *The European Nobilities*, vol. 1, pp. 195–7, 200–1, 221–4. For a case study of financial difficulties see Charles Jago, 'The "crisis of the aristocracy" in seventeenth-century Castile', *Past and Present* 84 (1979), 60–90.
14 Knud J. V. Jespersen, 'The rise and fall of the Danish nobility, 1600–1800' in Scott, *The European Nobilities*, vol. 2, pp. 48–9; Suzanne Desan, '"War between brothers and sisters": inheritance law and gender politics in revolutionary France', *French Historical Studies* 20 (1997), 597–634.
15 Peter McPhee, *A Social History of France 1789–1914* 2 ed. (New York, 2004), p. 104.
16 Joanne Baker, 'Female monasticism and family strategy: the Guises and Saint Pierre de Reims', *Sixteenth-Century Journal* 28 (1997), 1091–108; Karin J. MacHardy, 'Cultural capital, family strategies and noble identity in early modern Habsburg Austria 1579–1620', *Past and Present* 163 (1999), 36–75; Keith M. Brown, 'The Scottish aristocracy, anglicanization and the court, 1603–38', *The Historical Journal* 36 (1993), 543–76.
17 Caroline Castiglione, 'Accounting for affection: battles between aristocratic mothers and sons in eighteenth-century Rome', *Journal of Family History* 25 (2000), 39.
18 Pierre Bourdieu, *Outline of a Theory of Practice*, trans. Richard Nice, 19 ed. (Cambridge, 2005), p. 62.
19 Pierre Bourdieu, 'Marriage strategies as stategies of social reproduction' in Robert Forster and Orest Ranum (eds), *Family and Society. Selections from the Annales Economies, Sociétés, Civilisations*, trans. Elborg Forster and Patricia M. Ranum (Baltimore, 1976), pp. 122–3.
20 Margaret H. Darrow, *Revolution in the House: Family, Class, and Inheritance in Southern France, 1775–1825* (Princeton, 1989), p. 17.
21 For examples of failure and of success see Elie Haddad, *Fondation et ruine d'une 'maison': histoire sociale des comtes de Belin (1582–1706)* (Limoges,

2009); Jonathan Dewald, *Pont-St-Pierre* 1398–1789: *Lordship, Community, and Capitalism in Early Modern France* (Berkeley, 1987).
22 Scott, *The European Nobilities* vol. 2, pp. 274–91; F. L. Carsten, *A History of the Prussian Junkers* (Aldershot, 1989), chs 8–10; Dominic Lieven, *The Aristocracy in Europe, 1815–1914* (London, 1992); Madeleine Beard, *English Landed Society in the Twentieth Century* (London, 1989); Amanda N. Shanks, *Rural Aristocracy in Northern Ireland* (Aldershot, 1988); Roger Magraw, *France, 1815–1914: The Bourgeois Century* (London, 1983).
23 William Doyle, *Aristocracy and its Enemies in the Age of Revolution* (Oxford, 2009), p. 340.
24 The classic statement calling for attention to old landed nobilities is Arno J. Mayer, *The Persistence of the Old Regime: Europe to the Great War* (New York, 1981). David Higgs cites by way of example A. J. P. Taylor's description of late nineteenth-century nobles as sounding 'like an array of rich cream cakes'. He also offers some instructive suggestions as to why historians of modern France have avoided the study of nobility. Higgs, *Nobles*, pp. xv, 223.
25 For an illustration see the discussion of LeGouvé's essay 'Aristocratic and democratic politeness' in Nye, *Masculinity*, pp. 155–6. On changing notions of deference in the 1780s and 1820s see McPhee, *A Social History*, pp. 17, 155–6. On continuing respect for hierarchy see Higgs, *Nobles*, p. 220.
26 Elizabeth C. Macknight 'Why weren't they feminists? Parisian noble women and the campaigns for women's rights in France, 1880–1914', *European Journal of Women's Studies* 14 (2007), 127–41.
27 Anne Cova, 'Au service de l'église, de la patrie et de la famille': femmes catholiques et maternité sous la III République (Paris, 2000); Bruno Dumons, *Les Dames de la Ligue des Femmes Françaises (1901–1914)* (Paris, 2006), pp. 435–42.
28 Proust, *Time Regained*, p. 53.
29 Ralph Schor, *L'Anti-sémitisme en France pendant les années trente: prélude à Vichy* (Brussels, 1992); Michel Winock, *Nationalism, Anti-semitism, and Fascism in France*, trans. Jane Marie Todd (Stanford, 1998); Michael R. Marrus and Robert O. Paxton, *Vichy France and the Jews* (New York, 1981).
30 Mension-Rigau, *Aristocrates*, pp. 471–3; Christian de Bartillat, *Histoire de la noblesse française* vol. 2 *Les Nobles du Second Empire à la fin du XXe siècle* (Paris, 1991), pp. 427–30; Eugen Weber, *Action Française: Royalism and Reaction in Twentieth-Century France* (Stanford, 1962).
31 Urbain Gohier, *Droit de la Race supérieure* (1914) cited in Maurevert, *Fisc et blason*, pp. 61–2.
32 *Au Pilori* 8 July 1943 in AP 69/3 Fonds Béarn de Chalais.
33 Stuart Carroll, *Blood and Violence in Early Modern France* (Oxford, 2006).
34 Amy Livingstone, *Out of Love for My Kin: Aristocratic Family Life in the Lands of the Loire, 1000–1200* (Ithaca, 2010); Hans Medick and David Warren

Sabean (eds), *Interest and Emotion: Essays on the Study of Family and Kinship* (Cambridge, 1984).
35 David Cannadine, *The Decline and Fall of the British Aristocracy* (London, 2005), pp. 6–7.
36 Steven Ozment, *Ancestors: The Loving Family in Old Europe* (Cambridge, 2001), p. 108.
37 Henri Bordier, *Les Archives de la France* (Geneva, 1978), p. 356.
38 Jonathan Dewald, *The European Nobility* 1400–1800 (Cambridge, 1996), pp. 6, 186, 201.

Appendix

This appendix brings together information on the families and individuals whose *archives privées* were consulted in the course of research and whose names appear within the chapters. The relevant archives appear in the list of archival sources; where the *fonds* does not bear the name of the family I have indicated the name of the château in the entry below. The family's full patronymic name is used for the entry though the *fonds* may bear a shorter name (for example, the archives of the La Forest d'Armaillé family are called the Fonds de la famille d'Armaillé). Genealogical details have been kept to a minimum; further information on the various branches, titles, and generations of the families is contained in works such as the *Annuaire de la noblesse de France*. The abbreviations in brackets indicate the type of nobility (see the list of abbreviations) and/or whether the family belongs to the Association d'entraide de la Noblesse Française (ANF).

Albertas (d') The Albertas family (*extr.* ANF) originated from Provence. The marquis Félix d'Albertas (1789–1872) married Flavie Caussiny de Valbelle. This couple's eldest son, Arthur, married Angéline Tornielli di Borgolavezzaro.

Alexandry d'Orengiani (d') The Alexandry d'Orengiani family (*extr.* ANF) originated from Savoy. The baron Frédéric d'Alexandry d'Orengiani (1829–94) married Camille Cuillerie-Dupont. Frédéric was mayor of Chambéry in 1860, the year Savoy was annexed to France.

Astruc Gabriel Astruc (1864–1938) was an energetic impresario and outstanding contributor to European musical and theatrical culture. He was based in Paris and kept in regular contact with aristocratic patrons of the arts.

Bernard de Calonne (de) The Bernard de Calonne family (*extr.*) originated from the Belgian province of Hainaut and acquired lands in Artois through marital alliances with the Berghes and Delval de la Marche families. The vicomte Alphonse de Calonne (1818–1902) was an art critic, historian, editor of *Revue contemporaine*, and organiser of projects for the 1900 Exposition Universelle.

Berthier The Berthier family (*lett.* ANF) originated from Burgundy. Louis-Alexandre Berthier (1753–1815) received the titles of prince de Neuchâtel in 1806 and prince de Wagram in 1809. His eldest son, Napoléon-Alexandre (1810–87), married Zénaïde Clary. This couple had three children including a son, Alexandre (1836–1911), who married Berthe de Rothschild. Alexandre and Berthe had three children: Alexandre (1883–1918), Élisabeth, and Marguerite.

Bertier de Sauvigny (de) The Bertier de Sauvigny family (*par ch.* ANF) originated from Burgundy. Louis de Bertier de Sauvigny, killed on 22 July 1789, had four sons and seven daughters by Marie-Josephe Foullon. Among this couple's grandchildren were Alexis (1814–83), Ferdinand (1813–93), Charles (1817–1905), and Alphonse (1830–94).

Bonaparte, Lucien and his descendants Lucien Bonaparte (1775–1840) and his second wife, Alexandrine de Bleschamp, had nine children. In 1870 their son Pierre (1815–81) shot and killed a journalist. Pierre was acquitted then moved to England with his family. Pierre's daughter, Jeanne (1861–1910), married the marquis Christian de Villeneuve. Pierre's son, Roland (1858–1924), married Marie Blanc and this couple had one daughter, Marie Bonaparte (1882–1962).

Bonaparte, Napoléon Napoléon I's youngest brother, Jérôme, had three children by his second wife, Catherine de Wurtemburg: Jérôme-Napoléon (1814–47), Mathilde (1820–1904), and Napoléon (1822–91). The latter Napoléon married Marie-Clothilde, daughter of Victor-Emmanuel II, and this couple had three children. The eldest son Victor, prince Napoléon (1862–1926), married Clémentine, princesse de Belgique.

Briet de Rainvillers The Briet de Rainvillers family (*extr.* ANF) originated from Picardy; archives relating to this family were kept at the château de Boismont. Louis Briet de Rainvillers (1900–45) was arrested and deported in 1942 for helping an English pilot to hide from the Gestapo.

Castellane (de) The Castellane family (*extr.* ANF) originated from Provence. The comte Boni de Castellane (1867–1932) was the son of Henri de Castellane and Pauline de Talleyrand-Périgord. Boni married Anna Gould (1878–1961) in 1895; the couple divorced in 1906.

Caulaincourt (de) The Caulaincourt family (*extr.*) originated from Picardy. The marquis Armand de Caulaincourt (1773–1827) received the title of duc de Vicence in 1808. Augustine Louise de Caulaincourt (1774–1832) married Christophe de Mornay-Montchevreuil. This couple were the grandparents of Philippe de Mornay-Soult (1831–93).

Caumont La Force (de) The Caumont La Force family (*extr.* ANF) originated from Guyenne and was primarily Protestant. In 1876 Bertrand de Caumont La Force married Blanche de Maillé de La Tour-Landry. This couple's eldest son, Auguste, 12th duc de La Force (1878–1961), was elected to the Académie Française in 1925.

Clérel de Tocqueville The Clérel de Tocqueville family (*extr.* ANF) originated from Normandy. Hervé Clérel de Tocqueville received the title of comte in 1820; Alexis de Tocqueville (1805–59) was his son.

Clermont-Tonnerre (de) The Clermont-Tonnerre family (*extr.* ANF) originated from Dauphiné. Philibert, 8th duc de Clermont-Tonnerre (1871–1940), married Élisabeth de Gramont (1875–1954); the couple divorced in 1920.

Coëtnempren de Kersaint (de) The Coëtnempren de Kersaint family (*extr.* ANF) originated from Brittany. The comte Henri de Coëtnempren de Kersaint (1881–1949) had three sisters: Claire, Anne-Marie, and Blanche. The family lived on the estate of Versigny.

Courson de La Villeneuve (de) The Courson de La Villeneuve family (*extr.* ANF) originated from Brittany. The vicomte Aurélien de Courson de La Villeneuve (1808–89) was a historian; he married Pauline Le Jumeau de Kergaradec.

Courtin de Neufbourg The Courtin de Neufbourg family (*lett.* ANF) originated from Lyonnais. Guy Courtin de Neufbourg (1888–1986) was a member of the Académie des Inscriptions et Belles-Lettres.

Croÿ (de) The Croÿ family (*extr.* ANF) originated from Picardy. Rodolphe Maximilien de Croÿ, 11th duc de Croÿ-Dulmen (1823–1902), had nine siblings, including Alexis Guillaume (1825–98) and Georges Victor (1828–79).

Durrieu Antoine-Simon Durrieu (1775–1862) (XIX) received the title of baron in 1830. After his death, the title passed to his nephew, Alfred Durrieu (1812–77), who was deputy governor then governor of Algeria and married Blanche Dufour.

Espagnet (d') The Espagnet family (*par ch.* ANF) originated from Provence. The marquis Félix d'Espagnet (1821–99) married Valentine Girard du Demaine.

Espivent Archives relating to several branches of the Espivent family, including the Espivent de la Villeboisnet branch (*extr.* ANF), were kept at the château de l'Escuray. Henri Espivent de la Villeboisnet (1813–1908) received the title of comte from the pope in 1876 and it was authorised in France in 1877.

Estienne de Saint-Jean (d') The Estienne de Saint-Jean family (*par ch.* ANF) originated from Dauphiné. The vicomte Ludovic d'Estienne de Saint-Jean married Marie-Charlotte de Tourtoulon de La Salle. This couple's home, the château du Grand Saint-Jean, was badly damaged in an earthquake on 11 June 1909.

Faucigny-Lucinge (de) The Faucigny-Lucinge family (*extr.*) originated from Savoy. The Italian title of prince de Lucinge was authorised in France in 1828. Charles, 2nd prince de Lucinge (1824–1910), married Françoise de Sesmaisons (1839–1901) and this couple had five sons. The title passed to Ferdinand (1868–1928), 3rd prince de Lucinge.

Fialin de Persigny   Jean Gilbert Victor Fialin (1808–72) served as aide-de-camp to Louis-Napoléon and received the title of duc de Persigny in 1863. In 1852 he married Eglé Ney de la Moskowa, granddaughter of maréchal Ney. This couple had a son, Jean-Michel-Napoléon (1855–85).

Foresta (de)   The Foresta family (*extr.* ANF) originated from Provence. The marquis Marie-Maxence de Foresta was the comte de Chambord's chief representative in and around Marseille from 1871 to 1883. Marie-Maxence married Eugénie de Bully. This couple's eldest son, Henri (1855–1944), married Thérèse de Bonet d'Oléon.

Frotier de La Messelière   The Frotier de La Messelière family (*extr.* ANF) originated from Poitou. The vicomte Henri Frotier de La Messelière (1876–1965) was the author of numerous works on the Breton nobility.

Galard de Brassac de Béarn (de)   The Galard de Brassac de Béarn family (*extr.* ANF) originated from Béarn. Henri de Galard de Brassac de Béarn (1874–1947), known as the prince de Béarn de Chalais, married Béatrice Winans. This couple had a daughter in 1906 and a son in 1907.

Galliffet (de)   The Galliffet family (*extr.*) originated from Provence. The général marquis Gaston de Galliffet (1830–1909) served as Minister of War under Waldeck-Rousseau.

Gavini de Campile   Adeline de Raymond (1830–1909) was the daughter of the comte de Raymond (1783–1863), mayor of Agen. The Raymond family (ANF) originated from Guyenne. Adeline married Denis Gavini de Campile who was deputy for Corsica from 1876 to 1886.

Geouffre de La Pradelle (de)   The Geouffre de La Pradelle family (*extr.*) originated from Limousin. Albert de Geouffre de La Pradelle (1871–1955) was a jurisconsult to the Ministère des Affaires Étrangères.

Gouvello (de)   The Gouvello family (*extr.* ANF) originated from Brittany. The marquis Amédée de Gouvello married Octavie de Grouchy and this couple had four children. Their son, Paul (1855–1933), married Adèle de Tailfumyr de Saint-Maixent in 1887 and this couple had four children, none of who survived into adulthood. Paul later married Mathilde de Mengin-Fondragon.

Goyon de Feltre   Général Henri Clarke, of Irish noble descent, received the title of duc de Feltre in 1809. Clarke's granddaughter, Oriane de Montesquiou-Fezensac, married the comte de Goyon (1803–70). The title passed to this couple's son, Charles de Goyon, 3rd duc de Feltre (1844–1930). Charles married Léonie de Cambacérès (1858–1909). Their son, Auguste, married Helen Seton.

Gramont (de)   The Gramont family (*extr.* ANF) originated from Bigorre. Agénor, 11th duc de Gramont (1850–1925), married Isabelle de Beauvau-Craon who died giving birth to Élisabeth (future duchesse de Clermont-Tonnerre). In 1878 Agénor made a second marriage to Marguerite de Rothschild (1855–1905) and this couple had a son, Armand, duc de Guiche, later 12th duc de Gramont (1879–1962). Armand was internationally renowned for his research on optics and aerodynamics. He was president of the Académie des Sciences in 1956.

Grassis   Jean Gras was ennobled in 1632 by Victor-Amédée I. Over time the family name was amended to Grassis. In 1888 Mathilde Grassis, a nun at Sacré-Coeur in Bourges, wrote memoirs about her mother.

Greffulhe   The Greffulhe family (XIX) originated from Languedoc. Jean Greffulhe (1774–1820) received the title of comte in 1818. Jean's grandson, Henri (1848–1932), married Élisabeth de Caraman-Chimay (1860–1952). This couple had one daughter, Élaine (1882–1958), who married Armand de Gramont.

Harcourt (d')   The Harcourt family (*extr.* ANF) originated from Normandy. Bernard d'Harcourt, marquis d'Harcourt d'Olonde (1842–1914) married Marguerite de Gontaut-Biron in 1871. Bernard's brother, Louis (1856–1946), married Marie-Juliette Lanjuinais (1865–1949).

Isoard-Vauvenargues (d')   The Isoard-Vauvenargues family (*par ch.*) originated from Provence. Aloïs Joachim d'Isoard-Vauvenargues married Marie-Alexandrine de Coriolis. This couple's son, Jean Gonzague (1838–1913), married Marguerite de Rougé.

Jaucourt (de)   The Jaucourt family (*extr.*) originated from Champagne. The comte Jean-François-Charles de Jaucourt (1826–1906) was a deputy of the Corps Législatif under the Second Empire.

Kergorlay (de)   The Kergorlay family (*extr.* ANF) originated from Brittany. The comte Hervé de Kergorlay (1803–73) was president of the Société Centrale d'Agriculture and a deputy of the Corps Législatif under the Second Empire.

La Croix de Castries (de)   The La Croix de Castries family (*extr.* ANF) originated from Languedoc. René de La Croix de Castries, 5th duc de Castries (1908–86), was a historian; he was elected to the Académie Française in 1972.

La Forest d'Armaillé (de)   The La Forest d'Armaillé family (*extr.* ANF) originated from Brittany. Joseph de La Forest d'Armaillé (1783–1872) married Alexandrine de Robethon and this couple lived on the estate of La Ménantière. Pauline de La Forest d'Armaillé (1851–1928) married Victor, 5th duc de Broglie (1846–1906). This couple's daughter, Pauline, married the comte Jean de Pange.

Lannes de Montebello   The Lannes de Montebello family (XIX ANF) originated from Gascony. Jean Lannes (1769–1809) received the title of duc de Montebello in 1808. Following the death of Charles (1836–1922), 5th duc de Montebello, the title passed to his grandson, Napoléon.

La Rochefoucauld (de)   The La Rochefoucauld family (*extr.* ANF) originated from Angoumois. The comte Xavier de La Rochefoucauld (1867–1942) was a co-director of Action Libérale Populaire. During the First World War he was in charge of the hospital of Bizy at Vernon.

La Tour d'Auvergne Lauraguais (de)   The La Tour d'Auvergne Lauraguais family (*extr.* ANF) originated from Languedoc. Henri de La Tour d'Auvergne Lauraguais (1823–71) had a diplomatic career and received the papal title of prince in 1853; his brother, Charles-Amable (1826–79), was archbishop of Bourges. Henri de La Tour d'Auvergne Lauraguais (1876–1914) married Élisabeth Berthier de Wagram (1885–1960).

Le Borgne de Boigne   The Le Borgne de Boigne family (ANF) originated from Savoy and their titles are of Italian and Sardinian origin; the title of comte de Boigne was authorised in France in 1865. Ernest de Boigne (1829–95) married Delphine de Sabran-Pontevès and this couple had eight children.

Lecoq de Boisbaudran The Lecoq de Boisbaudran family (*par ch.*) originated from Angoumois and was primarily Protestant. Most of the family's fortune was lost between the Revocation of the Edict of Nantes and the 1789 Revolution. Paul-Émile (known as François) Lecoq de Boisbaudran (1838–1912) was a distinguished chemist who discovered gallium.

Lenoncourt (de) The Lenoncourt family (*extr.*) originated from Lorraine. It made a key marital alliance with the Sublet d'Heudicourt family in the seventeenth century. Odelric de Lenoncourt married Marguevite de Suremain in 1882.

L'Escale (de) The L'Escale family (*extr.* ANF) originated from Lorraine. Antoine de L'Escale (1847–1907) married Anna Sidonie du Verger de Cuy de Poulmic.

L'Estourbeillon (de) The L'Estourbeillon family (*extr.* ANF) originated from Brittany. The marquis Régis de L'Estourbeillon (1858–1946) was a historian, founder of the *Revue historique de l'Ouest*, and deputy for Morbihan from 1898 to 1919.

Luppé (de) The Luppé family (*extr.* ANF) originated from Gascony. The marquis Pierre de Luppé (1861–1934) married Albertine de Broglie.

Mackau (de) The Mackau family (*extr.*) originated from Ireland and came with James II of England to France where they settled in Alsace. The baron Armand de Mackau (1832–1918) married Mathilde de Maison (1837–86).

Mahuet (de) The Mahuet family was ennobled by Charles III and originated from Lorraine. The comte Antoine de Mahuet (1866–1958) married Yvonne-Marie-Joséphine Le Preud'homme de Fontenoy (1870–1955). This couple had two sons.

Molette de Morangiès (de) The Molette de Morangiès family (*extr.* ANF) originated from Auvergne. Christophe Théodore de Molette de Morangiès sold the château de Saint-Alban in 1821 owing to the family's financial debts. The comte Louis-Napoléon de Molette de Morangiès (1860–1914) had a military career and married Marguerite Bouchard d'Aubeterre.

Montesquiou-Fezensac (de) The Montesquiou-Fezensac family (*extr.* ANF) originated from Gascony. Marie de Montesquiou-Fezensac (1834–84) married Joseph, 18th prince de Chimay (1836–92). Thierry de Montesquiou-Fezensac and Pauline de Roux had three sons: Gontran (1847–83), Aimery (1853–73), and Robert (1855–1921).

Montgrand (de) The Montgrand family (*par ch.* ANF) originated from Languedoc. The marquis Claude de Montgrand (1616–1706) had three sons who were responsible for establishing the family in Provence. Later descendants who inherited the title included Charles (1825–1912), Joseph (1872–1958), and Charles (1913–2000).

Montholon and Sémonville The Montholon family (*par ch.*) originated from Burgundy. Following the death of Mathieu de Montholon in 1789 his widow married Charles-Louis Huguet de Sémonville (1759–1839). Louis-François-Alphonse de Montholon-Sémonville (1808–65) married Marie-Jacqueline-Sidoine de Moreton de Chabrillan and this couple had one son, François.

Mornay and Soult Jules de Mornay (1798–1852) married Hortense Soult who was the daughter of the maréchal Nicolas Soult, duc de Dalmatie. This couple's eldest son, Philippe de Mornay-Soult (1831–93), married Marguerite-Élisabeth-Alice Le Grand de Villers.

Mugnier The abbé Arthur Mugnier (1853–1944) was in close contact with aristocratic families in Paris and gave religious instruction to noble girls.

Mun (de) The Mun family (*extr.* ANF) originated from Bigorre. The comte Albert de Mun (1841–1914) was elected as monarchist deputy for Pontivy in 1876. He was a co-founder of the Cercles Catholiques d'Ouvriers.

Murat The Murat family (XIX ANF) originated from Guyenne. Joachim Murat (1767–1815) received the title of prince in 1806 and succeeded Joseph Bonaparte as king of Naples. Descendants include Joachim Murat IV (1834–1901) and his son Joachim Murat V (1856–1932) who married Cécile Ney d'Elchingen. Charles Murat (1892–1973) was the fifth child of Joachim Murat V. Charles and his American wife, Margaret Rutherford, lived in Morocco.

Ney d'Elchingen   Michel Ney (1769–1815) (XIX) received the titles of duc d'Elchingen, prince de la Moskowa in 1813. He married Aglaé-Louise Auguié. From this marriage there were four boys. The eldest son, Léon (1803–57), married Albine Laffitte and this couple had a daughter, Églé (future duchesse de Persigny).

Noailles, de Beaumont, de Grossolles-Flamarens (de)   The Noailles family (*extr.* ANF) originated from Limousin. Adrien-Maurice de Noailles (1678–1766) had two sons: Louis, duc de Noailles (1713–93), and Philippe, duc de Mouchy (1715–94). One of Philippe's great grandsons, Alfred, married Marie de Beaumont in 1852; the Beaumont family originated from Dauphiné. The Noailles were also connected by marriage to the Grossolles-Flamarens family from Guyenne. In 1897 the comte Mathieu de Noailles married Anna de Brancovan (1876–1933) who was a celebrated poet.

Orléans (d')   The Orléans family (*extr.* ANF) originated from Orléanais. Philippe d'Orléans, comte de Paris (1838–94), became pretender to the French throne following the death of the comte de Chambord. The Orléans family archives belong to the Maison de la France collection; there are some further documents relating to this family in the archives of the château de Lavilletertre.

Pérusse des Cars   The Pérusse des Cars family (*extr.*) originated from Limousin; archives relating to this family were kept at the château de Malesherbes. The vicomte Jean-Augustin des Cars (1821–60) married Alexandrine de Lebzeltern. This couple's daughter, Zénaïde, became a Carmelite nun.

Ploeuc (de)   The Plouec family (*extr.*) originated from Brittany. The marquis Alexandre de Plouec (1815–88) was one of the founders of the Banque Ottomane and of the Union Générale. He was responsible for the Banque de France during the Paris Commune.

Régnier de Massa   Claude-Ambroise Régnier (1746–1814) (XIX) received the title of duc de Massa in 1809. He married Charlotte Lejeune (1748–1835) and this couple had four children. Their eldest son Sylvestre (1783–1851), 2nd duc de Massa, married Nancy Macdonald, the daughter of maréchal Macdonald, duc de Tarente. After Sylvestre's death the title of duc de Massa passed to Alfred, then Jean then André.

Révérend   The vicomte Albert Révérend (1844–1911) was director and editor of the *Annuaire de la noblesse de France et des maisons souveraines de l'Europe* from 1890 to 1911.

Robien (de)   The Robien family (*extr.* ANF) originated from Brittany. The comte Louis de Robien (1888–1958) had a diplomatic career and married Laure du Pont de Gault Saussine. This couple had two children, Élisabeth and Anne-Thibault.

Rozières (de)   The Rozières family (ANF) originated from Lorraine and were given the title of gentilhomme de Laveline by René II, duc de Lorraine. Charles de Rozières (1827–93) married Louise-Caroline de Klopstein and this couple had six children. Their eldest son, Antoine (1858–1932), married Louise Pernot-Dubreuil and this couple had five children.

Saint-Exupéry (de)   The Saint-Exupéry family (*extr.* ANF) originated from Guyenne; archives relating to this family were kept at the château d'Arasse. The marquis Balthazar-Joseph de Saint-Exupéry (1815–76) married Louise de Laurière de Moncaut. This couple's son, Guy (1848–1914), married Marthe de Castillon.

Ségur (de)   The comte Louis Philippe de Ségur (1753–1830) had two sons: Octave was the father-in-law of the children's author, the comtesse de Ségur (née Rostopchine), and the other son, Philippe (1780–1873), was a military general. Philippe had three children by his first wife, Mademoiselle de Luçay; she died and Philippe then made a second marriage to the comtesse Greffulhe (née Vintimille du Luc), a mother of three children, with whom he had another three children.

Suchet d'Albuféra   The Suchet d'Albuféra family (XIX ANF) originated from Lyonnais. Louis-Gabriel Suchet received the title of duc d'Albuféra in 1813. His son, Napoléon, married Malvina Schickler (1822–77) who had a close friendship with Adolphe Thiers (1797–1877).

Talleyrand-Périgord (de)   Augustin-Hélie de Talleyrand-Périgord, duc de Périgord (1788–1879) married Apolline-Marie-Nicolette de Choiseul-Praslin in 1807. The archives of the château de Chalais contain documents on the Talleyrand-Périgord (*extr.* ANF) and Lafitte families.

Théas de Caille de Thorenc (de) The Théas de Caille de Thorenc family originated from Provence and was aggregated to the nobility in the late seventeenth century. François de Théas, comte de Thorenc (1719–94), and his descendants owned properties in and around Grasse; archives relating to this family were kept at the château de Mouans Sartoux.

Tredecini de Saint-Séverin The Tredecini de Saint-Séverin family (*extr.*) originated from Savoy. The marquis Charles-Félix Tredecini de Saint-Séverin (1827–1903) married Marie-Anne-Inès de Sabran-Pontevès (1836–74). Their younger son, Henri Elzéar (1858–1906), married Jeanne Françoise Marie de Roussy de Sales.

Vogüé (de) The Vogüé family (*extr.* ANF) originated from Languedoc. The marquis Melchior de Vogüé (1829–1916) was an archaeologist and diplomat. His son, Louis (1868–1948), married Louise d'Arenberg and this couple had ten children, including Marguerite.

List of archival sources

The *fonds* listed below were selected because they include documents from the period of the Third Republic. There are more *fonds* relating to aristocratic families in French archives but the documentation they contain does not necessarily extend to 1870. Inventories exist for the AP series and may be consulted at the Archives nationales in Paris. A few of the *fonds* in departmental archives were still awaiting classification at the time of consultation so there was no inventory available. Archival box numbers for cited documents appear in the notes for each chapter. A concise introductory guide to the subject of French nobility is Philippe du Puy de Clinchamps, *La Noblesse* 5 ed. (Paris, 1996).

Archives nationales, Paris

Série archives privées
AP 22 Fonds Kersaint et Coëtnempren
AP 31 Fonds Murat
AP 31 (II) Fonds Charles Murat
AP 36 Fonds Ségur
AP 44 Fonds Persigny
AP 69 Fonds Béarn de Chalais
AP 77 Fonds Thiers-Albuféra
AP 80 Fonds Bertier de Sauvigny
AP 86 Fonds de La Maison de Jaucourt
AP 88 Fonds Faucigny-Lucinge

AP 95 Fonds Caulaincourt
AP 97 Fonds Kergorlay
AP 101 (I) Fonds Gramont (le comte Greffulhe)
AP 101 (II) Fonds Gramont (la comtesse Greffulhe)
AP 103 Fonds Lucien Bonaparte et ses descendants
AP 107 Fonds Galliffet
AP 111 Fonds Noailles, de Beaumont, de Grossolles-Flamarens
AP 115 Fonds Montholon et Sémonville
AP 137 Fonds Ney
AP 142 Fonds Xavier de La Rochefoucauld
AP 154 Chartrier de Tocqueville
AP 156 (I) Fonds Mackau
AP 173bis Fonds Maréchal Berthier
AP 229 Fonds Durrieu
AP 258 Fonds Chanoine Mugnier
AP 272 Fonds Ploeuc
AP 278 Fonds Bernard de Calonne
AP 279 Fonds Massa
AP 300 (III) Fonds Maison de la France
AP 300 (IV) Fonds Maison de la France
AP 306 Chartrier de Castries
AP 349 Fonds Montesquiou-Fezensac
AP 353 Fonds Caumont La Force
AP 359 Fonds Clermont-Tonnerre
AP 378 Fonds Albert de Mun
AP 380 Fonds d'Harcourt
AP 384 Fonds Suchet d'Albuféra
AP 399 Fonds du château de Malesherbes
AP 400 Fonds Napoléon
AP 402 Fonds Mornay et Soult
AP 409 Fonds Gabriel Astruc
AP 427 Fonds Robien
AP 461 Fonds Montebello
AP 567 Fonds Vogüé
AP 616 Fonds Castellane
AP 644 Fonds La Tour d'Auvergne Lauraguais

Série AB XIX Papiers d'érudits
AB XIX 2644–84 Fonds des référendaires au Sceau de France
AB XIX 2979–3035 Fonds du vicomte Révérend

Archives départementales

Archives départementales des Alpes-Maritimes, Nice
25J Archives du château de Mouans Sartoux

Archives départementales des Bouches-du-Rhône, Marseille and Aix-en-Provence
3E 241 Fonds de la famille d'Estienne de Saint-Jean
3E 242 Fonds de la famille d'Espagnet
31E Fonds de la famille d'Albertas
103J Fonds de la famille d'Isoard-Vauvenargues
140J Fonds de la famille de Foresta
197J Fonds de la famille de Montgrand

Archives départementales de la Charente, Angoulême
J1044–1401 Fonds Galard, Brassac, Béarn, Chalais
4J Fonds Lecoq de Boisbaudran
10J Fonds du château de Chalais

Archives départementales de la Corrèze, Tulle
54J Fonds Raymond de Geouffre de La Pradelle

Archives départementales des Côtes-d'Armor, St Brieuc
19J Archives de Courson
60J Fonds Frotier de La Messelière
127J Fonds Goyon de Feltre

Archives départementales de la Loire, St Étienne
4J Archives de la famille Courtin de Neufbourg

Archives départementales de la Loire Atlantique, Nantes
9J Fonds Régis de L'Estourbeillon
186J Fonds du château de l'Escuray

Archives départementales de Lot-et-Garonne, Agen
1J 1009–13 Fonds Gavini de Campile
25J Fonds Luppé
83J Fonds du château d'Arasse

Archives départementales de la Lozère, Mende
4J Fonds Molette de Morangiès et Moré de Charaix

Archives départementales de Maine-et-Loire, Angers
17J Fonds de la famille d'Armaillé

Archives départementales de Meurthe-et-Moselle, Nancy
2J Archives de la famille de Mahuet
13J Archives de la famille de Lenoncourt
18J Archives de la famille de L'Escale

Archives départementales du Morbihan, Vannes
31J Archives du château de Kerlévénan – Fonds Gouvello

Archives départementales du Nord, Lille
26J E2508 Papiers de la famille de Croÿ

Archives départementales de l'Oise, Beauvais
35J Fonds du château de Lavilletertre

Archives départementales de la Savoie, Chambéry
29F Fonds d'Alexandry d'Orengiani
46F Fonds Tredecini de Saint-Séverin
8J Fonds de la famille de Boigne
20J Fonds Grassis

Archives départementales de la Somme, Amiens
2J Archives de la seigneurie de Boismont

Archives départementales des Vosges, Épinal
41J Fonds de la famille de Rozières

Index

Note: Where a noblewoman is listed under her married surname with a title, her first name and original surname are given in brackets

abortion 1, 149, 227
ageing 25, 106, 139, 190, 196, 201
Albertas family 233
Albuféra *see* Suchet d'Albuféra
Alexandry d'Orengiani family 233
Alexandry d'Orengiani, Fréderic d' 47–8, 134–5, 233
Almanach de Gotha 24, 29, 31–2, 36
archivists 9, 211–12, 229
Arenberg, Auguste d' 45, 186
Ariès, Philippe 6
Armaillé *see* La Forest d'Armaillé
Armaillé, comtesse d' (Marie de Ségur) 100, 198
Association d'entraide de la Noblesse Française 21, 29, 233
Astruc, Gabriel 8, 234

Béarn *see* Galard de Brassac de Béarn
Béarn, princesse de (Cécile de Talleyrand-Périgord) 22, 153–4, 185, 208, 210
Beauvau-Craon, Charles-Louis de 57
Bernard de Calonne family 234
Berthier, Alexandre, 3rd prince de Wagram 84, 95, 106–7, 109

Berthier, Alexandre, 4th prince de Wagram 174–5
Berthier family 84–5, 95, 109, 174, 180, 234
Berthier, Napoléon-Alexandre, 2nd prince de Wagram 97, 99, 109
Bertier de Sauvigny family 234
Bibesco, Georges 57, 179
Bibesco, princesse (Marthe Lahovary) 53, 57, 179
Boigne *see* Le Borgne de Boigne
Bonaparte family 30–2, 234
see also Napoleon
Bonaparte, Jeanne 41
Bonaparte, Lucien 30–1
Bonaparte, Marie 32, 150
Bonaparte, Roland 30–1, 170, 184–5
Bonneval *see* Val de Bonneval
Bourdieu, Pierre 3–4, 118, 193, 225
Bourgeois, Léon 75, 87
Bourget, Paul 72, 87, 191
Breteuil, Henri de 46, 72, 181
Breteuil, marquise de (Constance de Castelbajac) 44, 177–8
Briand, Aristide 135
Briet de Rainvillers family 108, 235
Broglie family 1, 100, 174, 182, 187–8

INDEX

Caraman-Chimay, Joseph de 47, 204
Caraman-Chimay, princesse de (Marie de Montesquiou-Fezensac) 162, 202–4
Cassatt, Mary 153
Castelbajac family 177–8
Castellane, Boniface de 48–9, 59, 69–70, 107, 176–7, 199
Castellane family 176, 235
Catholic Church 2, 50, 131–4, 136, 159, 181, 191, 222
Catholic women's organisations 146–7, 163–4, 222–3, 227
Caulaincourt family 235
Caumont La Force, Bertrand de 129, 131
Caumont La Force family 235
Chalais, prince de 21–2, 24, 26, 28, 37, 209
Chambord, Henri, comte de 125–7, 222
Chancellery 19, 24, 26
Charles V, Holy Roman Emperor 16, 36
childbirth 130–1, 149–51, 219
Civil Code 41, 87, 136
Clarke, Général Henri 238
Clérel de Tocqueville family 235
 see also Tocqueville, Alexis de
Clermont-Tonnerre, duchesse de (Élisabeth de Gramont) 47, 69, 151, 162
Clermont-Tonnerre family 235
Coëtnempren de Kersaint family 235
colleges 131, 183–6
Confédération générale du travail 235–6
Courtin de Neufbourg family 236
cousins 44, 84, 186
Croÿ family 236

death 21, 27, 97, 202–9, 221
Declaration of the Rights of Man and Citizen 17
des Cars *see* Pérusse des Cars
divorce 41–2, 49–51, 149
Dreyfus Affair 220, 227
Durrieu family 236

elections 119, 121, 125, 127–8, 139, 222
Elias, Norbert 106
endogamy 44–5, 224
engagement 52–3, 60

ennoblement 16, 222
Espagnet family 236
Espivent family 236
Estienne de Saint-Jean family 236
exile 44, 222
extraction 16, 34

Faucigny-Lucinge family 112, 236
Ferry, Jules 117–19, 131–2, 134, 222
fertility 51–2, 147–9, 221
Fialin de Persigny family 237
fief 85, 117, 167
First World War 35, 76, 78, 111, 145, 147, 152, 164, 175, 227
Foresta family 185, 191–2, 237
Foresta, Marie-Thérèse de 182
Foresta, Maxence de 185, 191–2
Franco-Prussian War 48, 133, 145, 183, 206, 208, 220
Frotier de La Messeliere family 237
Furtado-Heine, Cécile-Charlotte 60, 70

Galard de Brassac de Béarn family 25, 173, 186, 237
Galard de Brassac de Béarn, Gaston de 22, 29–30, 185, 209
Galard de Brassac de Béarn, Henri de 21–4, 26–9, 36–7, 173, 185, 208, 211
Galliffet family 237
Galliffet, Gaston de 189–91
Gavardie, Henri de 136–7
Gavini de Campile, madame (Adeline de Raymond) 237
Geouffre de La Pradelle family 237
Goué family 183
Gould, Anna 47–9, 69
Gouvello, Amédée de 124, 137
Gouvello family 137, 237
governess 99, 154, 160, 172–3, 225
Goyon de Feltre family 238
Gramont, Armand de 55, 158–9, 238
Gramont family 238
grandparents 130, 177–80, 184, 196, 225
Grassis family 238
Greffulhe, comtesse (Élisabeth de Caraman-Chimay) 45, 50, 53, 55–7, 68, 100–1, 107, 111, 155

Greffulhe, Élaine 54–5, 151, 155, 158–9, 173, 187
Greffulhe family 45, 238
Greffulhe, Henri 53, 55–6, 100–1, 107, 135–6, 151, 186–7, 201–3
Guiche, duc de see Gramont, Armand de
Gyp 72, 180

Harcourt, Emmanuel d' 132–4
Harcourt family 45–6, 93, 97, 107–8, 238
Harcourt, François-Charles d' 82, 96, 106
Helleu, Paul-César 171
Hozieres, Charles-René d' 15, 25

income tax 65, 75–6
infidelity 49, 56–8, 199
in-laws 58–9, 179, 181
Isabella, Queen of Spain 27
Isoard-Vauvenargues family 238

Jaucourt family 238
Jesuits 131, 146, 183–4

Kergorlay family 239

La Croix de Castries, René de 15–16, 239
Lafitte family 209–12
La Forest d'Armaillé family 239
L'Aigle, Marie de 186–7
L'Aigle, Robert de 151, 186
languages 48, 156, 160–1, 172–3
Lanjuinais family 45–6
Lannes de Montebello family 86, 239
La Nouë family 183
La Rochefoucauld, comtesse de (Isabelle du Val de Bonneval) 80, 213–16
La Rochefoucauld family 97, 112, 239
La Rochefoucauld, Solange de 111
La Rochefoucauld, Xavier de 79–81, 111, 213–16, 239
La Tour d'Auvergne Lauraguais family 175, 239
Law on Associations 2, 139
Le Borgne de Boigne family 239
Lecoq de Boisbaudran family 240
Lenoncourt family 240
Leo XIII, Pope 2, 137

Leopold I, Holy Roman Emperor 36
L'Escale family 240
L'Estourbeillon family 240
Louis-Philippe, King 77
Louis XIII, King 22
Louis XIV, King 15, 26
Louis XVI, King 198
Louis XVIII, King 17, 18, 77
Luppé family 240

Mackau, Armand de 59, 132, 196–7
Mackau, baronne de (Mathilde de Maison) 58–9, 150, 153, 161, 196–7, 207–8
Mackau family 240
MacMahon, Patrice de 19–20
Mahuet family 240
Maillé de La Tour-Landry, Armand de 124–32, 138–40, 172, 175, 184
Maistre, Joseph de 206
majorat 65, 76–9, 223
Massa see Régnier de Massa
Mayer, Arno 5
meals 106, 108, 172, 187–9
Médici family 36
Molette de Morangiès family 240
Montesquiou-Fezensac family 240
Montesquiou-Fezensac, Mathilde de 189–91
Montgrand family 241
Montholon-Sémonville, François de 241
Morisot, Berthe 153
Mornay-Soult, Philippe de 241
Mugnier, abbé Arthur 8, 57, 150, 241
Mun, Albert de 132–3, 162, 241
Murat family 40, 70, 83, 241
Murat, Joachim, 5th prince Murat 40, 52–3, 60, 83, 93, 101, 122–3, 181, 221
Murat, princesse (Cécile Ney d'Elchingen) 40, 52–3, 93, 101, 111, 160–1, 181, 221

Nadar, Paul 55, 56, 102, 105, 190, 200
Napoleon I, Emperor 16–17, 31–2, 41, 65, 136, 139
Napoleon III, Emperor 18, 31
Ney d'Elchingen family 40, 241
Noailles, comtesse de (Anna de Brancovan) 83, 139, 181, 188–9

Noailles family 242

Order of Malta 24, 36
Orléans family 44, 47, 126–7, 179–80, 242
Orléans, Philippe d' 44
orphans 137–8

Pange, comtesse de (Pauline de Broglie) 1, 100, 182, 187–8, 205
Paris, comtesse de (Isabelle d'Orléans-Bragance) 179–80
peerage 16
Pérusse des Cars family 242
Pérusse des Cars, Zénaïde 182–3
Plouec family 242
Polignac, princesse de (Winnaretta Singer) 112
Potocki family 97
précepteur 146, 171, 174–6, 225
Proust, Marcel 20, 21, 45, 95, 104, 108, 112, 160, 187, 221, 227

Quinsonas, Humbert de 58–9, 196

Radziwill family 77
ralliement 2
Régnier de Massa, André 33–4
Régnier de Massa family 78–9, 242
Régnier de Massa, Jean 32–3, 78–9
religion 2, 48–9, 132–8, 146, 162–4, 181–2, 205–8, 222
religious orders 118, 131–2, 137, 162, 164, 182–3, 208, 222
René II, duc de Lorraine 243
Révérend, Albert 21–9, 243
Robien family 243
Rothschild, Carl de 95
Rothschild, Marguerite de 47
Rozières family 243

Sabran-Pontevès family 219
Saint-Exupéry family 243
Schickler family 80–1

Second World War 36, 192, 213, 219, 227
secularism 2, 118, 132–4, 159–60, 164, 223
Ségur family 100, 243
Separation of Church and State 2, 20, 133, 135–6, 163
sex 52–8, 104–5, 130–1, 148, 153
see also fertility; infidelity
shareholding 70
siblings 31, 84, 185–6, 201–2, 204–5
Suchet d'Albuféra family 154, 243

Talleyrand-Périgord, Élie Roger 22, 209
Talleyrand-Périgord family 29–30, 209–12, 243
tax on titles 65, 72–6, 223
Théas de Caille de Thorenc family 244
Thiers, Adolphe 154
Thompson, Edward P. 92, 94, 106, 108, 110
Tocqueville, Alexis de 72, 198, 235
Tredecini de Saint-Séverin family 244
Tudesq, André-Jean 4, 7

usurpation 20, 32–3, 226
Uzès, duchesse d' (Anne de Mortemart) 198–9, 205, 227

Val de Bonneval, Paule du 81
Victor-Amédée I, duc de Savoie 238
Victor-Emmanuel II, King of Italy 234
Victoria, Queen of England 47, 184
Villeneuve, Christian de 41
Vogüé family 155–7, 162, 244
Vogüé, Marguerite de 155–7, 162

Wagram, prince de *see* Berthier
Wagram, princesse de (Berthe de Rothschild) 95, 99, 103, 109
Waldeck-Rousseau, René 136–7
wet nursing 145–6, 152–3, 155, 157–8, 222
Winans family 23

Zamoyski family 77

EU authorised representative for GPSR:
Easy Access System Europe, Mustamäe tee 50,
10621 Tallinn, Estonia
gpsr.requests@easproject.com

www.ingramcontent.com/pod-product-compliance
Ingram Content Group UK Ltd.
Pitfield, Milton Keynes, MK11 3LW, UK
UKHW041937210426
5322IPUK00016B/222